Workings of the Spirit

**BLACK LITERATURE
AND CULTURE**
*A series edited
by Houston A. Baker, Jr.*

HOUSTON A. BAKER, JR.

Workings
of the Spirit

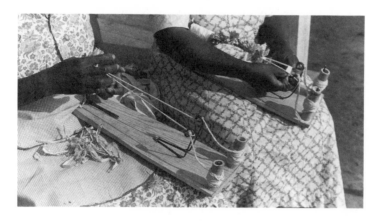

*The Poetics of Afro-American
Women's Writing*

*With a Phototext by Elizabeth Alexander
and Patricia Redmond*

THE UNIVERSITY OF CHICAGO PRESS

Chicago and London

Houston A. Baker, Jr., is professor of English and the Albert M. Greenfield Professor of Human Relations at the University of Pennsylvania, where he also directs the Center for the Study of Black Literature and Culture. His many publications include *The Journey Back, Blues, Ideology, and Afro-American Literature, Modernism and the Harlem Renaissance,* and *Afro-American Literary Study in the 1990s* (edited with Patricia Redmond), all published by the University of Chicago Press.

The University of Chicago Press, Chicago 60637
The University of Chicago Press, Ltd., London

Library of Congress Cataloging-in-Publication Data

Baker, Houston A.
  Workings of the spirit : the poetics of Afro-American women's writing / Houston A. Baker, Jr. ; with a phototext by Elizabeth Alexander and Patricia Redmond
    p.   cm.—(Black literature and culture)
  Includes bibliographical references.
  ISBN 0-226-03522-0 (cloth)
    1. American literature—Afro-American authors—History and criticism. 2. American literature—Women authors—History and criticism. 3. Afro-American women—Intellectual life. 4. Women and literature—United States. 5. Afro-American women in literature. 6. Afro-Americans in literature. I. Alexander, Elizabeth. II. Redmond, Patricia. III. Title. IV. Series.
PS153.N5B28   1991
810.9'9287—dc20   90-41980
                                                                    CIP

⊗The paper used in this publication meets the minimum requirements of the American National Standard for Information Sciences—Permanence of Paper for Printed Library Materials, ANSI Z39.48–1984.

C O N T E N T S

*This book is dedicated in love
and deep admiration to my mother,
Viola Elizabeth Baker, who was the
first to instruct me in the spirit's work.*

. . . A hearing of Afro-American woman's voice, an embodying for our era of a unique inscription of the Afro-American self as woman.

Like the dead-seeming, cold rocks, I have memories within that came out of the material that went to make me. Time and place have had their say.

—Zora Neale Hurston

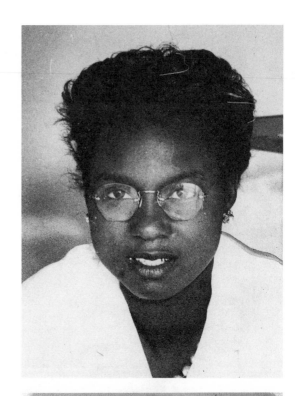

The Daughter's Departure: Theory, History, and Late-Nineteenth-Century Black Women's Writing

WE ARE ALWAYS embroiled with theory—even when the word itself is absent. It is an illusion to suppose that a non-theoretical subject position is possible. An inadequately, complacently, or self-deceptively *theorized* position: yes. But an untheoretical one: impossible. Our lives and works are always conditioned (if not overdetermined) by models that lead to definitions of the "I" who speaks for "me." These models do not simply rise to consciousness or arrive serendipitously and full-blown. (One reading—perhaps my own reading—of matters suggests that they only arrive unexpectedly as functions of specific autobiographical detailings. Certainly, they come, often, as the end of specific beginnings. At the conclusion of the present work I shall have more to say about the "I" and "me" of theoretical positions.) Theoretical models are always partial and shifting, tentative and reflexive, always hybrid installments on understanding. What would it signal to speak of *pure* Marxism? Or what would one intend by the phrase "uncorrupted deconstruction"? In addition to their omnipresence and multivalence, explanatory models are haunted by their own unoriginality—their communal necessity. If we are always embroiled with theory, we are never embroiled alone.

In our contemporary universe of literary studies, theory has competed with matters of gender and race for preeminence. Indeed, the decidedly political arrival of women and Afro-American studies, students, and faculty in the field of American literary and cultural studies has, I believe, occasioned our energetic contemporary quest for revised and more comprehensive theories. Afro-American women's expressivity and the analyses that it has prompted during the past two decades represent the most dramatically charged field for the convergence of matters of race, class, and gender today. And the material at hand is abundant, for in recent years there has emerged an indisputably brilliant cadre of black women writers. Their work has occasioned heated debates about race and gender. There has also emerged a remarkable community of Afro-American women critics and scholars to refine and theorize these lines of debate. The field constituted by Afro-American women writers and scholars, therefore, would seem patently to be one that not only demands theorization but also promises theorizations of race, class, and gender applicable at a general level.

But there has been a resistance to theory where Afro-American women's literary and cultural studies are concerned—a resistance that has come less from outside scholarly neglect or indifference than from the community of Afro-American women scholars, writers, and critics themselves. In part, this resistance is a warranted suspicion about the intentions of white men, white women, and black men who want "intellectually" to explain Afro-American womanhood and expressivity. Faced with such a prospect, black women might well experience the chill of Ole Sis Goose in Brer Fox's court. Their verbal response to the situation might echo Anna Julia Cooper's juridical report at the turn of the century: "The summing up of the evidence deposed, and the charge to the jury have been made—but no word from the Black Woman."[1]

Still . . . what if one were (hypothetically) to assume that not only are we always embroiled with theory but also that all have equal rights at the bar of theory? Then resistance would be less a justifiable response than a marked refusal to enter theoretical lists. Is this the case where Afro-American women's creativity and criticism are concerned? To a certain extent, I believe it is. The resistance, or refusal, makes the study of Afro-American women's expressivity both a charged and a demanding field of inquiry.

I come to the field in order to complete a critical trilogy that began with *Modernism and the Harlem Renaissance,*[2] a study followed by *Afro-American Poetics: Revisions of Harlem and the Black Aesthetic.*[3] My two previous works argue the inescapability of theory; they also develop an autobiographical sounding of Afro-American expressive culture predicated upon what I call "spirit work." The two studies that led to my present analysis of Afro-American women's writing began with my father and all the founding fathers who led to us. This study, however, is dedicated to my mother, and I hope, is coextensive with the work of a community of Afro-American
women scholars.

The quotidian rites of a black woman's passage through the world
(p. 63).

Theoretical engagement with Afro-American women's expressivity is scarcely a matter of mere personal choice for anyone who seeks a comprehensive understanding of literary and cultural studies. But, still, I do not want to convey the impression that I think of "theory" as an unforetold advance. Nor do I want to imply that I am a lone, original theoretical pioneer. Afro-American culture is, in a sense that I shall make clear, already advanced in theory. And I am scarcely alone, disconnected, or empirically isolated in my theoretical attention to Afro-American women's expressivity. Surely my efforts join those of many others with whom I shall now enter into dialogue.

What I wish to do at the outset of this study is to prepare the ground for an explicit treatment of theory and the poetics of Afro-American women's writing by assessing what seems to me the historical majority situation of current Afro-American women's literary criticism. Next, I want to read this situation as a reflex of turn-of-the-century Afro-American women's expressivity, which I analyze under a topos I have named "the daughter's departure." Let me turn first then to questions of originality and beginnings as a way of beginning.

~~~~~

In a postmodern world disillusioned with romantic individualism, a writer cannot hope to be either a lone pioneer or a bright original. Originality, in fact, under the impress of ideological analysis and European poststructuralism, reveals itself as a disguise—a veil shadowing myriad precedents, interconnections, and intertextual alliances. Where the criticism of Afro-American women's creativity is concerned, any new project is compelled to adknowledge an extensive field of influences.

These influences are constituted in the first instance by a strong line of Afro-American women's expressive production that includes handicraft, blues, culinary originality, quilting expertise, dynamic conjuring, brilliant oratory, superior storytelling, and belles lettres. Even if there had been no recent upheaval in cultural studies, a scholar dedicated to a project in Afro-American women's creativity would have found a basis within this tradition of production for formulating explanatory models.

Afro-American women artists—as opposed to self-differentiated critics, anthropologists, art historians, musicologists, and so forth—have always been a source of wisdom and practical insight about their own work. Literary critics, folklorists, and art historians are able to construct persuasive analyses of slave women's expressive culture, for example, because they can consult the narratives of slaves themselves— both artisans and audiences alike. Similarly, a present-day scholar of Toni Morrison's oeuvre has the author's own sophisticated critiques for guidance. In the world of Afro-American women's cultural practices, as in all cultural traditions, artists and artisans constitute a promising repository of critical and theoretical insight. Still, perhaps the most significant referential site for current scholarly projects is the prolific outpouring of commentary and criticism produced by the recently emergent community of professional, academic Afro-American women critics and theorists to which I have already alluded.

The names comprising this community are legion: Mary Helen Washington, Deborah McDowell, Nellie McKay, Barbara Christian, Hortense Spillers, Barbara Smith, Gloria Hill, Cheryl Wall, Valerie Smith, Hazel Carby, Mae Henderson, Gloria Wade Gayles, Thadious Davis, Trudier Harris, Frances Foster, Sherley Anne Williams, Joyce Joyce, Claudia Tate, and many others come instantly to mind. This list is, of course, only a selective one. It is indisputable, however, that the commentators represented on it have moved into the academy in recent years with amazing commitment and unstinting energy. They have challenged hegemonic patterns by insisting upon radically revised critical agendas and new pedagogical strategies. In addition, they have compiled anthologies, written books and articles, presented innumerable conference papers, and contributed endless consultative hours to promoting the understanding of Afro-American women's expressivity. *Sturdy Black Bridges, Home Girls, But Some of Us Are Brave, Midnight Birds, Blackeyed Susans, Invented Lives,* essays in leading periodicals, anthologized essays, probing interviews— these comprise but a selected representation of what this generation of academic critics has accomplished.[4] And such accomplishments gain in strength and relevance when we remember that they were a further realm added to the achievements in Afro-American women's cultural work that occurred under the aegis of the Black Arts Movement of the nineteen-sixties and early nineteen-seventies. The names and works of Toni Cade Bambara, Sonia Sanchez, Carolyn Gerald, Gwendolyn Brooks, Nikki Giovanni, Mari Evans, and others come to mind as forerunners for today's scholars. Today's scholars have extended their force further through coalitions with Anglo-American feminists. Together, these two constituencies have increased the availability of women's texts and enhanced the academic-political power of women. Coalition efforts have not been confined to Anglo-American mergers. *This Bridge Called My Back*[5] speaks eloquently, for example, of cross-cultural alliances between Afro-American and Third World women's political and expressive cultural concerns. Hence, a scholar who conceives a critical project in Afro-American women's creativity immediately feels the blessings of fellow travelers. There are now abundant textual resources[6] and an energetic community of scholars to consult.

~~~~~

But with blessings begins responsibility. The emergent community of Afro-American women scholars has implicitly issued its own manifesto in the form of admonitions, injunctions, and cautions to those who wish to share the open road. They have been liberally nonpartisan in such injunctions. All scholars who are not Afro-American women have been put on notice that new imperatives (new travel codes, as it were) are in effect, ones that can seldom be met by traditional or generally accepted models. White women scholars, for example, have been cautioned not to assume that their analytical canons developed for traditions of British and Anglo-American expressive culture are adequate for the study of black women's creativity. Alice Walker's condemnation of Patricia Meyer Spacks's *The Female Imagination* for the author's failure to include black women's work still dominates the stage where such matters are concerned.[7] And *This Bridge Called My Back* makes it abundantly clear that Afro-American women have joined Hispanic, Latino, and other Third World women in vigorously critiquing what they deem the exclusions and tactical misdirections of white, bourgeois feminism. Afro-American male critics have been warned by the Afro-American women's community to abandon such colonizing gestures as: (1) restricting participation of Afro-American women to token representation in conferences or on course syllabi; and (2) appropriating works or images of Afro-American women through a black, male "gaze": *viz.,* objectifying and commodifying black women for purposes of blackmale projects. (The use of the term "blackmale" serves to complement my employment of "whitemale" as a collective signifier. "Whitemale" gathers into its folds politics, history, ideology, and a visually-overdetermined field of racial discourse. For me it refers to a collective of human beings who are prismatically white and biologically self-identified as male and who feel entitled to brand all who are not like them as, in a word, "other." My experience of such collective "othering" began at an early age in a segregated city in the United States. I suspect that my experience mirrors that of millions of "others" around the globe. "Blackmale," by contrast, signals for me a site of an ever-present white offensive as well as the place of a necessary black self-inventiveness and self-defense. These terms have been used in those instances that seem to call forth such a collective response.)

In the world of Afro-American women's criticism, white men have generally suffered the fate that Toni Morrison ascribes to them at the hands of black women creative writers: they do not constitute a palpable focus.[8] "Palpable" is the key word here. For while there may be no *palpable* whitemale presence, there is often an implicit presence that marches in silent complicity with the texts of black women. To my knowledge, Barbara Smith's 1977 critique of whitemale hegemony in criticism—though more than a decade old—is still one of the boldest revisionary statements Afro-American women critics have produced.[9] In its advocacy of a specifically black, lesbian model of analysis, Smith's essay advertises its insurgent anomalousness. In counterpoint to her call, a majority of Afro-American women critics have employed traditional models of European, British, and Anglo-American male literary criticism. And this majority has usually remained silent about the complicity in hegemony implied by such tacit approval. A surprisingly small number of cautions, injunctions, and admonitions have been launched forcefully against whitemale intellectualdom.

What then is one to make of general road conditions for a blackmale scholar who wishes to journey in provinces of Afro-American women's expressivity? It seems fair to say that such a scholar can find a goodly share of company and useful information. He will also find cause to mind his steps in a demanding territory. I believe that the cautious anxieties of Afro-American women scholars as well as the blackmale scholar's necessity for caution are functions of the decidedly historical situation of Afro-American women's expressive cultural study since its recent academic emergence. Certainly, the anxieties of the majority of Afro-American women critics may be read as an almost inevitable reaction to the double founding in recent years of their scholarly project in the competing domains of Black Studies and Black Power.

On one hand, the Afro-American women's expressive cultural project can be read as a function of Black Power. In another reading, it can be thought of as an outgrowth of Black Studies. I want to suggest that the first site—Black Power—entails a relationship to what Hortense Spillers calls "the flesh."[10] This is a theoretical, minority position. The second site—Black Studies—contrasts with the first insofar as it signals an essentially historical relationship to the "body." Spillers gives resonance to these discriminations in her essay "Mama's Baby, Papa's Maybe: An American Grammar Book":

> But I would make a distinction in this case [of the slave trade] between "body" and "flesh" and impose that distinction as the central one between captive and liberated subject-positions. In that sense, before the "body" there is the "flesh," that zero degree of social conceptualization that does not escape concealment under the brush of discourse or the reflexes of iconography.

Spillers returns in her distinction via a metaphor of a seemingly essentialist cast to the moment before social erasure or appropriation of the African as an exchangeable body. Her return is both a considered figural risk and a canny challenge to culture. For her theoretical proposal invokes an African prehistory of European touch and opens dramatically a refigured Afro-American women's (and men's) subject position. I believe that her figurative energies recapitulate the revisionary discursive swerves executed more than a century ago by Frederick Douglass and his fugitive compeers moving through an American abolitionist grammar of "outside" and "in."

A standard feature of abolitionist meetings held indoors—frequently in churches and away from the quotidian signifying and busy passage of the world's signs—was what one commentator calls the "Negro exhibit."[11] The fugitive slave turned his back to the audience and displayed his wounds and scars from floggings at the stake of slavery. His or her body, in all of its marked and visible clarity of wounding, made affective the metaphors of moral suasion propounded by white abolitionists. The fugitive slave silently turned his back to the audience. The fugitive slave was a silent, partially naked body turning to a predominantly white audience. The silent, fugitive slave's body became an erotic sign of servitude in the social, liberational discourse of white abolitionists and their predominantly white audiences. Gasps and moans (of empathy? reassurance? relief?) followed.[12]

Douglass, like Harriet Tubman, Sojourner Truth, Harriet

Jacobs, and others was quick to realize that it was not by display, essentialist play, or bodily exhibition for private, indoor use that he could flesh out a tale of slavery. He—and other of his black compeers—came to understand that it was only through engagement with the public, symbolic order that he would be able to venture statements that would come legitimately to be defined as in/on the slaves' liberational behalf. By making themselves brilliantly ironic orators—self-reflexive masters of metaphor—Douglass and his fellow travelers were able to change the very definitions of both "social" and "public" in American life.

Refusing to speak Black English Vernacular as his white employers wished, Douglass assumed the dynamic role of black field-worker in the semantics of abolitionism. As he told the Massachussetts Antislavery Society, he wanted to craft and tell his own horrendous tale rather than serve as an illustration or mere exhibit in that society's inside tale-tellings. Eventually, he came to see that his alternatives were: inner silence or risky and resonant engagement with the inordinately complex significations of his era. Douglass's consciously crafted decision to become a floating signifier (like those ships he observed upon the Chesapeake as signs of freedom) carried him beyond abolitionist historical containment.

Valerie Smith offers an instance of the figurational possibilities that I have outlined for Douglass in her analysis of the work of another famous fugitive. Smith brings stunning insight to bear on Linda Brent's (Harriet Jacobs's) narrative entitled *Incidents in the Life of a Slave Girl*.[13] She asserts that Brent secured liberty by reversing and revising social and symbolic structures meant to confine her. The "slave girl," according to Smith, craftily contrived to slip from the stream of enslavement and the mainstream of literary conventions of her era: "From within her ellipses and ironies—equivalents of the garret in which she concealed herself for seven years—she [Brent] expresses the complexity of her experience as a black woman" (28). Brent's self-confinement and crafty choice of an "inadequate form" (the sentimental novel) for her experiences are, thus, converted to subversive acts of empowerment. The "slave girl," in effect, contests and revises conventions that would have kept her accessible to her master's lust, excluded from the Afro-American slave narrative's male heroics, and an anomaly in the chartings of the white (woman's) sentimental novel. In a word, Linda Brent converted her bodily confinement into expressive insurgency by working in the metaphorical interstices. One suspects that the energy that Smith as-

cribes to Brent is precisely the type of figurational power that
she recommends for those who want to enlarge the field of
Afro-American literary theory through considerations of
gender.[14] Out of ellipses and ironies, therefore, Smith, like
Spillers, summons a revisionary theoretical voice.

Spillers's decision to figure "the flesh"—like Douglass's
and Brent's decisions to get out—represents the siting that I
call *Black Power.* This "power," like all other power, is the
power of metaphor. Surely "Mama's Baby, Papa's Maybe,"
like Smith's analyses, represents one of the most interesting
refigurations of Afro-American womanist concerns to appear
in recent years. My citing of such exemplary work is not
meant as a gesture of either exclusion or appropriation. I do
not want to imply that there are no other examples or models
(such as the fine theorizing of Mae Henderson, Deborah
McDowell, or Cheryl Wall) available. Nor do I want to sub-
ordinate the work of Smith or Spillers to a narrowly self-
interested end. I cite their work out of deep admiration and
scholarly respect for the force it contributes to a siting of one
domain of Afro-American expressivity, one that I call Black
Power.

〜〜〜

If we return, however, to the inside, we encounter Black
Studies. I use this term as a marker for a discourse that seems
analogous in some ways to northern abolitionism. Abolitionism was a predominantly white reform movement made possible by the ever-fresh influx of black fugitives from the south.
In recent years in the United States, it was the new-left, academic radicals of the nineteen-sixties who welcomed a generation of black academicians (in from the cold) under the aegis
of Black Studies. Their welcome signaled a project and prospect very different from that of "the flesh."

Without fully rehearsing the history of the sixties and early
seventies, one might say that when a storm of law and order,
conservatism and right-wing reaction broke over America
two decades ago, a number of young liberationists retreated
into the shelter of the academy. Unlike their European counterparts who were battered by waves of reactionary State violence at approximately the same moment, America's academic
radicals did not set out intellectually to solicit the metaphysical foundations on which their country's symbols and rheto-
rics were perched. As a newly inside group, they resorted, for

the most part, to traditional American myths of pluralism and equal rights. (They adopted what Sacvan Bercovitch has termed a familiar form of American rhetorical and ideological *consensus*.)[15]

In the ears of this generation rang the sounds and songs of the Civil Rights Movement. In their mind's eye were images of confrontations between massed black demonstrators and assemblies of State police in myriad hamlets of America. Moved by these sounds and images, a generation of United States academic radicals made valiantly philanthropic efforts when Reverend Martin Luther King, Jr.'s assassination marked, unequivocally, the end of an era that gave promise of genuine equality. A new academic generation instituted "affirmative action" plans and gave its blessing to Black Studies.

Here is not the place to enter a critique of Black Studies under a more general critique of the historicizing defensiveness of a United States academy confronted with French antimetaphysics. It will suffice to say that the first impulse of the black men and women who came in from the cold with the new left to serve as drivers and students of Black Studies was to discover and expound *historical bases* for their right to subjecthood and subject status in university curricula. But even while Black and Women's Studies were being overpraised and underfunded in order to keep them plugging away at a grounded, linguistically clear, historical "excellence," an influential cadre of the whitemale academy turned to quite *nonhistorical* modes of theory and analysis.

My analogy for the state of affairs represented by this disjunctiveness (if not duplicity or hypocrisy vis-à-vis Black Studies) is the turn-of-the-century training of blacks for vocational/technical jobs that they could not possibly hope profitably to occupy in a segregated economy—an economy where even jobs that they were qualified for were rapidly becoming anachronistic. And it was at the very moment of what might be called Black Studies' historical double bind that Afro-American women's creative writing, criticism, and theory emerged. The founding era of Afro-American women's creativity and criticism was also the moment in which a generation of young blackmale poststructuralist critics (following the lead of white counterparts) became influential in the academy.[16] These blackmale literary critics had moved decisively to nonhistorical, theoretical modes of inquiry by the mid-seventies.

One interpretation of the intellectual succession implied by my brief account of early Black Studies moments suggests

that Afro-American male literary criticism and study, in effect, *displaced* Afro-American historical inquiry as an innovative scene of scholarship. But my account is not meant to
be so uncharitable. Certainly the efforts of historians such as
John Blassingame, Lawrence Levine, Nathan Huggins, Nell
Painter, Thomas Holt, Eugene Genovese, Winthrop Jordan,
Willie Lee Rose, George Rawick, and others provided insight
and grounds on which an emerging generation of black literary theorists built. But after the emergence of these theorists,
matters were irreversible; there could be no return, as it were,
to a *pure history*.

Hence a kind of critical lag marked the universe of discourse of Black Studies in the mid- to late-seventies. While
history and the body were of the essence of Afro-American
women's creativity and criticism, Afro-American male critics
and theorists were engaged in a furious battle of the signs—a
stormy passage to postmodernism that dropped many a Black
Historical, Black Arts, and Black Aesthetic male hero from
grace.

In criticism and theory, a first generation of Afro-
American women scholars began in the mid-seventies their
construction of a *historical* (as opposed to a "theoretical") basis
for subjecthood and curricular subject status. Though supported affectively by Women's Studies, Afro-American womanist endeavors found themselves primarily alone in the historical trenches—the proving ground and bastion of academic
defense for such verities as high seriousness, ease of comprehension, and "simplicity" and "clarity" of style. Afro-
American feminist scholars were praised and rewarded—
sometimes even by their sisters in Women's Studies—for
keeping the historical faith, for refusing to give way to the
complexities and demands of, say, deconstruction or other
theoretical modes of discourse. One might say that the historical situation of Afro-American women in Black Studies, as I
have described it, can be read as a latter-day instance of the
fugitive being asked to turn a scarred and essential back to a
white audience as proof both of the figutive's authenticity as
fugitive . . . and of the white audience's moral superiority and
intellectual complexity. The anxiety that such a situation entails is one of figural displacement. For what if conditions for
getting out of a comfortably essentialist and academically ap-
proved historical situation are precisely ones that returned the
historical occupant to a history that *hurts*—one that demands
not a mystifying self-certainty but an empowering, figural
self-renewal?

Confronted by such a choice—a choice that mandates rigorous, engaged, theoretically informed critiques of black and white male and white women's hegemonic self-certainties—a Black Studies majority is likely to follow the course of those who prefer not to *theorize*. I don't think this refusal in the instance of Afro-American women scholars represents an act of bad faith so much as a faithful refusal to act "bad": i.e., to figure forth and flesh out the funkiness that reveals a traditional and embodied history and historiography as the prison house of an inside containment.

By enforcing the methodically historical mode of Black Studies, the majority of Afro-American expressive cultural scholars have anxiously avoided all charges of, say, a libidinously inappropriate, or fleshly, theoretical offensive(ness). A stolidly scholarly and amply historical "body" has served to represent a new order of Afro-American women's intellectual (as opposed to, say, "fleshly") being. The irony of this embodiment is that it does not actually effect what it sets out to assure. For, regarded in its ironically willing subjection to historical incorporation, the majority becomes an appropriable site for a dominant tradition's discourse of desire. It is, finally, precisely such discourse that always masquerades (and marauds) as "history."

A reliance upon even a "modern" historiography in an ahistorical, postmodern world is equivalent, I believe, to Ole Sis Goose investing her juridical faith in Brer Fox's court. How many historical facts, examples, out-of-print texts will suffice radically to alter the rhetorical power ratios between Afro-American women's traditions and those of a white, theoretically dominant cohort? Although Afro-American advocates of a historical Black Studies positionality will be enthusiastically promoted and held up as examples by hegemonic discourses, such approbation based on theoretical silence can be no more than a cynical gesture of co-optive self-empowerment by the theoretically powerful. It suggests a scene in which Brer Fox assures Sis Goose that there is no need to worry herself about the finer points of Fox Law.

For Afro-American women's expressive cultural criticism to maintain an exclusively historical situation is for it to remain silently and complicitously accessible to the *touch* of Euramerican discourse. The metaphor for such a condition is represented as a theoretically silent body, as an exchangeable object of desire, or, in expressive terms, as a faint echo of her masters' voice. The refiguration of such grammars of desirous silence and historical echolalia are, I believe, the aim of Spillers and others of a Black Power disposition. The surest warrant for attributing such an aim is, of course, the nature of what I have called Black Power discourse itself.

~~~~~

In a sense, the Black Power or fleshly constituency—though in the minority—has taken a necessary step beyond the anxieties of subjecthood that worry, worry, worry about the approbation of a white other. They have refused to please, appease, or seek historical justification. And they have offered resonantly informed and imagistically reverberant portrayals of possibilities that lie beyond any received "history." The anxieties of the historical majority and their resultant injunctions to all and sundry are perhaps then, voicings of a last-instance, defensive protest. However, I believe this majority is composed of writers who are destined, despite their protest, not to repeat or to re-embody history, but to be catapulted beyond it through the figural energies of Black (theoretical) Power.

The intriguing aspect of the current situation in Afro-American women's expressive cultural study is that it so strikingly recapitulates the moments of pre- and postmodernity characterizing turn-of-the-century Afro-American women's expressivity. The desire of Afro-American women critics who comprise today's historical majority is not unlike that of turn-of-the-century Afro-American daughters who sought to incorporate themselves comfortably into an essentialist, northern, history. And the momentousness of theoretical returns upon the flesh that constitute Zora Neale Hurston's "modernity" (or "postmodernity," perhaps) is surely a precursor for today's theoretical minority. Hence, a survey of the nineteenth-century expressive terrain of the daughters' departure helps to clarify today's critical anxieties and inaugurates the present study's analytical mapping of Afro-American women's imagistic figurations of departure and return in American economies of desire.

~~~~~

Departure is a well-rehearsed configuration in a literature that commences with fugitives. Only a sentence or two is required to evoke its resonances. Harriet Jacobs's *Incidents in the Life of a Slave Girl* (1861) records the topos as follows:

The next day I was on the deck as soon as the day dawned. I called Fanny to see the sun rise, for the first time in our lives, on free soil; for such I *then* believed it to be. We watched the reddening sky, and saw the great orb come up slowly out of the water, as it seemed . . . We looked at each other, and the eyes of both were moistened with tears. We had escaped from slavery, and we supposed ourselves to be safe from the hunters.[17] (163–64)

Fanny, the daughter of Old Aggie (a tenant on the property of Linda Brent's grandmother), and Brent herself have revised Douglass's mere "gaze" at ships on the Chesapeake. They have actually sailed those waters to the harbors of Philadelphia. But in the chapter following their sunrise encomium, Reverend Jeremiah Durham of Philadelphia's Bethel Church conveys to Brent the conditions of the black woman's northern, discursive options. When she tells the story of her concubinage and childbearing out of wedlock, Reverend Durham responds:

"Excuse me, if I have tried your feelings . . . I did not question you from idle curiosity. I wanted to understand your situation, in order to know whether I could be of any service to you, or your little girl. Your straightforward answers do you credit; but don't answer every body so openly. It might give some heartless people a pretext for treating you with contempt." (166)

Brent's response: "That word *contempt* burned me like coals of fire." She is completely undone. Unable to talk, she goes wearily to bed. A sleep of silence ensues.

The question that rises from this scene of silencing is: What tale can the daughters tell without incurring *contempt?* Male fugitives like Douglass can represent themselves in their narratives as participants in moments of successful northern industry and heroic abolitionist oratory. Brent, by contrast, can only become—and this by the best of fortunes—a surrogate mother and maid to a kindly white New York family named Bruce. Douglass is named in the North for a Scottish hero; Brent becomes a domestic to *the Bruces.* The energy and subversion of the slave girl's cunning letters in the South are reduced to an orderly record of indignities encountered at sites catalogued during her travels in the North. We have a literate *Our Nig,* without the more brutal physical assaults.[18]

The community of women—black and white, mistresses and

slaves, cooks, healers, and concubines—so energetically drawn by Brent in the South disappears; it is replaced by a company of white patronesses and black domestics. To an extent that perhaps even Brent (Jacobs) herself would have been reluctant to confess, it is precisely a fear of *contempt* from such white patronesses as the wives of Mr. Bruce that conditions the texts of the daughters' departure.

Incidents states its goal as arousal—"to arouse the women of the North." What better tale for such arousal than one of concubinage unredeemed by marriage—sexual taboo violated without the expiation of death? Such arousal represents more than simple embodiment. It is embodiment with a purpose. *This,* it seems to declare, my historicized body is given unto you as a willed object of exchange.

The return upon this fugitive investiture is aid, forgiveness, and acknowledgment by white women of the North that the storyteller and her Afro-American sisters have evolved beyond a black, southern bestiality. White desire wants only the flash dance of the scarred black body; the dance should be followed by an altogether domestic tranquillity. There is, thus, no white audience demand for a resonant fleshing or figuring out of the black body's story. A dance of the veils, then, keeps the black body's drama distanced. The only desirable presence is a domesticated one. And the affective consequences of even this presence are physically problematic. One thinks, for example, of Miss Ophelia's tactile aversion in *Uncle Tom's Cabin* to even a sanitized and penitent Topsy. The issue here with respect to the Afro-American daughters is one of audiences and authorial sitings.

When Brent first tells her story of concubinage, her audience is an eponymous "reader": "And now, reader, I come to a period in my unhappy life, which I would gladly forget if I could. The remembrance fills me with sorrow and shame" (54). This telling ends with the narrator's own evaluation and judgment of her conduct: ". . . I feel that the slave woman ought not to be judged by the same standards as others" (56). Despite this superbly courageous endorsement of situational ethics, *Incidents* waffles with respect to "white women of the North." There is no scene, for example, in which Brent confesses her story of concubinage to the first Mrs. Bruce. Rather, it is Mrs. Bruce's intelligent conversation and her provision of opportunities for the fugitive to read—combined with the black woman's own growing affection for her white infant charge—that cement an affectional, intellectual bond between the northern white mistress and the black northern domestic. There is no great space here for tales of concubinage and resistance, conjure and southern women's community. Jacobs maintains "reader" interest by ignoring the fact that her son and daughter are entirely free—manumitted by Mr. Sands's purchase of them and his bestowal of their certificates of manumission before Brent departs the South. But the fugitive slave Jacobs secures the Mrs. Bruces' interest—in a strictly fiduciary sense of the term—by refusing to return to or to dwell figuratively upon the conditions of productivity and expression that have secured her northern mistresses' "readerly" and philanthropic interest in the first place. Rather than a more liberated teller of a southern story, Brent becomes a passive reader of white women's texts; this black domestic reading acts as a sign of the fugitive's *non-contemptible* northern gentility. Brent seems, therefore, self-consciously to depart from the role of subversive and communally oriented *writer* that she so effectively assumed in the South.

During months of correspondence with her white patron and eventual editor, Lydia Maria Child, Harriet Jacobs knew that the most arresting and significant actions of the majority of blacks in the United States were unfolding in the South. But these actions we grasp only by indirection; they constitute only a shadow text from distant provinces in the last third of *Incidents*. Finally, it is Brent/Jacobs as a northern domestic paragon and not even her historicized shadow text that is literally *bought* by the second Mrs. Bruce. Though Brent says she feels only contempt for herself (for her complicity in chattel economics) and for a country that endorses slavery, Jacobs, as author, is not reluctant to conclude her narrative on triumphal notes of purchased and freed mother/child bonding: "I and my children are now free!" And at the same instant there are: "Love, duty, gratitude . . . [that] bind me to . . . [Mrs. Bruce's] side. It is a privilege to serve her who pities my oppressed people, and who has bestowed the inestimable boon of freedom on me and my children" (207). The dissonance between *being* free and having freedom *bestowed* is, at least, the conflict between the flesh and the body. A domestic's freedom is, perhaps, always a bestowal on the body. The *being* of freedom resides, by contrast, in an insistent figurative return upon the flesh, a return in which mothers' and grandmothers' texts are resonant. There is, however, no genealogical textuality at the conclusion of *Incidents*. There is only a sentimental and naturalizing amnesia: "[T]ender memories of my good old grandmother [come to me] like light, fleecy clouds floating over a dark and troubled sea." And: "I would gladly forget . . . ['dreary years I passed in bondage'] if I could" (208).

My return in this critique of Brent to a mulatto aesthetics

is not intended as a facile condemnation of "bourgeois" black authors. It is not, of course, meant to recuperate either Robert Bone's condescension toward turn-of-the-century Afro-American texts or Addison Gayle's black aesthetic condemnation of them *tout d'un coup*. Rather, I am concerned to figure forth the seemingly insistent desire for the FATHER that finds its way into the discourse of the colonized. Cultural production under the sign of the FATHER always lives a politically contingent life. Nineteenth-century Afro-American texts that are now being reissued and lavishly praised for their "cultural" merit are often the very texts that during the past century of Afro-American intellectual discourse have been placed under assimilationist quarantine. Why have such bans been lifted today? One answer is that they have been lifted in order to provide a historical lineage for late-twentieth-century Afro-American women's subjecthood. However, actual violence against such subjecthood is precisely what these newly circulating texts often seek so forcefully to transform into marks of beautiful distinction. Present-day critics and theorists of turn-of-the-century texts frequently go everywhere in their commentary but to the texts themselves as they seek grounds for fulsome evaluations. Finally, these critics are trapped, I think, by a law of historical conservatism. They are caught up, that is to say, in saving a literarily textualized "past" because they, like the turn-of-the-century daughters, willfully refuse to conceptualize a southern, vernacular ancestry as a site of both consuming violence and discrete value. My working hypothesis is that only by "speaking on" the FATHER's violence and the cultivated transvaluation of African value that it occasions in the northern daughters' texts can we make a return upon the flesh. There are, to be sure, other strategies. But uncritical, historically conservative revivalism simply reinvests the capital of patriarchal production in a bankrupt fund. The idea of my present critique is to begin a new account.

Of course, there can be no forgetting the grim details of so many incidents in the brutal life that Jacobs narrates; they form the crux of the first two-thirds of *Incidents*. Nonetheless, the picture of departure is an evolutionary one. There is veritably a new order of northern being that embodies itself as a literate, historically verifiable, black progress. Dignified womanhood, socially acceptable companionship, moral rectitude, intelligent converse, fidelity to job descriptions, patriotism, racial awareness, missionary zeal on behalf of the benighted southern sectors of the race—this is a loose, arbitrary set of characteristics describing a new embodiment of black

life in the North. It certainly cannot be viewed with contempt. While Brent's text merely adumbrates such characteristics, Pauline Hopkins's *Contending Forces* (1900) figures them
forth in full detail.[19]

In *Contending Forces,* the drama of the British Montforts'
tragic fate at the hands of South Carolina vigilantes is, we are
assured, old history. In the novel, the Montfort drama serves
merely to set bloodlines of mulatto adventure flowing. Shadowy southern moments of blood-violence and vicious white
crackerdom recede. They are reflected, finally, only on the
brow and in the evil heart of John P. Langley. They are also
recalled briefly in Lycurgus (Luke) Sawyer's fiery speech that
provides ancestral keys to Sappho Clark's origins. (Lycurgus?
Sappho? We seem to witness not only a new, but also a classical order of black, northern being.)

If the first consequence of departure is a shadowing of the
South, then a second is the ironic transmutation of the mark,
sign, and act of concubinage (read: "rape") into a symbolic
black code of beauty, grace, intelligence, and historically embodied prominence. In *Contending Forces,* Sappho Clark enters
a room crowded with respectable churchgoing black north-
erners:

> With modest self-possession she moved to Mrs.
> Smith's side, and soon found herself being presented to
> the occupants of the parlor. For a moment or two there
> was an unbroken hush in the room. Tall and fair, with
> hair of a golden cast, acquiline nose, rosebud mouth,
> soft brown eyes veiled by long, dark lashes which
> swept her cheek, just now covered with a delicate rose
> flush, she burst upon them . . . (107)

Burst, indeed, Sappho does—bearing no sulfurous taint of the
southern whitemale hell in which she was repeatedly raped,
first by a step uncle, and then by others. Burst she does, ov-
erawing the room, looking for all the world like a very "white
woman of the North" herself. " 'Lord,' said Ophelia Davis to
her friend Sarah Ann, 'I haven't see enything look like thet
chile since I lef' home' " (107). The black and comedic (virtually minstrel) laundresses are overwhelmed by the bright irradiance of Sappho—a Sappho whose name does not refer
textually to anomalous sexual proclivities, but only, one assumes, to a classical mastery of the word. Ironically, such
mastery for a mulatto woman in nineteenth-century Boston
does not yield an island poet, but a clerk typist. Still, Sappho
is resplendent. And so, too, is her landlady, Mrs. Smith:

Thick bands of snowy hair, falling in natural waves,
were curled closely at the back of a well-shaped head.
Her clear olive complexion contrasted pleasantly with
eyes large, soft, and black, heavy black eyebrows and
long curling lashes. An acquiline nose, thin lips and
delicately shaped ears gave her a very pleasing countenance. (369)

The sign of white, patriarchal hegemony is recuperated by
the departed daughters as a "pleasing" set of features. The
shadowy story of a brutalizing South can, in fact, be read in
the mulatto's "countenance." But the interpretetive judgment
of this shadowed narrative is a black northern fondness, awe,
approbation, and approval.

Professor Hazel Carby's *Reconstructing Womanhood: The
Emergence of the Afro-American Woman Novelist* presupposes a
rather more Kantian view of the daughters' literary act than
my own reading.[20] *Reconstructing Womanhood*'s analyses are
based on deep-contextual, authorial intentionality rather than
on actual literary consequences. Assuming the mulatto as a
medium of interracial mediation, Carby infers a great deal
more social effect and liberating reader response from the
works of Pauline Hopkins, Frances E. W. Harper, and others
than their actual reception histories seem to warrant. The case
that Carby constructs for turn-of-the-century daughters is,
thus, predicated more on a golden humanistic mean of critical
behavior than upon a theory of liberational, expressive empowerment for Afro-American women.

Subjecthood in the nineteenth-century daughters' texts
comes to imply, it seems to me, more than simply a literate
mediational voice; it finally comes to mean an implicit approval of white patriarchy inscribed in the very features of the
mulatto character's face. The nineteenth-century daughters'
departure recapitulates, then, the dynamics of the daughters'
seduction. Undone by an uncle, Sappho first gets herself to a
nunnery, but in *Contending Forces,* she eventually marries the
Harvard- and Heidelberg-educated mulatto Will Smith. Will
is a W. E. B. DuBois look-alike, *sans* radical politics. At a
public meeting held in response to a southern lynching, he
speaks as follows:

> "My friends, it is going to take time to straighten out
> this problem; it will only be done by the formation of
> public opinion. Brute force will not accomplish any-
> thing. We must *agitate.* As the anti-slavery apostles
> went everywhere, preaching the word fifty years be-
> fore emancipation, *so must we do to-day.*" (272)

In Will's call for gradualism and agitation, we grasp what is, perhaps, the most significant consequence of the daughters' departure. The suppression of southern horror and the transmutation of patriarchal seduction into a new, classical species of intelligent colored life are, finally, in the service of the cultivation of *an approving white public opinion*. The daughters' departure is, thus, a propaganda topos for a progressive historical reading of African life in America. The topos is sent forth into the world (to paraphrase Richard Wright's "Blueprint for Negro Writing") as a courteous ambassador—or, a trial balloon.[21] Brent arises from her sleep of silence dedicated to a type of white-faced minstrelsy that, she hopes, will forestall contempt.

"Let us show you what a show we can put on in whiteface," seems to be the daughters' prelude. While the blackfaced minstrel stage and its archetypes and icons were thriving at the turn of the century, the daughters countered with their own whiteface revels, designed, presumably, to rouse *anyone* who might lend aid in the North to what Brent calls "a realizing sense of the condition of two million women at the South, still in bondage, suffering what I suffered, and most of them far worse" (xiv). The daughters' strategy shares a history with Booker T. Washington's manipulations of minstrel discourse. But it is to be distinguished from Washington's mastery of form insofar as it refuses the split-subject position that comes from inhabiting the black-faced minstrel mask. For the nineteenth-century daughters chose, finally, a moralizing and discursively subservient disguise. Perhaps the distinction between *their* makeup and the mastery of form can be represented by the space between fiercely straightened hair and dreadlocks disguised as pickaninny plaits.

Contending Forces stages a show of Colored Women's Clubs and committed church communities acquiring property, expressing social concern, paying mortgages. There are accommodating and altogether self-sacrificial black southern educators like Arthur Lewis, who is joined in his service by Will's sister Dora. There are judges and even mulatto British M.P.s to inspire confidence in a new northern race in whiteface. Moreover, there is a narrative energy and topical comprehensiveness in *Contending Forces* that make the novel a virtual curiosity cabinet of its era. Phrenology, racial politics, Klondike gold discoveries, British manumission, feminism, occultism, and myriad other topics make the pages bristle. It is as though the narrative mind of the text wishes to sound its repleteness,

its comprehensive intelligence as a fit complement for the

Photographer's caption: "Aunt Susan frying—two pots kept going."

novel's whitened faces. The admixture is intriguing, even if it fails finally to provide a purchase on ameliorative strategies for the "contending forces" said to be ruining the Negro in America: "conservatism, lack of brotherly affiliation, lack of energy for the right and the power of the almighty dollar which deadens men's hearts to the sufferings of their brothers" (256).

Finally, Hopkins's rendering of the daughters' departure is a courtesy book for a new era. Robert O'Meally claims, in a fine essay devoted to Douglass's *Narrative,* that the fugitive's text was "meant to be preached." [22] After Dora Smith has delivered herself of a short speech on the necessity for judging all sisters according to Christian codes of forgiveness, Sappho responds: "You are a dear little preacher . . . and if our race ever amounts to anything in this world, it will be because such women as you are raised up to save us" (101). On this northern rock of departure, the Afro-American nineteenth-century daughters erected their didactic church. Their gospel is strict moral rectitude, white-faced mannerliness, and black northern achievement.

Hopkins does not ignore the South altogether. Madame Frances (as alter ego and guardian for Sappho's child) is very much a prophetic presence in the novel—a "spiritualist soothsayer and marvellous mind-reader" (197). Further, Hopkins seasons her mulatto stew with the high jinks of Mrs. Ophelia and Dr. Abraham Peters—a "magnetic physician." But at the text's conclusion, it is mulattos in service to a higher spirituality who are traveling, not South to redeem the masses, but to Europe to establish an institution in the Old World for the training of colored men. Even Dr. Lewis joins some readers of *Contending Forces* in the opinion that Will Smith's project is "Chimerical and quixotic" (389).

〜〜〜

Historically, of course, there was a great deal of quixoticism in the ranks of that army of Afro-American women who formed clubs, ran newspapers, lobbied, agitated, and fought valiantly for a new black woman's subjecthood at the turn of the century. In *When and Where I Enter: The Impact of Black Women on Race and Sex in America,* Paula Giddings writes:

> A profile of 108 of the first generation of [Afro-American] clubwomen revealed that most had been born in the South between 1860 and 1885 and had moved north before the mass migration of the late

nineteenth century. Historian Carter G. Woodson observed that the group of Blacks who left the south in
the earlier period were among the most talented. Many
of the clubwomen had been reared to respect discipline, thrift, and piety—values that were confirmed by
their teachers, in many instances imbued with New
England Missionary zeal. About 67 percent of the
clubwomen were teachers themselves.[23]

Names like Ida Wells-Barnett, Mary Church Terrell, Margaret Murray Washington, Olivia Davidson, and others signal
the power of the clubwomen's movement in the United States
and make clear the strength that led to its motto: "Lifting
as We Climb." According to historian Evelyn Brooks-
Higginbotham, the uplift provided or dreamed by Baptist
women's organizations came as a "gospel of education, cleanliness, and Victorian morality. They conducted mothers'
training schools, women's meetings, and mothers' conferences among poorer ex-slave women, in order to teach
'proper' childrearing and marital duties."[24]

The intended recipient of such services was a black majority population in the south—a majority under siege at the turn
of the century by brutal economic, legal, and psychological
forces that led Vernon Logan to define the era as "the nadir"
of race relations in America. In *Labor of Love, Labor of Sorrow,*
the historian Jacqueline Jones writes:

> By the end of the nineteenth century, nine out of ten
> Afro-Americans lived in the south, and 80 percent of
> these resided in rural areas, primarily in the formerly
> slave Cotton Belt . . . In 1910 fully nine-tenths of all
> southern blacks who made their living from the soil
> worked as tenants, sharecroppers, or contract la-
> borers.[25]

Under the impoverished circumstances marked by this description, those "millions" of black women foreshadowed by
Brent and addressed by middle-class black clubwomen were
required, in a phrase, to make a way out of no way. Setting up
households in filthy, cramped tenant shacks with no money in
hand, children to feed, and virtually no material possessions,
these *millions* were compelled—for the sake of survival—to
do "a man's share in the field, and a woman's part at home"
(Jones, 85).

Faced with "the nadir," it scarcely seems anomalous that
black clubwomen interposed their version of a social gospel
between an utter black despair, on one hand, and a sublime

white indifference on the other. Seizing the mantle of their tutelage in New England cleanliness, godliness, and duty, they preached and ministered to those furthest down. They combined their social gospel with a politics of agitation which they hoped would lead to the formation of sympathetic white public opinion.

But if the daughters as clubwomen in a woman's era were moved—no matter how chimerically—to an actional form of didacticism, their era counterparts as authors were unable to produce more than a preacherly shadow text of the nadir. Which is to say: a nineteenth-century black women's vernacular southern culture in the heroism of its economic survival, and then in the resonances of its quilts, gardens, conjuration, supper-getting-ready songs, churched melodies, woven baskets of Charleston wharves, and culinary magnificence, is a *great absence* in the texts of the escaped, northern daughters *as authors*. The virtues of the vernacular—in its multifaceted textuality and "forms of things unknown"[26]—are obscured by the overwhelming question (a haunting and redacted query of *concubinage*): "Are black women who are not northern, in whiteface, and bearing Greek attributes capable of moral virtue?" Summoning to view black southern mothers—even in their gardens or at the frames of their patchwork quilts—was for the daughters at the turn of the century taboo. For such a summons could only evoke a place of inescapable erring and difficulty whose representation might well bring *contempt* and not the fiercely sought sympathetic white public opinion. Hence, rather than return to a southern place, the daughters chose to dream dreams and project visions of a universal white-faced American *noplace*—a mulatto utopia.

One questions, though, how many utopian generations might be required to whiten the black masses of women to the point where they could enter this imagined utopia as Sappho, or as Iola Leroy? Ophelia Davis in *Contending Forces* and Aunt Linda in *Iola Leroy*[27] are not hopeful signs of such impending entry by the darker masses:

> Aunt Linda: "How did I know yer? By dem mischeebous eyes, ob course. I'd knowed yer if I had seed yer in Europe."
> Robert Johnson: "In Europe, Aunt Linda? Where's that?"
> Aunt Linda: "I don't know, I specs its some big city somewhar." (153)

Of course, in Frances Harper's *Iola Leroy,* from which this exchange is quoted, women in general—save the heroine and her brother's dark-complexioned helpmeet—do not fare well on the field of intelligence:

> Eugene Leroy:"Yes, Marie, let them [the children, Iola and Harry] stay North. We seem to be entering on a period fraught with great danger. I cannot help think and fearing that we are on the eve of a civil war."
> Marie: "A civil war!" [she] exclaimed with astonishment. "A civil war about what?"

~~~~~

Of course, the daughter Iola can escape such womanly stupidity and backwardness and get on with the construction of a mulatto utopia. Poor self-sacrificial, dialect-speaking Tom says of Iola: "My! but she's putty. Beautiful long hair comes way down her back; putty blue eyes, an' jis ez white ez anybody's in dis place. I'd jis wish you could see her yoresef" (38). We are told that Tom worships Iola, whose freedom he secures, "[a]s a pagan might worship a distant star" (40).

Yes, and that is rather the story for us all in respect to *Iola Leroy* the novel. Like low-spirited realists, we view its endless pages of exposition and lofty sentiment—its creakingly mechanical and entirely predictable plot—with a kind of detached wonder, knowing that its author was both abolitionist lecturer and journeyer in the South. And we can only grasp the "behold the star" quality of the text and not quite believe in it other than as a less engaging version of the daughters' departure than *Contending Forces*.

Iola Leroy's true ideal is not the offspring of Eugene and Marie, but Robert Johnson—the standard-English-speaking, clever mulatto youth whom we encounter at the beginning of the book. Robert eventually becomes the Duke, as it were, of C＿＿ (*sic*), North Carolina. He is the white patriarch as mulatto—a new organizer of the former slaves. Like Will Smith's of *Contending Forces,* his is the chimerical plan concluding the novel: The in-progress transformation of former slaves will be completed under Robert's largesse in a communal dukedom. This dukedom will be a utopian southern place where Iola and her brilliant physician husband, Dr. Latimer (a mulatto, of course), will ensure education and health. Rejecting her white physician suitor, Dr. Gresham (who balks at the idea of mulatto offspring), Iola sets her future among colored people of the South.

Finally, *Iola Leroy* describes no significant orbit. It begins and ends in C_____, North Carolina. Its energy resides in its status as a forum. Characters do not act, they talk—endlessly. They stage debates and even *conversazione* on, primarily, economic, political, and social aspects of the race question in America. What emerges from their polemics—in addition to a call for racial uplift—is an essentially conservative appeal to white public opinion.

Harper, like Hopkins, can be considered the author of a courtesy book intended for white reading and black instruction. While Dr. Gresham is a whitemale advocate for literacy and the power of the pen, it is, finally, merely an extended form of abolitionist moral suasion that carries the weight of *Iola Leroy.* Like *Contending Forces,* Harper's text seems bent on winning approval by embodying a subjecthood that has little reflective power at a mass black southern, vernacular level. Aunt Linda as the chief black woman and southern spokesperson spends most of her words comically condemning the tomfoolery of her people, whom she labels "niggers." The novel speaks of a movement from the "old oligarchy of slavery into the new commonwealth of freedom" (271), but the scene looks a lot like *Cabin in the Sky,* overseen "after de War" by industrious mulattos. There seems altogether too much William Lloyd Garrison and too little Marx, Freud, DuBois, or Washington in *Iola Leroy.*

The quest for subjecthood in what seemed to turn-of-the-century black women writers a new era of freedom was not a simple matter, and the search for an effective historical embodiment of the *black-woman-as-subject* was equally problematic. Standing under the whiteman's historic burden of concubinage and the silence enforced where such matters were concerned, black women creators were hard-pressed for a credible subject position. Linda Brent writes:

> The secrets of slavery are concealed like those of the Inquisition. My master was, to my knowledge, the father of eleven slaves. But did the mothers dare to tell who was the father of their children? Did the other slaves dare to allude to it, except in whispers among themselves? No, indeed! They knew too well the terrible consequences. (34)

Taking up residence in the North, the departed daughters of such silence attempted to avoid the weight of an "old oligarchy" by founding a new voice and image. Unfortunately, their articulations echoed preeminently the didactic embodiments of white abolitionism, ignoring black southern sound-

ings, preferring instead a soothing mulatto utopianism. Economics, politics, sociology, and even religion were left out of
account. In their place, the daughters inserted a bright Victorian morality in whiteface.

~~~~~

But, then, there is the crown jewel of these turn-of-the-
century black women's attempts at subjecthood. It is represented by Anna Julia Cooper's *A Voice from the South by a Black
Woman of the South* (1892).[29] Cooper's text seems in its title to
promise a sharp swerve from the almost exclusively New England ethics that blow like drafts from Graylock through *Contending Forces* and *Iola Leroy*.

A Voice is clearly the work of a member of DuBois's "Talented Tenth." Its author is at ease with Latin, German, science, mathematics, Matthew Arnold, and the classics. She is
as familiar with the work of Andrew Crummell as with that
of Sappho. In many respects, she is a full match for the founding editor of *The Crisis*. *A Voice* differentiates itself from the
work of Harper and Hopkins in its clear attention to the "Colored Girls of the South." "Oh, save them, help them, shield,
train, develop, teach, inspire them," the text pleads (24–25).
Frankly taking up issues of concubinage and lynching,
Cooper makes an appeal on behalf of a beleaguered black
southern womanhood.

On initial view, then, it seems the daughters' departure
must be credited with at least one found voice of protest, as
distinguished from genteel syllables of moral suasion. Finally,
though Cooper is less interested in specific lines and features
of black southern womanhood than in a general, essentialist
set of claims on behalf of True Woman: "[W]hile we do not
unfrequently see women who reason, we say, with the cool-
ness and precision of a man, and men as considerate of help-
lessness as a woman, still there is a general consensus of man-
kind that the one trait is essentially masculine and the other is
peculiarly feminine. That both are needed to be worked into
the training of children, in order that our boys may supplement their virility by tenderness and sensibility, and our girls
may round out their gentleness by strength and self-reliance"
(60–61). Cooper is so absorbed with this dual, essentialist
symmetry of masculine/feminine that she extends it to all
walks of life. America, she argues, in a rhetorical act of sheer
perversity, *needs* a race problem in order to avoid the domi-
nance and deterioration that result in cultures when a single

racial ideal holds sway. America needs the subject position and voice of Anna Julia Cooper because her testimony represents a complementary and, as yet, unheard black woman's voice.

And her voice is one that surely devastates William Dean Howells's *An Imperative Duty* for that novel's myopic assumption that a polite mulatto woman would find no suitable companionship among any given assembly of black people. Cooper's is also a voice that easily assumes the New England actuarial exactness and authority of a customhouse and delivers a costs/benefits analysis of the Afro-American situation. The voice is an ironic, informed, caustic, engaging, intimidating witness by a District of Columbia wizard. What precisely it is not, however, is "a voice from the South."

Unlike Aunt Linda, Anna Cooper *knows* exactly where Europe is and mines its stores for all they rhetorically are worth. Her intellectual hauteur is as apparent as her *contempt* for, say, the mass religion of southern black folk. Listen to her voice: "Thinking colored men almost uniformly admit that the Protestant Episcopal Church with its quiet, chaste dignity and decorus solemnity, its instructive and elevating ritual, its bright chanting and joyous hymning, is eminently fitted to correct the peculiar faults of worship—the rank exuberance and often ludicrous demonstrativeness of their people. Yet, strange to say, the Church, claiming to be missionary and Catholic, urging that schism is sin and denominationalism inexcusable, has made in all these years almost no inroads upon this semi-civilized religionism" (34). So much for "organic intellectual" claims for this "voice from the South."

Cooper's is the voice of a strong, feminist advocacy; it is at its best in the ironic mode—especially in its biting critique of the white women's movement. While *A Voice* provides an acerbic narrator worthy of the company of Mary Church Terrell, however, the work remains an essentialist compendium, implying that an affective, intellectual mulattoization of "the Race" is an altogether desirable goal. At heart, Cooper is not a DuBoisian but a Washingtonian. Episcopalianism and manual labor are her recommendations for the souls of black folk. These are to be overseen by a blackmale elite, who, in the preservation of a staid symmetry, will receive instructions in *mercy* from their college-bred wives.

~~~~~

The daughters have gone. They have set up residence in the North. Their departure is recorded as an essentialist, historicizing moment in whiteface. Their departure recuperates an abolitionist, pre–Civil War moment at exactly the nadir of American race relations—an epoch when all vestiges of anti-slavery sentiment are under erasure among policy-making whites. The daughters' departure is, thus, a religio-humanist misreading of events rather than an energetic refiguration meant for tricky, Gilded Age times. But can one lose sight of the fact that works such as *Contending Forces, Iola Leroy,* and *A Voice from the South* were the sole on-shelf alternatives to whitemale signs that advised: "Nigger, read this and run!"[30] No, we should never forget that the author rolls of Afro-American are seldom overfull.

Furthermore, it seems advisable to look upon the daughters' departure as instructive. First, we must consider the inescapable question of influence, noting, for example, that both Nella Larsen and Jessie Fauset—well-known Harlem Renaissance authors—are bone of the bone descendants of their departed turn-of-the-century precursors.

Larsen and Fauset operate a transformation of the daughters' mulatto utopia under the sign "passing." Rather than a vision of communal, white-faced self-containment and race leadership, the Harlem Renaissance writers experiment with the narrative possibilities of moving even closer to the patriarchal source of concubinage. They dream of redeeming "shame" in the name and under the flag of *(in)corporated white rights.* While the phrase is a complex substitute for "passing," it signals, I believe, the genuine complexity of Larsen's and Fauset's authorial decisions to release the mulatto woman from a round of clubwomen's honorifics, rural teaching, European exile, and clerk typery. Their decisions required, at least, a more syntactically complex discourse than the mere term "passing" seems to suggest.

The narrative courses of Helga Crane, Clare Kendry, Angela Murray of, respectively, *Quicksand, Passing,* and *Plum Bun* represent adventurous attempts by Fauset and Larsen to stretch a white patriarchal envelope of American meanings.[31] But the risks of such attempts are signaled by the protagonists' final statures. Helga becomes an infidel and voluntaristic invalid. Clare dies. Angela is in European exile at the conclusion of her tale, in the company of her own Luke Sawyer, named in *Plum Bun* Anthony Cross (or Cruz).

The mulattoization of Afro-American that marks the daughters' departure, thus, gives way to the novel of "passing."[32] The movement from one to the other is not, however, overly encouraging. Black southern vernacular energies remain an absence.

Yet, there is some advance. Helga, Clare, and Angela—

unlike their predecessors—seek less to court white public opinion than to sample it. *Quicksand, Passing,* and *Plum Bun* are not so much "and when . . . ," or utopian projections, as "what if . . ." texts—provocative dancings at the very borders of social and sexual taboo. If abolitionism operates the discourse of a first daughterly generation, then desire operates a second. The unity of the two consists in their common appeal to a presumed white *goodwill.* Their unity, in this respect, would seem to suggest a common naïveté in response to possible *contempt.*

For one is never "incidentally," "adventurously," or "utopianly" mulatto. And it is not *goodwill* that erases the "shame" occasioned by the mulatto's appearance in a white audience or that transforms that appearance itself into an effective prognostication of nonracial utopias.

"White public opinion" may well be soothed by the mulatto's embodied ambassadorship, but it will never be effectively *moved* to more than sentimental tolerance. And that very tolerance disappears if the mothers' southern texts are summoned figuratively to view. What remains absent, then, in the daughters' texts, as I have already indicated, is a fleshing out of both the southern, vernacular, communal expressivity of black mothers and grandmothers, *and* a portrayal of the relentless whitemale hegemony—the very site of violence—that threatened ceaselessly to eradicate such expressivity.

"Mulatto," in a word, is a sign of the legitimacy and power of—in its American instance—whitemale patriarchy: an economically, politically, and socially maintained authority. That authority is so high, low, and wide that there is no easy evasion of it, and its door is marked: "For white men only." "Goodwill" has no place whatsoever in this architecture.

A critique of the proto-situation of Afro-American women commences, then, not with a departure that leads to the valorization of mulatto signs of concubinage and high hopes for white approbation. Nor can it begin with a projection of onanistic fantasies played out with Axle Olson, Roger Fielding, and other whitemale models. The critique begins, instead, with a figurational return of daughters to southern gardens. This return is *not* to the mother's body, but to her texts. It is not real petunias, finally, that one is after, but an inversive, revolutionary, symbolic spirit that enables one theoretically to refigure the mothers as both victims and executioners, precursors who can be read as women who had no choice but to flesh out their own survival.[33]

The notion of "return" returns us to Spillers's figurative return upon the socialized body—to her fleshing out of an American (male) grammar of white mythology. And our topic is still "theory." For the most difficult moment to activate is not, finally, departure. The challenge, instead, is disruption, or, in Toni Morrison's phrase, "eruption." [34] What Morrison depicts as eruptions of funk, Spillers calls figurations of the flesh. I call the process "theory." Theory is a powerful black figurative negotiation of a blackmothered past. It is a reclamation of the energies of those who knew that daughters fathered upon them by white men were but "yellow wasted" if they did not sing and bring about the type of communal empowerment that marks the work of, say, Baby Suggs in *Beloved*. [35]

> "Here," she said, "in this here place, we flesh; flesh that weeps, laughs; flesh that dances on bare feet in grass. Love it. Love it hard. Yonder they do not love your flesh. They despise it." . . . She stood up then and danced with her twisted hip the rest of what her heart had to say while the others opened their mouths and gave her the music. Long notes held until the four-part harmony was perfect enough for their deeply loved flesh. (88–89)

To achieve the fleshly, communal effect of Baby Suggs is to move beyond the historical essentialism of the turn-of-the-century daughters and their Harlem Renaissance successors into a refigured space, place, and time of black women's creativity. This *beyond,* however, is not a detour around, but a journey *through* theory. The journey is a theoretical return beginning with definition and debate and leading to a poetics of Afro-American women's expressivity. Such a return seeks, not a refurbished historical room of one's own, but a vibrantly refigured expressive world.

CHAPTER ONE

Theoretical Returns

A THEORY IS an explanation. Successful theories offer the possibility of global description and a predictive adequacy. Their goal is an order of understanding different from common sense or mere appreciation. They begin where such modes of thought end or at least where these modes fail to address questions that require for answer more than enumeration, cataloguing, impressionistic summary, selective list, or nonce formulation.

Proposed responses to the question "What is Afro-American literature?" might include anthologies, literary histories, bibliographies, survey courses, or reading lists. These responses—as useful as they may be—are not theory. For theory is occupied preeminently with assumptions, presuppositions, and principles of production rather than with the orderly handling of material products represented by anthologies and survey courses. Theory's relentless tendency is to go beyond the tangible in search of *metalevels* of explanation. A concern for metalevels, rather than tangible products, is also a founding condition of Afro-American intellectual discourse.

Africans uprooted from ancestral soil, stripped of material culture, and victimized by brutal contact with various European nations were compelled not only to maintain their cultural heritage at a *meta* (as opposed to a material) level but also to apprehend the operative metaphysics of various alien cultures. Primary to their survival was the work of *consciousness,* of nonmaterial counterintelligence.

The primacy of nonmaterial transactions in the African's initial negotiations of slavery and the slave trade led to a privileging of the roles and figures of medicine men, griots, conjurers, priests, and priestesses.[1] This emphasis on spiritual

38

leadership (and leadings of the spirit) was embodied in at least one form as the founding institution of African American group life—the church, which in its very name sometimes expresses the spiritual syncretism of its founding: "African Methodist Episcopal."

The generative conditions of diasporic African life that privilege spiritual negotiation and the work of consciousness also make autobiography the premier genre of Afro-American discourse. Bereft of material, geographical or political inscriptions of a state and a common mind, diasporic Africans were compelled to seek a personal, spiritual assurance of worth. Their quest was analogous to Puritan religious meditations, such as Jonathan Edwards's *Personal Narrative*,[2] in the mainland British colonies of North America. For, like their Puritan fellows in deracination and forced immigration, Africans were compelled to verify a self's being. They were forced to construct and inscribe unique personhood in what appeared to be a blank and uncertain environment. Afro-American intellectual history, therefore, is keenly theoretical because it pays compulsory attention both to metalevels of cultural negotiation and to autobiographical inscription. Our intellectual history privileges the unseen and the intangibly personal. The trajectory of this process is from what might be called the workings of a distinctively syncretic spirit to autobiographical inscriptions of spirit work. Two images suggest themselves as illustrations of this trajectory.

One is the frontispiece of Phillis Wheatley's *Poems on Various Subjects Religious and Moral* (1773).[3] Clad in servant's clothing, the young and distinctively African-featured poet Phillis holds pen in hand and looks meditatively ahead, concentrating on something that remains invisible for viewers of her portrait. But the pen in her hand has obviously been at work. There are lines written on the parchment that we see. Perhaps they are the following ones:

> The happier *Terence* all the choir inspir'd,
> His soul replenish'd, and his bosom fir'd;
> But say, ye *Muses,* why this partial grace,
> To one alone of *Afric's* sable race:
> From age to age transmitting thus his name
> With the first glory in the rolls of fame? (4)

We do know that Phillis inscribed these lines in her poem "To Maecenas." In doing so, she wrote her male precursor African's name (Terence) into the discourse of eighteenth-century heroics. Further, she comes to us in these lines as African successor to Terence's precursorial spirit. She calls the question on the muses as it were—with her pen. That question, finally, is one of metalevels and canonicity. What is it, Phillis queries, that privileges Terence's name and why is there a situation of "partial grace" and perpetual exclusion?

The second image, this time from Frederick Douglass, reads as follows:

> The hearing of those wild notes always depressed my spirit, and filled me with ineffable sadness. I have frequently found myself in tears while hearing them. The mere recurrence to those songs, even now, afflicts me; and while I am writing these lines, an expression of feeling has already found its way down my cheek. To those songs I trace my first glimmering conception of the dehumanizing character of slavery. I can never get rid of that conception. Those songs still follow me, to deepen my hatred of slavery, and quicken my sympathies for my brethren in bonds.[4]

Here the precursors are legion, but it is their *sound* that marks an expressive lineage. A self-conscious narrator of African ancestry can be envisioned staring straight ahead in the manner of Wheatley, hearing again from a position analytically outside the circle of song an informing sound. The tear on "these lines" is the unifying affective bond between a spirited and singing text and the written autobiography of Frederick Douglass. Theory's intangible province is captured in the image of the narrator writing black, lyrical first principles that he has extrapolated from his meditations on song. "Slaves sing most when they are most unhappy." Unhappiness, the tear, a soul-killing institutionalization of the African body bring the narrator's present writing and the songs' past sounding together under the controlled pen of African autobiographical genius. We might say the spirit comes through; the vernacular resounds in brilliant coalescence with the formally literary. The metalevel prompting the African slave impulse (an expressive impulse) to song is made readable.

The conflation of past and present, ineffable and readable, marked by Douglass's passage prepares the way for an entirely self-conscious translation of "unhappiness" in a soul-killing institution that brings the narrator into portrayed, pen-in-hand harmony with the Wheatley of *Poems on Various Subjects:*

> I had no bed. I must have perished with cold, but that, the coldest nights, I used to steal a bag which was used for carrying corn to the mill. I would crawl into this bag, and there sleep on the cold, damp, clay floor, with

my head in and feet out. My feet have been so cracked Theoretical with frost, *that the pen with which I am writing might be* Returns *laid in the gashes.* (my emphasis; 72)

Deprivation, theft, commodification, the burlap (wool?) pulled over the slave's eyes, a sleep of reason that produces wounds ("cracked . . . gashes")—all of these merge in the meditation of a present narrator who has pen in hand. The spiritual bankruptcy of American slavery is expressed as the wounded and commodified ("a bag which was used for carrying corn to the mill") body of the African. The spiritual significance of such a scene emerges only through the pen laid, as poultice and portrayal, in the wound. The spirited response suggested by the pen's work is anticipated, however, by the counter-capital rebellion involved in "stealing" the bag. Finally, though, it is a single fissure ("gashes") that gives rise to written signification of immense proportions as Douglass, like his precursor Wheatley, calls the question.

The images of Wheatley and Douglass are images of Afro-American theory in its autobiographical resonance. They could be multiplied tenfold through a survey of Afro-American literary and critical traditions. One thinks of W. E. B. DuBois's autobiographical situation at the close of his "Forethought" to *The Souls of Black Folk*. One summons to mind the autobiographical positioning of Richard Wright in "The Literature of the Negro in the United States," or of James Baldwin's narrator in the "Autobiographical Notes" that serve as prelude to *Notes of a Native Son*. There are, as well, Ralph Ellison's autobiographical "Introduction" to *Shadow and Act* and Amiri Baraka's introductory, autobiographical essay "Cuba Libre" in *Home*. Such enumerations, however, are not theory. They are certainly metatheoretical, though, in a way that will, one hopes, clarify the project in Afro-American intellectual traditions at work here. For the examples serve to adumbrate a lineage of autobiographical, metalevel negotiations that constitute Afro-American discourse in its most cogent form.

~~~~~

At present in the United States, there seems to have occurred quite a remarkable reversal of and aversion to this lineage. Imagistically, this reversal displays itself in the person and voice of Afro-American critics, with pen in hand, suggesting that theory is *alien* to African American discourse. Such critics claim that black discourse is most aptly character- *41* ized not as complexly theoretical, but as univocally humanistic and unambiguously moral. Critics such as R. Baxter Miller and Joyce Joyce want, in fact, to suggest that Afro-American discourse *must* be taken as the output of a loving, moral creature known as Man, or more charitably and inclusively, Humankind.[5] Implicit in the claims of Miller and Joyce is the notion that Homo Africanus is somehow comprehensible by standards of scholarship and fields of rhetoric that are not implicated in the sphere of metalevels, or "theory." For Joyce, Miller, and their compeers, an adequate picture of Afro-American discourse can be achieved only via assumptions of a traditional humanism and methods of standard disciplines such as social history, philosophy, and group psychology. Such claims situate their proponents with debunkers of a project in literary and expressive cultural study that has been disruptively influential for at least the past two decades in American, French, and British universities. It also situates them, I believe, at some remove from discernible contours of African American literary and critical traditions as I have tentatively envisioned them.

What I want to suggest is that the African American's negotiation of metalevels, in combination with his or her propensity for autobiography as a form of African survival, has always enabled him or her to control a variety of levels of discourse in the United States. Such control has placed African Americans in a position that refutes, it seems to me, any claims for a simplistic humanity, humanism, or affective purity of discourse.

The most forceful, expressive cultural spokespersons of Afro-America have traditionally been those who have first mastered a master discourse—at its most rarefied metalevels as well as at its quotidian performative levels—and then, auto-biographically, written themselves and their *own* metalevels palimpsestically on the scroll of such mastery. Their acts of mastery have sometimes moved hostilely *against* claims of a traditional humanism, and they have seldom been characterized by any sentiment that might unambiguously or simply be designated "love."

A case in point from black discourse is resonantly before us in this time of celebration of the Constitution of the United States. When the writer David Walker issued his *Appeal* in 1829, in the form of a revolutionary document containing a "preamble" and four "articles," and maintained throughout that document an autobiographical voice, he accomplished the type of founding black theoretical negotiation I have in mind. As a document that, in a sense, writes itself on the enslaved body of the African, the Constitution of the United States contains both a foregrounded story of freedom and a variety of backgrounded narratives of suppression and en- slavement. David Walker, like all theoretically adept Afro- American spokespeople, had absolute knowledge of one set of suppressions, and he took as his task an appealing writing (or re-righting) of the African body in the very foreground of the Constitution. Walker, in Henry Louis Gates's sense of the word,[6] *signifies* with, on, in the very face of the *meta* and per- formative levels of a founding (constitutive) discourse of Eu- ramerican culture. He knew, of course, that such discourse as the Constitution had to be survived and syncretically refi- gured if African freedom and community were to become a United States of America reality.

Now, whether Walker was more loving, humanistic, con- vivial, or inherently humane than, say, the average white Bos- ton citizen of his day, is a stunningly irrelevant issue where Afro-American expressive cultural theory is concerned. What is important is that Walker was both autobiographically astute and strikingly brilliant with respect to the foregrounded sto- ries of such white citizenry. (His very title, in its long form, refers to colored *citizens*—a truly African heretical invocation of 1789.) He was, in short, a successful Afro-American theo- rist who knew that simplistic assertions of a distinguishable African American cultural and discursive practice would yield nothing. He knew that he had to *master* the very forms of en- slavement in order to *write,* let us say, "African flesh" in em- powering ways.

Walker's act, thus, constitutes an autobiographical revolu- tion, an explosive superliteracy that writes, not in the terms of the other, but in lines that adumbrate the suppressed story of *an-other.* His *Appeal* emerges as a new covenant, a new con- stitution. It repudiates a hypocritical Constitutional human- ism and urges a robust hatred of slavery. Theory understood in terms of David Walker's *Appeal* is, I believe, of the essence of Afro-American intellectual traditions.

What most discourages readers about "theory"—specifi- cally, as it has manifested itself in the academy in recent years—is its aloofness, difficulty, and refusal to supply mate- rial examples and enumerations that make for general recog- nition. Theory, in such a manifestation, seems merely self- indulgent, an endless spinning of solipsistic webs, or a cease- less construction of what Elizabeth Bruss calls "beautiful theories."[7] Not only do such efforts fail to yield material ex- amples or general reading, they may seem, finally, to have no practical consequences whatsoever, refusing to translate complex expressive cultural texts into enumerative, catalogued, or syllabused forms.

There is much to be said in support of the suspicion and charges of theory's detractors. There exist, for example, forceful, comprehensive, and usable accounts of expressive texts that derive from such seemingly "theory free" accountings as psychological and sociohistorical explanatory narratives. Still, the disparagement of theory in the expanded form in which it actually exists today seems slightly bizarre when it comes from Afro-American scholars. For it is surely theoretical discourse—conceived as autobiographical cultural commentary—that is the discursive foundation of Afro-American intellectual life in the United States. The incendiary deconstruction, defamiliarization, and signifying within the master discourse represented by Walker's *Appeal* or DuBois's *Souls* or Baraka's *Home* (full as that text is of Wittgensteinian analytic philosophy) constitute a foundational writing and informed ritualization that is indispensable in any fleshing out of an African story in America.

Finally, it is not theory, I think, that Afro-American detractors mean when they attack the Afro-American literary theoretical project, but rather the *politics of theory* as they have unfolded. Afro-Americans have been the very first radically to call the question on the traditional exclusiveness of the American academy, and they have called it in traditionally Afro-American theoretical ways. At Yale, Cornell, and San Francisco State, for example, such workers as Armstead Robinson, Roy Bryce Laporte, Michael Thelwell, James Turner, Sonia Sanchez, and Nathan Hare astutely, personally (writing, talking, and thinking out of their own lives) adduced a different idea of the *real* story of higher education in the United States. Their endeavors were under the aegis of Black Studies. We might say that where the founding of Black Studies was concerned, the personal was the theoretical. The results of Black Studies initiatives have included new courses, revised canons of study, and the creation of possibilities for myriad formerly suppressed or backgrounded discourses to take to the open air in their unique significations. Still, Black Studies represented only an initial move. No matter how culturally specific its motivations, they were, nonetheless, subject to institutional constraints of an academy that demanded an historically grounded blackness. Only by achieving an academic superliteracy has Black Studies become Black (theoretical) Power. I have already discussed the theoretical distinctions between the two enterprises and want here merely to emphasize what might be termed an initiatory autobiographical energy Theoretical marking Black Studies' inaugural instances. Returns

From black actional autobiography, as it were, the academy has moved, on one hand, to other "studies" such as Women's, Chicano, Gay, Asian American, Lesbian, etc. On the other hand, the actively revisionist and committedly political energies that produced Black Studies have been recuperated by disciplines such as "English" as occasions for esoteric, leisurely "readings" of the same books by the same whitemale authors who have marked syllabuses for decades. The traditionally privileged (as with the New Historicism's cast of authors and critics) maintain their access and control through renomination. A "new" academic generation in its thirties, forties, and fifties, therefore, looks almost as white—if not as male—as its forebears.

Represented in the manner that I have chosen, theory does seem somewhat useless, and Afro-American scholars who are academic theorists must appear traitors to a nativist purity, humanism, and love.

Still, neither the remissness of white academicians—men or women—nor the entrepreneurial or careerist motives of black academicians, men or women, should compel us to desert the most active traditions of *Afro-American theory* in our own intellectual lives. We must continue to seek—in our own currently possible negotiation of academic metalevels—to extrapolate from "theory" what is actionally and autobiographically necessary and useful *for us*. Only by doing so will we be able to move the founding and always resonantly in-action analytical project of our own culture beyond, let us say, the facile renominations within an academic elite's commodified, careerist pleasure dome.

In short, the task seems to me one of negotiating the unseen, presuppositional domains of current popular white theorizing in much the same way that Walker, Douglass, Wheatley, DuBois, or Baraka negotiated their respective eras—pen in hand, listening to sounds of African precursors, mastering (both intellectually and rhetorically) the public symbolic orders of the day. Like the workers of our cultural past, we must be fully informed—indeed brilliant—strategists of metalevels, trusting our own autobiographical impulses in a world that implores or intimidates us to a stolid historical essentialism.

There are several objections that I can envision to my proposals. First, there will arise the familiar and always paradoxical—considering its normal source—query about "exclu-

sion." Does an autobiographical condition of existence and authenticity exclude non–Afro-American (say, "white") commentators from Afro-American expressive cultural theory? The answer is a painful No. Painful because the incumbency for the non–Afro-American critic is to finger the grains of a brutal experience in which—if he or she is white—he or she is historically implicated. In response to a white student's objection that James Baldwin's work was too full of "hatred," the author replied: "Your objection shows exactly why we need a white history month. Only when there is such education will we achieve a new moral vocabulary." "Autobiographical," in my proposal, means a personal negotiation of metalevels—one that foregrounds nuances and resonances of *an-other*'s story. The white autobiographer who honestly engages his or her own autobiographical implication in a brutal past is as likely as an Afro-American to provide such nuances. What has usually been meant, however, in raising the objection of "exclusion" is that a vaguely specified "WE" should be concerned more with the universal (whatever that means) than with the autobiographical. Which brings us to the second possible objection: The situation of theory in the realm of autobiography seems to privilege delimited personal "experience" as a category of observation and analysis rather than general systematic, objective, empirical considerations of variables. The objection brought by practitioners of the latter against the "personal" is normally launched in the names of both moral and scientific objectivism. Morality and science (read: "rational truth") demand *transcendence* of the personal. Here, I think, we might enter a brief meditation on the *personal* as a way of addressing the objection and as a prelude to considerations of a poetics of Afro-American women's writing.

〰〰〰

There are few moralists who fail to discover in their own lives indisputable evidence of an unimpeachable morality. Similarly, there are few scientific theorists who do not find in their work evidence of a stunning fidelity to the "spirit" of their subject. Neither the moralist nor the scientific theorist, however, is likely to see his or her evaluations as self-congratulatory. Governed by standards of a general virtue or a universalist objectivity, neither wishes to acknowledge the determinancy of language, vested interests, privileged interpretive postures, or a will to power in their analyses. At least since Samuel Taylor Coleridge's reservations in the *Biographia Literaria* about the merely idiosyncratic features of Wordsworth's verse—or, perhaps, it is at least since Socrates set the ideal vision of the State against the idiosyncratic and merely personal reveries of the poets—moralists, poets, and analysts have been cautioned against the personal. We listen for a moment to T. S. Eliot: "One error, in fact, of eccentricity in poetry is to seek for new human emotions to express; and in this search for novelty in the wrong place it discovers the perverse. . . . Poetry is not a turning loose of emotion, but an escape from emotion; it is not the expression of personality, but an escape from personality."[8] Eliot not only brings the classical argument home with full force but also states precisely the criteria by which any autobiographically situated project would be disqualified as standard or classical poetry and, perhaps, aptly characterized as "perverse." But before rushing to his judgment, we might attempt a series of counterclaims: Theorists follow, always, a purely personal line. In their most self-aware moments they have no doubt about the specifiable personal determinants of each of their essays, reviews, lectures, and pedagogical utterances. Now if they choose never to be "personal," that simply means they have made an entirely "personal" choice. Who, after all, in our most self-directing moments stands over us, saying "Now, you'll probably want to perform a search-and-replace operation when you're finished with the present essay, changing all 'I's to 'one's"? There are, to be sure, institutional conventions, career and market constraints, that serve as implicit censors for us. But, finally, we make our own choices and are seldom deceived, I think, about the "personal" determinancy of our work. The search-and-replace operation that normally forestalls recognition (sometimes even self-recognition) of the *personal* is the substitution of *human* or *universal* for what actually operates any given theoretical enterprise: *VIZ. my* values. The substitution of *human* or *universal* is always in the service of powerful interests (one's own included) that seek to maintain the *status quo* in the name of *la condition humaine*. But as the theorist normally works—even under such rigorously political circumstances as those of, say, Mikhail Bakhtin—the *condition* closest to hand is a very personal and interested one.

Thus, for a theorist to acknowledge autobiography as a driving force is for him or her to do no more than tell the truth. When I "analyze," for you my reader, a poem or a novel, or set forth a large-scale topos (e.g., "the daughters' departure") for an entire expressive domain, I am merely offering you a determinate recall of my experiences under the conventions of criticism, or theory—a peculiar and covering style, as it were. Now this is not to plump down squarely for a return to journeys of sensitive souls among the masterpieces. Both "sensitive" and "masterpieces" were overdetermined in that form of impressionism.

No, what "recall" implies here is a narrative, which begins, as Barbara Herrnstein Smith argues in *On the Margins of Discourse,* with the founding condition "something happened."[9] My critical position or theoretical project is a personal posture marked by the narration of what happened, *to me.* The decisive emphasis (mine) on "to me" suggests, of course, the work of Walter Pater and others. In *The Renaissance,* Pater says that Matthew Arnold's injunction to see *the* object "as in itself it really is" demands qualified restatement. The aim for Pater was to see *a* particular, unique object as it is *to me.* I am not, finally, advocating more than an autobiographical allowance that transforms *the* critic or theorist into *a* critic—a very particularly constructed and accounted-for figure.

～～～～

Where Afro-American women's expressivity is concerned, the particular construction and accountability of the critic must allow him or her to negotiate metalevels of space, place, and time in order to figure forth a new expressive world. Like the autobiographical meditations of Wheatley and Douglass, the critic's work must be consciously theoretical if it is to be adequately figurative, and vice versa. The most thorough and persuasive work is that which is marked by a fit converse between consciousness and the figurative. Surely such converse is what Spillers implies when she calls us imaginatively to negotiate a presocial moment of the African "flesh"—to take back or secure a pre-European return upon African expressive energies silenced by an enslaving trade in our bodies. It is also such converse that Gaston Bachelard has in mind when he defines a phenomenological project in poetics. The convergence of poetics and Afro-American women's expressivity not only promotes a refiguration but leads, as well, to the revision of all American stories in the person of the "theorist"—say, a teller of metalevels such as Janie Crawford Killicks Starks Woods, who poetically refigures everyday black women's life in her own conscious autobiographical accountings. Bachelard's project is a resource with which we might enhance our

general theoretical store in a way that enables us successfully
to follow the world-renewing example of Hurston's protagonist.

Conditioned by Bachelard's allegiance to a phenomenology of the imagination, the "Introduction" to *The Poetics of
Space* reads as follows:

> The image offered us by reading the poem now be-
> comes really our own. It takes root in us. It has been
> given us by another, but we begin to have the impres-
> sion that we could have created it, that we should have
> created it. It becomes a new being in our language, ex-
> pressing us by making us what it expresses; in other
> words, it is at once a becoming of expression, and a
> becoming of our being. Here expression creates
> being.[10] (xix)

This statement implies a virtually shimmering instant when
objective reality and all indicative experience are bracketed,
compelling a reader to inhabit and to be inhabited by *the being*
of the poetic image. For Bachelard, poetic images are the origin of consciousness. As reverberating products of poetic reverie, they enhance language and renew both us and the world
in which we live.

More importantly, poetic images such as *house* serve as
analytical tools. They allow us not only to map a topography
of intimate human space but also to follow moments of human consciousness to the very functions (signaled by the verb
"to inhabit") of intimacy and protection that are coextensive
and coterminous with an image such as *house*. The "objective," "remembered," or "retained" corner of a childhood
house is less important for an understanding of corners than
felicitous images of *corner* presented by poetic reverie.

Hence, when he uses the word "poetics," Bachelard does
not intend a peculiar set of conventions, rules, and procedures
for the composition or analysis of creative writing. "Poetics"
signals images and the consciousness-work through which
they constitute the origin and foundation of a human world.
"Space," for example, is conceivable only in terms of poetic
images (such as *house* and *corner*) that figure it forth from and
intersubjectively to human consciousness.

Bachelard wages a polemic against psychology and psychoanalysis because these disciplines strive to explain the
"cause" or meaning of poetic images. For Bachelard, nothing
prepares or "causes" a poetic image; its appearance and presentation are entirely new. Further, no psychobiography of a

poet can make more effective the shimmering import of even one of his or her felicitous images.

The felicitous poetic image is, for Bachelard, not an objective phenomenon, but a reverberant event of consciousness that one enters in the office of renewal, comprehension, and liberation:

> A great verse awakens images that had been effaced, at the same time that it confirms the unforeseeable nature of speech. And if we render speech unforeseeable, is that not an apprenticeship to freedom? What delight the poetic imagination takes in making game of censors! (xxiii)

Bachelard's poetics and an effective criticism of Afro-American women's writing converge at the site of the felicitous poetic image.

One of the most important essays on the efficacy of Afro-American women's expressivity in the United States is Alice Walker's "In Search of Our Mothers' Gardens,"[11] in which the author recalls:

> I notice that it is only when my mother is working in her flowers that she is radiant, almost to the point of being invisible—except as Creator: hand and eye. She is involved in work her soul must have. Ordering the universe in the image of her personal conception of Beauty. (241)

This description—in its shimmering irradiance of subject and object—captures the splendid intersubjectivity detailed by Bachelard. The word "invisible" suggests a pure reverie in which the intuitively imaged *garden* is created as spiritual and eternal form.

Neither *flowers* nor *mother* is as important, finally, as an implied aboriginal creation in the *garden*. In a word, Walker as both reader and poet discovers through the image *garden* how the world is made anew.

By phenomenologically recovering her mother's vernacular *garden* and presenting it as literate poetic image (in the manner of Wheatley's "Terence" or Douglass's "songs"), Walker opens the field of Afro-American women's consciousness in its founding radiance and claims for herself an enduring spiritual legacy. Beginning her essay with a discussion of Jean Toomer's *Cane,* a book in which Afro-American women are tragically mute in their repressed spirituality, and Virginia Woolf's "A Room of One's Own," which discusses the traditional repression of women's creativity, Walker discovers

rejoicing, celebration, and hope in her mother's imaged *gar-*
den. If Bachelard's and Walker's formulations are combined,
the prospect emerges for a theoretical approach to Afro-
American women's writing called a "poetics."

~~~~

But even as we project such an approach, the questions
arise: "Why phenomenology in a poststructuralist world?
How can the deployment of phenomenology be reconciled
with adherence to a postmodernist problematic of sign production?" (These questions do not arise with equal interest to
all, and the nonphilosophically disposed reader should know
that he or she can avoid my proposed answers in this and the
next section without losing the thread of my general argument. For those interested in the philosophical and, specifically, the Derridean strands of the thread, the two sections are
indispensable.) After all, phenomenology seeks to move transcendently beyond indicative signs that govern "ordinary"
communication. As a rationalist enterprise or method, it seeks
its source of explanation in consciousness. For phenomenology objective validity is a function of intuition, not an "effect"
of sign production. It is the quiddity or "what is" of phenomena, that is to say, that concerns phenomenology. Husserl's
attempt to make philosophy "scientific" constitutes an inaugural move of the project.[12]

By "scientific," Husserl intended a status that would be
methodologically adequate for certifying the unique givenness to consciousness of objectively valid knowledge. "Objectively valid" means *givenness as such*—in a manner adequate to
demonstrate that the object of an intuition could not have been
given otherwise. The phases of the *epoche* (or bracketing of the
contingent), *reduction* (clearing away of phenomenal residue),
and *ideation* (a perspectival "turning" or induction) are well
known as Husserl's distinctive elaborations of method. The
importance of his work is that it constitutes a critique of prior
practices of philosophy. It attempts to escape metaphysics and
the positivism of natural sciences that were contemporaneous
with his *Logical Investigations*. Like Frege, Wittgenstein,
Whitehead, Russell, and others at the beginning of the twen-
tieth century, Husserl was concerned to start all over again, to
solicit Western metaphysics and the traditional rationalism
subsumed under the heading of "philosophy." It is the spirit
of critique that makes his project compelling.

Taking philosophy as the science of being, he sought to

provide a method for investigating absolute knowledge of absolute being. Such a method could only begin with the consciousness of the rational subject and the phenomenal data
presented to that consciousness. For the only true being of
objectivity is being in consciousness (*Bewusst-sein*), and the
phenomenological description that reveals this being is objectively valid only insofar as it is valid for all time and all possible subjects.

Philosophy, thus, becomes a methodical reflection on consciousness as revelatory of being. Husserl designates the process implied here as "knowledge theory" and suggests that
such theory

> investigate[s] the problems of the relationship between
> consciousness and being, . . . [and] can have before its
> eyes only being as the correlate of consciousness, as
> something 'intended' after the manner of conscious-
> ness: as perceived, remembered, expected, represented
> pictorially, imagined, identified, distinguished, be-
> lieved, opined, evaluated, etc. It is clear, then, that the
> investigation must be directed toward a scientific essen-
> tial knowledge of consciousness, toward that which
> consciousness itself 'is' according to its essence in all its
> distinguishable forms.[13]

Subsequent to Husserl, Heidegger defined the same
"knowledge theory" or phenomenological method as a leading back or re-duction of the investigative vision from a
naively apprehended being to being.[14] But phenomenology,
according to Heidegger, must not be confined to the pure ne-
gativity of a re-duction or retreat from *beings* (*res extensa*) toward being. It must also include a leading forward toward
being. "Being does not become accessible like a being. We do
not simply find it in front of us. As is to be shown, it must
always be brought to view in a free projection. This projecting of the antecedently given being upon its being and the
structures of its being we call *phenomenological construction*"
(21–22). And there is yet a third component of phenomenological method that, according to Heidegger, involves the dis-
entanglement of traditional concepts of philosophy from their
historical situatedness and overdetermination:

> [A]ll philosophical discussion, even the most radical at-
> tempt to begin all over again, is pervaded by tradi-
> tional concepts and thus by traditional horizons and
> traditional angles of approach, which we cannot as-
> sume with unquestionable certainty to have arisen

originally and genuinely from the domain of being and
the constitution of being they claim to comprehend. It
is for this reason that there necessarily belongs to the
conceptual interpretation of being and its structure,
that is, to the reductive construction of being, a *destruc-*
tion—a critical process in which the traditional concepts, which at first must necessarily be employed, are
de-constructed down to the sources from which they
were drawn. Only by means of this destruction can
ontology fully assure itself in a phenomenological way
of the genuine character of its concepts. (22–23)

What prevails in my selective account is an air of critique.
Phenomenology's aims seem to be a new rigor, a disentangle-
ment or *deconstruction* of received tradition, an escape from
metaphysics, and an order of explanation that provides objectively valid knowledge. Essential to this project is a rejection
of the causality of natural sciences based on laws governing *res*
extensa. *Res cogitans* and a language to fit them are preeminent.

In order to achieve its ends, phenomenology attempts to
situate itself transcendently beyond the limitations of ordinary
language. It rejects indication and communication in favor of
expression and presentation. And it is in this linguistic aspect
of its work that it is overtaken by the influential deconstruc-
tionist critique of Jacques Derrida in *Speech and Phenomena:*
Introduction to the Problem of Signs in Husserl's Phenomenology.[15]

Derrida's monograph is one of the most influential poststructuralist interrogations of phenomenology. But his project is less a refutation, I think, than an inversion. Its most decisive move is privileging *nonbeing* and *absence* as, at least,
philosophically coimplicated in all investigations of being and
presence. His topsy-turvydom sounds as follows:

> To think of presence as the universal form of transcen-
> dental life [as phenomenology does] is to open myself
> to the knowledge that in my absence, beyond my em-
> pirical existence, before my birth and after my death,
> *the present is. . . .* I have a strange and unique certitude
> that this universal form of presence, since it concerns
> no determined being, will not be affected by it. The re-
> lationship with *my death* (my disappearance in general)
> thus lurks in this determination of being as presence,
> ideality, the absolute possibility of repetition. . . . The
> I *am,* being experienced only as an I *am present,* itself
> presupposes the relationship with presence in general,
> with being as presence. . . . Therefore, I *am* originally
> means I *am mortal.* (54)

The nonbeing of *death* is, thus, thematized by Derrida in terms of language as *différance*. In a word, Derrida reminds us that repetition alone maintains presence, and repetition's motivation is preeminently a system of signs whose very possibility is founded in absence. A *sign* is a sign only insofar as its signifier and signifieds are systematically independent of a present speaking subject. The birth of the sign is precisely the death of the subject.

Signs are founded in difference—distinctions marked by phonemes and the infinite deferral of *meaning,* which is always indeterminately suspended between past and future.

To the extent that signs provide our only access to "repetition" and "presence," they can never be bracketed as contingent and inessential. The metaphysical paradox of phenomenology's quest for "present" "objective validity" of consciousness arises from its attempts at such bracketing.

Derrida, thus, argues that phenomenology forwards its project through an (at best) naive or (at worst) metaphysical privileging of voice, which the project deems an antithesis to the contingency of signs. (The original French title of Derrida's monograph was *La Voix et le phénomène.*) But this turn to voice is a dissimulation, since the verbal or spoken is already fissured, *differed,* as it were, by the *ur*-conditions of signification. The *différance, trace, supplément* that define the sign are anterior to and determinative of any possibility of "meaningful" voice or speech.

Hence, Derrida concludes that phenomenology's impulse to write a scientific philosophy free of metaphysics is betrayed by the project's own metaphysical privileging of a primordial expressive voice. The "metaphysics of presence"—with its formal, logical requirements and teleological desire for truth—is palpably inscribed in phenomenology.

The phenomenologist, then, responds with questions of his own: "Is there life after Derrida? Or only death? Must phenomenology be abandoned in favor of its inversion? On what revised or expanded terms might one continue?"

~~~~~~

If ideality, consciousness, being, and quiddity continue to interest us as themes of a project that contains, at least, the possibility of an escape from metaphysics, then I would think phenomenology remains of interest. It is, after all, precisely within the tradition of phenomenology that Derrida differs and defers: i.e., has any significance and import for us

through a diacritical critique. Further, if we hope to avoid the
optimistic existentialism of (natural) scientific explanation
and the skeptical, sometimes tedious hermeneutics of representation, then we are compelled to investigate being and consciousness in the uniqueness of their constitution and relationships.

The Derridean critique of phenomenology is, in effect, the difference within that project that alerts us to both its vulnerabilities and possibilities. The "voice," as it were, of Derrida is like the hearing of itself of phenomenology. "Hearing oneself speak is not the inwardness of an inside that is closed in upon itself; it is the irreducible openness in the inside; it is the eye and the world within speech." [16]

Derrida's phenomenological *mundus inversus* is the site of intersection between phenomenology and its *différance*. It is a phenomenology of phenomenology that is in accord with Heidegger's specifications of a third moment in the project's method. Derrida's critique is the *deconstruction* of phenomenology that is always implicit in the project's goals—already anticipated, even invited. I think it is the aporia signaling, not an occasion for abandonment, but an opportunity for beginning again. But commencing not in a spirit of voluntaristic denial.

Derrida's dark auguries of death, closure, and endings cannot be willed out of account. Nor can they be considered sanctions for passive abandonment of the themes of phenomenology. Being, knowledge, consciousness, quiddity do arise to mind when we struggle to articulate the "whatness" and its mode of being of a tradition such as Afro-American women's expressivity. And metaphysical, historical, psychological, and positivistic models seem less promising than the possibility of an account that endeavors to discover the conditions and objects of consciousness of this expressivity.

Such an account would, in my estimation, be both metaphysical and Derridean. It would be "metaphysical," however, in a Johnsonian sense of yoking seemingly radically dissimilar projects together; Derridean insofar as radical dissimilarity reveals itself as the grounds of being (as well as the certainty of mortality) of the quest for being itself. A too simple way of stating the matter is to say that a phenomenological poetics proceeds today as a project whose "irreducible openness" has made available a methodologically tensioned mode of analysis that may lead to, at least, a semblance of both knowledge and theory.

If we continue to forward a phenomenological project *through* Derrida, then, we shall have done no more than seize

upon the implications of what, to me, is the most significant
utterance in *Speech and Phenomena:*

> [T]o restore the original and nonderivative character of
> signs, in opposition to classical metaphysics, is, by an
> apparent paradox, at the same time to eliminate a con-
> cept of signs whose whole history and meaning belong
> to the adventure of the metaphysics of presence. This
> also holds for the concepts of representation, repeti-
> tion, difference, etc., as well as for the system they
> form. For the present and for some time to come, the
> movement of that schema will only be capable of
> working over the language of metaphysics from
> within, from a certain sphere of problems inside that
> language. No doubt this work has always already be-
> gun. (51–52)

Derrida is precisely that beginning for phenomenology, and,
in a sense, all we do when we forward the project is read and
re-read Derrida as a propaedeutic to a method of talking
(again) about the themes of phenomenology.

In expressive cultural analysis, phenomenology offers a
site that foregrounds the sign without minimizing the possibilities of unique access to and processing of being by human
consciousness. Phenomenology does not augur a mimetic
(sociohistorical, reflective, or "influence") theory of expressive culture, nor does it give place to pseudoscientific–new-
critical models and allegories of reading. Rather, it assumes
spirit and consciousness as agent and agency—through
signs—of human expressive cultural production. It does not
eradicate the material in its analyses, but seeks to constitute
the being of the material in terms of a preeminent spirit work.
If the sign is the limit of a *material ideality* or *mortal immortality,*
then "the material" is the limit case coimplicated with spirit
work.

Just as neither representation (v. presentation), reflection,
nor deconstructive "reading" can upstage the consciousness of
phenomenology, so the material itself takes its place not ahead
of but onstage beside consciousness—paradoxically half-
perceived and half-created through the very materiality of the
sign. Signifying on a striking figure of Husserl's, Derrida locates the scene of his own phenomenology of phenomenology
in the Dresden gallery:

> The gallery is the labyrinth which includes in itself its
> own exits: we have never come upon it as upon a par-
> ticular *case* of experience—that which Husserl believes
> he is describing. It remains, then, for us to *speak,* to

make our voices *resonate* throughout the corridors in
order to make up for [*suppléer*] the breakup of presence. The phoneme, the *akoumenon,* is the *phenomenon
of the labyrinth.* This is the *case* with the *phone.* Rising
toward the sun of presence, it is the way of Icarus.
(104)

Derrida, of course, retains flight (sight toward the sun) in
the face of the repeated (as myth) possibilities of failure. And
so, of course, does the expressive cultural critic seeking the
"essence" or "being" of Afro-American women's creativity.
Although writing, difference, supplement, and the sign may
be always already determining, still the agency of spirit and
consciousness motivates our analytical quest beyond a passive
curator's desk and toward an investigation and sounding of
corridors and works that are productions of an inferable and
inspirited past.

The "stage" of the Dresden gallery, like the work of the
expressive cultural critic, summons the question of *communication*—that signal heat likely to dissolve the wings of Icarus.
For of what use is an investigation of being that cannot be
communicated?

The foundering place of phenomenology has, tradition-
ally, been easily located at the site of *intersubjectivity.* In a foot-
note devoted to temporalization, Derrida writes,

> [D]etermination of "absolute subjectivity" would also
> have to be crossed out as soon as we conceive the pre-
> ent on the basis of difference, and not the reverse. The
> concept of *subjectivity* belongs *a priori and in general* to
> the order of the *constituted.* This holds *a fortiori* for the
> analogical appresentation that constitutes intersubjec-
> tivity. Intersubjectivity is inseparable from temporali-
> zation taken as the openness of the present upon an
> outside of itself, upon *another* absolute present. This
> being outside itself proper to time is its *spacing:* it is a
> proto-stage [*archi-scene*]. . . . There is no constituting
> subjectivity. (84–85)

And yet, Derrida realizes—even as Icarus must—that a denial
of the sun is possible only in a flight toward it. To assert the
negation is to open the possibility (in consciousness, at least)
of the affirmation of a constituting subjectivity. The paradox
of that subjectivity's claims *for itself* is what is at issue at the
site of intersubjectivity. Quentin Lauer describes the paradox
as follows:

> In a phenomenological context the problem of com-
> munication is really a double one. Though it is true

that any cognition recognized by the subject as "objectively valid" will be recognized as being necessarily such for any possible other subjects, communication can be significant only if there are actual other subjects. The first problem, then, is that of knowing other actual subjects, in a framework where nothing is known unless it is constituted subjectively as an object of cognition. Thus the other subject must be an object constituted as a subject (i.e., as constituting its own subjects, including subjects other than itself).[17]

One way of characterizing this stumbling block is to call it the problem of a *staged,* monadic intuitionism. Rather than taking refuge from the logical paradox thus presented in paralyzing skepticism or solipsistic idealism, we can simply take the stance "nevertheless it moves."

That is to say, while we will have to qualify all claims to the absolute, and certainly to absolute and objectively valid "truth," we may nevertheless note that our phenomenological investigations move us beyond the tedious cleverness of skeptical "readings" that take comfort in a commitment to absolutely "nothing."

What we, in spite of our siting in a solitary self-consciousness, must communicate is a spirited, if tentative, sounding of culture work.

The paradox of constituting "other subjects" seems less formidable, perhaps, for an Afro-Americanist tradition in which the very spirited order of consciousness in and for itself, as either extant or *being,* has always already had to be constituted against a dominant culture's persistent "othering" and "objectifying." The pragmatic character of methodological *effect* tends—even through paradox—to win the day in Afro-American culture over logical completeness. Phenomenology may not communicate *all* that we wish to know—precisely because, as Derrida has demonstrated, it is locked into a communicative relationship to the world. But it is capable of providing a pragmatic and forceful accounting of Afro-American culture work. It succeeds, paradoxically, by acceding to the claims of its own deconstruction as to a treaty, let us say, with *différance.*

Hence, Bachelard's phenomenology and poetics of space should be impossible as moving cultural analysis, yet they move as persuasively as any account that one can imagine. Further, specifications for the intersubjectivity of poetic images should be impossible, yet they accord (even in an age of sophisticated cultural semiotics) well with what we know, or feel, or intuit of the workings of the expressive spirit in Afro-American culture. Phenomenology, then, seems to succeed in spite of itself—in conjunction, one might say, with its very paradoxes. Certainly it makes available, through a qualified deployment of Bachelard, a poetics for sounding Afro-American women's expressivity.

~~~~~

The "poetics of Afro-American women's writing" signals, then, a theory that seeks to arrive at the guiding spirit, or consciousness, of Afro-American women's writing by examining selected *imagistic fields*. Space, as conceived by Bachelard, is an imagistic field. It is a function of images (e.g., *house* or *corner*). We come to know space through an examination of such images. Furthermore, human space has attached to it both "protective value" and "imagined values, which soon become dominant" (xxxi–xxxii). By examining imagistic fields that compose space, therefore, we also come to apprehend values and beliefs that govern our lives. Our cultural geographies are, thus, comprehensible through images.

The word "cultural" must be taken as an independent variable. For Bachelard's approach is only effective, I believe, when it is combined with examinations of culturally specific creative or imaginative fields such as Walker's "In Search of Our Mothers' Gardens." A general or universal field such as space is, finally, only a motivating area of examination—one hypothesized as constitutive for all cultures.

We assume, for example, that space, place, and time as universal fields are, indeed, rife with images that Afro-Americans have both inhabited and been inhabited by. At the same time, we assume that there is a field of "particular" or vernacular imagery unique to the Afro-American imagination.

The task of a poetics, then, is to operate a universal category or imagistic field through a culturally specific field in order to enhance both. The project is, one might say, akin to the application of a course in general linguistics to the specifics of, say, Black English Vernacular. Again, it might be likened to the examination of Afro-American expressive culture under the prospect of general theories of textual production and performance. The axiological results of such operations include accessing the general, framing images and values of a culture as well as foregrounding the quite specific values or instances that modify and expand a general field.

For example, one might attempt to show how a "poetics of Afro-American women's expressivity" applied to a text such a Toni Morrison's *Sula*[18]—a text determined by *place* from its opening phrase "In that place"—sharply modifies and expands the field of *place* and, at the same time, foregrounds distinctive values and aspects of an Afro-American expressive field. *Place,* in a poetics of *Sula,* differentiates into European and Afro-American. Within the Afro-American, it undergoes further gender discrimination into a "standard" male province and a woman's cosmetological territory.

Correlatively, "the Bottom," which serves as *Sula's* vernacular setting, becomes a field where specifically Afro-American women's places—Eva Peace's and Helene Wright's houses, Edna Finch's Mellow House, and Irene's Palace of Cosmetology—offer an energetic figuration of patterns of purity and danger, order and inversiveness in Afro-American life. The shack, or place, of Ajax's mother—where seven sons are taught respect, love, and admiration for women as well as the spiritedness of the art of conjure—becomes a generative image in the field of place and a foregrounded place of potential for spatial rearrangements of Afro-American life.

〰〰〰

If one measure for determining the success of a poetics of Afro-American women's writing is the type of expansiveness and foregrounding just discussed, then surely another measure—indeed, one implicit in any project conditioned by phenomenology—is a palpable or felt "shift" of critical horizons. A theorist may always feel that his or her work has been successful in producing such a shift, but the essentialness of the shift can be confirmed only by the response of another. An example of the type of intersubjectivity that I have in mind occurs at the conclusion of Zora Neale Hurston's *Their Eyes Were Watching God,*[19] when Pheoby, the friend to whom Hurston's protagonist, Janie, tells her autobiographical story, responds:

> "Lawd, . . . Ah done growed ten feet higher from just listen' tuh you, Janie. Ah ain't satisfied wid mahself no mo'. Ah means tuh make Sam [my husband] take me fishin' wid him after this. Nobody better not criticize you in mah hearin'." (284)

A sense of growth and change, a sense of dissatisfaction with the previously given are combined in Pheoby's words with a resolution to pursue a different course of action. Here, it seems to me, is one clearly figured success of poetics.

For, in a sense, what Janie has done—in a fictive and precursorial foreshadowing of Walker—is transform the quotidian rites of a black woman's passage through the world into a series of figures or images that are so resonant that they catapult Pheoby into new consciousness. Janie's revealed images become occasions for Pheoby to both read and write the world in new and liberating ways.

The type of intersubjective response that I have in mind is analyzed in Afro-Americanist terms by Michael Awkward in his fine work *Inspiriting Influences*.[20] Awkward views the process as akin to call-and-response—a necessarily communal communicative mode motivated by Afro-American double consciousness. As a split subject of slavery's "othering," the Afro-American strives for a participatory expressive return to wholeness or, in Awkward's term, "(comm)unity" (49–50). My suggestion is that the mode is coextensive with a general philosophical project and that project's projection of what might be called *image work*.

The life of Hurston's protagonist has its origins in the derogation and sexual exploitation of her grandmother and mother. The life itself is essentially a meditative one. It is recuperated in its potential, however, by an imagistic, autobiographical telling that receives attentive response. From two unfulfilling marriages and a tragically brief and fleetingly happy third one, Hurston's protagonist creates a poetics of Afro-American woman's everyday life.

What might be called Janie's "poetics" are of inestimable transformative value. To make Sam take her fishing is for Pheoby to alter expected relationships, transforming the black woman from worker (mule) of the world to a participant in male, ludic rituals that provide leisure and a space for spiritual growth. (We have but to recall how powerfully instructive for culture the one-day fishing expedition is in Hurston's *Mules and Men*.) For Pheoby to forestall "criticism" of Janie is for her to exemplify a potential for the renewal of Afro-American tolerance and communality that is always immanent in black women's expressivity.

~~~~~

The correlations between universal and particular, critic and audience, that constitute measures of success for a poetics of Afro-American women's expressivity also suggest a third

measure. Successful analyses, in their concentration on the essential spirit or immanent potential of Afro-American wom-
en's expressivity, move the criticism and theory of black
women's writing beyond merely interested readings. Hereto-
fore, the potentially liberating effects of Afro-American
women's expressivity—like the poetic potential of Janie's
autobiographical recall—have been hampered by the self-
interested approaches of critical camps so busy, in Janie's
phrase, "wid talk" that they have failed to provide the kind of
comprehensive hearing offered by Pheoby.

As early as the appearance in the 1970s of Gayl Jones's
Corregidora[21] and Toni Morrison's *The Bluest Eye*,[22] some
blackmale critics insisted that Afro-American women's writing was but an Amazonian show of divisiveness, despair, and
violence.[23] Such critics were particularly distressed by what
they considered the exuberant blackmale-bashing of black
women writers. This earlier critical impulse to a self-inter-
ested concentration on aversive images in black women's writings persists in recent criticisms of Alice Walker's hugely successful *The Color Purple*.[24]

In response to such male criticism have come equally interested feminist responses suggesting that Afro-American
women's writings are more amenable to feminist than to other
kinds of critical readings.[25] The sound of this criticism is suggested by the guiding claim of one of Barbara Smith's notable
essays: "Black women's existence, experience, and culture and
the brutally complex systems of oppression which shape these
are in the 'real world' of white and/or male consciousness beneath consideration, invisible, unknown" (157). Here, a phenomenological "unintelligibility" or inaccessibility to other
than committed feminist critics is assumed as a ground for
privileging radical feminist readings of black women's writings.

Finally, there are interested readings by both theorizing
ideologues and rhetoricians (our new Sophists). The interested reading here is, perhaps, the most colonizing form of
all. It shows no allegiance or obligation to the field of Afro-
American particulars. Practitioners are often critics who feel
that it is unnecessary for them to read an entire text before
delivering sweeping critical judgments. They also feel no obligation to inform themselves, through even minimal study,
of Afro-American culture or expressive consciousness before
holding forth on novels, poems, essays, and short stories that
are, at least in part, functions of such culture and consciousness.

But surely nothing could be more intensely "interested" than pointing to the limitations and excesses of critical orientations different from my own, and a poetics of Afro-American women's expressivity, as I advocate it, is indeed an interested enterprise. First, it proceeds from a theorist who began work under the aegis of the Black Aesthetic and whose nationalist orientation remains strong. Second, it derives from a male critic who has a decided interest in theory. These interests, obviously, condition my sense that there is a *sui generis* cultural spirit at work in quite specific ways in Afro-American woman's expressivity and that this spirit can be elucidated through theoretical analysis.

But having acknowledged the interestedness of my own orientation (a subject position about which I shall have more to say later), I want still to claim that the success of a poetics of Afro-American women's expressivity should be measured by the extent to which the project avoids limitations of an exclusive self-interestedness and offers broadly comprehensive analyses of the guiding spirituality to be discovered in the imagistic fields of black women's creativity. And by "interestedness" I intend a preeminently defensive and ideological cast of mind that refuses to question the relativity of its judgments or to figure itself as figuring in an "open" field of inquiry. "Interestedness" marks, therefore, a negative limitation of the "self" rather than the type of inversive, challenging, autobiographical expansiveness that operates the most powerful theoretical analyses.

The spirit work that is imagistically projected by Afro-American women's expressivity is, I think, like what is called by the religion of voodoo *The Work.* In women's narratives such as Morrison's *Sula,* Zora Neale Hurston's *Mules and Men,*[26] and Ntozake Shange's *Sassafras, Cypress and Indigo,*[27] spirit work is frequently imaged by the space, place, and time of the Conjure Woman. One might say, in fact, that a poetics of Afro-American women's writing is, in many ways, a phenomenology of conjure. In any case, the field most decisively analyzed by such a poetics is decidedly not one where pathological or aversive images dominate. Rather, what are revealed are felicitous images of the workings of a spirit that is so wonderfully captured by "In Search of Our Mothers' Gardens." Describing the task of her generation of Afro-American writers, Alice Walker asserts:

> We must fearlessly pull out of ourselves and look at and identify with our lives the living creativity some of our great-grandmothers were not allowed to know. I

stress *some* of them because it is well known that the
majority of our great-grandmothers knew, even without "knowing" it, the reality of their spirituality, even
if they didn't recognize it beyond what happened in the
singing at church—and they never had any intention of
giving it up. (237–38)

Walkers's is a felicitous, as opposed to an "aversive," image
not because it is visual or complimentary. "Felicitous" signals
"well chosen, apt, appropriate," and I would add, *comprehensive*. What such an image entails is less a visual survey than a
comprehensive hearing as in the case of Pheoby and Janie.
"Comprehensive" signals a necessary attention to discordant
or problematic cultural notes. After all, Walker's own *epoche*
and *reduction* leading to her mother's garden begins not with a
joyful noise but with a brutalizing and enforced silence. "Felicitous," then, signals an objectively valid act of consciousness that is sanctioned by all possible subjects' acquiescence in
the *givenness* of the image. "Aversive," by contrast, suggests,
perhaps, an exploitatively melodramatic or sensationalistic
image in the service of a profitable ideology of shock. I believe
Afro-American women creators have traditionally sought felicitous and multisensory images. Mae Henderson has also
suggested to me in conversation that such images are "multi-
metaleveled," since they encode not simply explicitly racial
but also complex gender negotiations of space, place, and
time. Henderson believes that the specific "character" of the
imagistic experience is dependent upon *both* the image as
given and consciousness as giver and receiver. "Knowing" an
image as felicitous or aversive, therefore, is a matter of a field,
as it were, of consciousness that has always to be recon-
structed, learned anew, renewed in manifold (as opposed to
binary) ways.

My emphasis on "image," as I hope the extensiveness of
my foregoing discussion suggests, is not intended as an appropriation of black women's expressivity through a colonizing gaze. Rather, a theory of the felicitous image suggests a
comprehensive, conscious audition of the soundings of black
women's expressivity in its intended fullness. One might say
mine is an attempted listening to such expressivity in its very
well-chosenness.

Hurston's "conjure" is one of the most well-chosen images
of space that I know, and it unfolds its field of signification
with persuasive energy in *Mules and Men*. The order of presentation of the poetics I wish to propose begins with space
because Hurston has figured this field—in a striking return to

southern territories of mothers and grandmothers—with poetic grandeur. The order also begins with space because Bachelard's siting of this category provides an account whose general specifications are both enhancing for and enhanced by Hurston's soundings and significations.

Workings of the Spirit: Conjure and the Space of Black Women's Creativity

[N]o one may approach the Altar without the crown, and none may wear the crown of power without preparation. *It must be earned.* And what is this crown of power? Nothing definite in material. Turner crowned me with a consecrated snake skin. I have been crowned in other places with flowers, with ornamental paper, with cloth, with sycamore bark, with egg-shells. It is the meaning, not the material that counts.

Mules and Men

Conjure: conspiracy, *c*1540 Surrey *Ecclesiastes* iv.41 And by conjures the seed of kings is thrust from state.
Conjurement: The exercise of magical or occult influence.
Conjurer: One who performs tricks with words.

Oxford English Dictionary

THE WORD "CONTEXT" carries a certain intimacy, bearing always nuances of enclosure and stability. "Meaning," by contrast—especially in critical and theoretical arenas marked by a poststructuralist sensibility—carries visions of openness, uncertainty, indeterminancy. The human metaphysical and analytical inclination is to conceive "context" as a determinable place that stands in causal relationship to an always elusive "meaning." Context, thus, becomes, out of a bent for certainty, the meaning of meaning.

Attempting to discover why these somewhat comforting
speculations on matters left me irreducibly uncomfortable, I
realized that at the root of such thinking was what Bachelard
calls the "lazy certainties of the geometrical intuitions."[1] Geome-
trism, according to Bachelard, seeks always a symmetry of
oppositions. For example, if one cannot control or apprehend
the meaning of an expression, one can, at least (and some
would argue more importantly), determine the context (often
labeled "historical") that generates, gives birth to, or produces
the expression. An "outside" uncertainty is, thus, geometri-
cally balanced by comforting images of contextual containment. Analytic and historicized interiors protect one, as it
were, from immense reaches and troubling figurative ex-
teriors.

What I find helpful about Bachelard's formulations, however, is not a facile or tendentious condemnation of geom-
etrism, but rather, their promotion and investigation of the
poetic image. The poetic image for Bachelard is a means of
liberation from a reductive dialectics of order. The poetic image disrupts, exaggerates, transgresses, transforms. Its unpredictability makes us aware of possibilities of freedom.

The phenomenological arguments adduced by Bachelard,
as I have already suggested, are not without their contradic-
tions and valorizations of the "speaking subject." Nonetheless, his stance enables him to localize the dialectics of inside
and outside, open and closed, in language. They permit the
image to stand in contrast to meaning. "And language," he
asserts, "bears within itself the dialectics of open and closed.
Through meaning it encloses, while through poetic expression it opens up" (222). Confining consciousness to language,
he sees, nonetheless, imagistic means for consciousness to escape oppositions that accompany language as a sign of closed
self-sameness. The image is contrastive to an oppositional order that pits a masterful "I" against a subjugated "other," a
civilized "inside" against a wild "exterior." The poetic image,
rather than creating or fostering division, relies on and promotes transubjectivity:

> When I receive a new poetic image, I experience its
> quality of inter-subjectivity. I know that I am going to
> repeat it in order to communicate my enthusiasm.
> When considered in transmission from one soul to an-
> other, it becomes evident that a poetic image eludes
> causality. Doctrines that are timidly causal, such as
> psychology, or strongly causal, such as psychoanalysis,
> can hardly determine the ontology of what is poetic.

For nothing prepares a poetic image, especially not culture, in the literary sense, and especially not perception, in the psychological sense. I always come to the
same conclusion: The essential newness of the poetic
image poses the problem of the speaking being's crea-
tiveness. (xx)

Extrapolating from Bachelard, one might claim that the
poetic image is coextensive with the poetic trope.[2] It is a pivotal and reflexive surface that defies a rigorous opposition of
subject and object. It absorbs energies of its creator as subject,
but is effectively sonorous only through the matching subjectivity of its recipient. Its force is felt in its disruptive effects, in
its liberation of creator and recipient alike from boundaries of
conceptual overdeterminations.

One can suggest, in fact, that the poetic image is a reverberant space of habitation. One may also suggest that it is a
locus of value characterized by the function of inhabiting.
Writing of the poetics of corners, Bachelard says:

> For to great dreamers of corners and holes nothing is
> ever empty, the dialectics of full and empty only corre-
> spond to two geometrical non-realities. The function
> of inhabiting constitutes the link between full and
> empty. A living creature fills an empty refuge, images
> inhabit, and all corners are haunted, if not "inhabited."
> (140)

Creation, apprehension, re-creation comprise the process that
makes the image habitable space. The process involves passage, for creativity is not an individualistic and radically material endeavor, but a passage of the liberating spirit summoned by the image through the image's inhabitant.

One problem with this statement as a possible model for
the study of expressive culture is that it requires a definition
of *space*. For what, after all, does it mean to designate an image as a space or to invoke the vocabulary of inhabiting? In
Space and Place,[3] the writer Yi-Fu Tuan offers the following
definition:

> In experience the meaning of space often merges with
> that of place. 'Space' is more abstract than 'place.'
> What begins as undifferentiated space becomes place as
> we get to know it better and endow it with value. Ar-
> chitects talk about the spatial qualities of place; they
> can equally well speak of the locational (place) qualities
> of space. The ideas 'space' and 'place' require each
> other for definition. From the security and stability of

place we are aware of the openness, freedom, and threat of space, and vice versa. Furthermore, if we think of space as that which allows movement, then place is pause; each pause in movement makes it possible for location to be transformed into place.(6)

On the basis of Tuan's observations, we might say that *space* is the condition of possibility of movement, a possibility that can be affirmed by sight or vision and confirmed by touch. Place, as a complement, is a locational pause contoured by distinguishable interests. Hence, place, insofar as interests mark its boundaries, may be thought of as "a focus of value, of nurture, and support" (29).

The relational semantics of Tuan's formulation enable us to define the poetic image as a space offering conditions of possibility for movement. Those who take up and perpetuate the image and leave behind records of their encounters provide pauses, locational moments, that enable us to define the image as what Bachelard terms "eulogized space."

Space that has been seized upon by the imagination cannot remain indifferent space subject to the measures and estimates of the surveyor. It has been lived in, not in its positivity, but with all the partiality of the imagination. Particularly, it nearly always exercises an attraction. For it concentrates being within limits that protect. In the realm of images, the play between the exterior and intimacy is not a balanced one. (xxii)

Eulogized, imagistic space "exercises an attraction" through its potential to liberate us. Our freedom is a function of our ability to mine locational pauses—*places* of record within space—that comprise instances of passage or moments on a space-place continuum that are sites of interest.

What I want to claim within the spatially imagistic frame sketched is that Zora Neale Hurston's *Mules and Men* (1935)[4] is a *locus classicus* for black women's creativity. The work assumes this status through its *instantiation* (a word that marks time and suggests place) of the conjure woman as a peculiar, imagistic, Afro-American space. Hurston's collection constitutes a locational moment of perception and half-creation within the space comprised by the voodoo doctor, the hoodoo fixer, the two-headed bearer of wisdom in Afro-America. To make clear the type of classical/spatial relationship I have in mind I want to invoke two universes of discourse—architecture and literary criticism.

Space is perhaps the architect's primary consideration. Architecture is an abstract art risking dreadful banality when it
resorts to representational designs like ice-cream cones, hot
dogs, brown derbies, and golden arches. Abstraction demands not concretization or reification but relation and relationship. The idea must be translated through appropriate
communicative channels and set in just relationship to features
comprising the space into which it is to move. Material is important in translation or communication, but the "material"
can be virtually immaterial. Air, light, and space, for example, are all elements of architectural design. The dissolving
of boundaries between traditionally material and immaterial
phenomena that marks the architectural enterprise is similar
to the transformation of space that constitutes architectural relationship. Any building project must decide to seek harmony
with the extant landscape, or to disrupt that harmony through
counter-spatial design, or to combine these strategies, adding
new dimensions while, at the same instant, preserving fidelity
to the existing landscape. We can think of successful architectural projects in terms mapped for literary classics by T. S.
Eliot's justly famous essay "Tradition and the Individual Talent."[5] Speaking of a literary succession from Homer to his
own century, Eliot writes:

> The existing monuments form an ideal order among
> themselves, which is modified by the introduction of
> the new (the really new) work of art among them. The
> existing order is complete before the new work arrives;
> for order to persist after the supervention of novelty,
> the *whole* existing order must be, if ever so slightly, al-
> tered; and so the relations, proportions, values of each
> work of art toward the whole are readjusted; and this is
> conformity between the old and the new. Whoever has
> approved this idea of order, of the form of European,
> of English literature will not find it preposterous that
> the past should be altered by the present as much as the
> present is directed by the past. And the poet who is
> aware of this will be aware of great difficulties and re-
> sponsibilities. (5)

The terms of Eliot's description are spatial and abstract. He
invokes "relations," "proportions," and "values" in his effort
to suggest how classics are created and sustained.

I want to suggest that a relationship of identity exists between the successful architectural project and a classic work of
verbal expressiveness because both are spatially constituted.
Their material inscriptions are less important than the cultural

dynamics they encompass and facilitate. Rather than simple reifications of ideas of their individualistic creators, they are transmitters of cultural dynamics. And they must accomplish their transmission in historically harmonious, yet contemporaneously efficacious, ways. A *classic* in any culture, one might say, is a space in which the spirit works. The very sign "classic" denotes an absence of temporal and material boundaries and suggests the accomplishment of effects through means outstripping the tangible and immediate.

If one seeks the classical in Afro-American expressive culture, one discovers without great difficulty a mode of discourse or performance that I call "mythomania."[6] Mythomania is the classical spirit work of Afro-America. Zora Neale Hurston's *Mules and Men* is simply one instance within this world of production. Mythomania is most aptly defined as: "a compulsion to embroider the truth, to exaggerate, or to tell lies." The French scholar Ernest Pierre Dupré in his attempt to describe psychic states achieved in voodoo rituals labels such a compulsion a *"pathologie de l'imagination,"* a sickness of the imagination and feelings.[7] Louis Mars, by contrast, in describing the authentic crisis of possession accompanying seizure by a *loa* in voodoo ritual (and paying close attention to the work of Dupré) distinguishes between the affectivity of possession and the compulsions of mythomania.[8] According to Mars, a person possessed by a *loa* (a spiritual intermediary between human and supernatural) loses all control of a first person and personality to the possessing spirit. The mythomaniac, by contrast, is, in Mars's account, akin to the hysteric.

In one definition, "the hysteric lies mostly with his body."[9] The distinction that interests Mars is between an emotive-kinetic mysticism and an objectivized fiction in which a mythomaniac tells, mimes, and performs with his or her own physical and mental personality. The distinction resides in the degree of conscious control separating the possessed from the performer. Hence, mythomania can be taken out of a strictly mythic domain and employed as a sign for any Afro-American "fabricating" performance designed for encounters with and manipulations of the Afro-American cultural anima, or spirit. And it might, possibly, be renamed as "mythophilia" in the estimate of the Nigerian poet Niyi Osundare, who recently made the suggestion to me in Ibadan. Such a renaming would accord very well with the process I have in mind, lending to it a fully affirmative cast. For the present, however, it seems wise to maintain "mythomania" as a marker of the

tradition of commentary on "voodoo" or "conjure" in which
this discussion is situated.

A primary component of what might be termed "classical" Afro-American discourse is "soul." In more sacral dimensions, this component is labeled "spirit." Soul motivates; spirit moves. The generative source of style in Afro-America is soul; the impetus for salvation is spirit. *The spirit* is the origin of species, one might say, for countless black generations who did not choose material deprivation, but who were brutally denied, as I have suggested earlier, ownership or control of *material* means of production. If these generations had not possessed nonmaterial modes of production, there would have been no production at all. Their situation would have been equivalent to the possession of "luck" in the blues: "If I didn't have hard luck, I wouldn't have *no* luck at all."

The preeminent question vis-à-vis Afro-America's classical performances designed to move the spirit is: How is spirit work accomplished? The answer is that spirit creativity, like *spirit* itself, is an ever innovative production. In psychoanalytical definition, spirit is an active projection. It is desire's objectification of a something other, a secondary inhabitant of a cosmos that it both constitutes as primary material and infuses. A topos bringing together both psychoanalytical and literary expressive deployment of the spirit appears in a quatrain from James Weldon Johnson's "The Creation."[10]

> And God stepped out on space,
> And he looked around and said:
> I'm lonely ——— I'll make me a world. (17)

God's smile rolls up darkness; light stands shining on the far side. The topos reveals not only the production of a "secondary inhabitant," but also the deployment of the spirited word to move from singularity and aloneness to the birth of light. And this topos is as variable as the spirit creation—the fabricating performance—that sets it in motion. The words of Professor Eleanor Traylor encoding Robert Hayden's magnificent poem "Runagate Runagate" come to mind as a variation on Johnson's topos.[11] That which "Runs falls rises stumbles on from darkness into darkness"[12] in Hayden's poem, according to Traylor, is Afro-American cultural anima. It is unbounded spirit moving "over trestles of dew, through caves of the wish" (77) to light.

In classical Afro-American discourse, the spirit may assume various guises. For the classically successful performance is contingent upon the ability to fabricate outrageously,

to improvise and embroider in outlandish fashion. The
"power" of classical strategies in black America resides in
one's ability to provide the nonce lie. For example, the arch
impostor of Ralph Ellison's college scene in *Invisible Man* is
President Bledsoe.[13] When the protagonist of the novel insists
that he is in trouble because he followed a white trustee's orders, Bledsoe responds, "He *ordered* you. Dammit, white folk
are always giving orders, it's a habit with them. . . . My God,
Boy! You're black and living in the South—did you forget
how to lie?" (136). If being "in the South" is taken as a metaphor for a traditionally oppressed or bounded situation, if it is
a sign that gestures, for example, toward the closures of overdetermined *meanings* in language, then one understands "the
lie" as a performance designed to forward the cultural anima's
always already impulse toward freedom or liberation. And in
such culturally grounded and always poetic performances,
distinctions between matter and spirit, form and content,
written and spoken are dissolved.

Spirit work, mythomanic (or, *pace* Osundare, "mytho-
philic") fabrication, is kaleidoscopic, and its variations reflect
a limitless cultural repertoire. A trickster rabbit, for example,
like a funky blues singer, makes impossible a clear distinction
between the singer and the song, the artful dodger and the
dodge. Furthermore, genre in classical Afro-American spirit
work is noncategorical; spaces that might be deemed "separate" are dissolved in the general medium of the spirit. Rather
than rigid formal categories and a restricted economy of content, Afro-American spirit work is as boundless in its efficacy
as the gift in Marcel Mauss's classic formulation.[14] For in
Afro-America what are traditionally defined as *gifts of the
spirit*—discernment, prophecy, and healing—are frequently
functions of work that transmits *spirit* in an efficacious manner. Such transmission preserves the spirit's gifts alive through
continual circulation. (Bob Nesta Marley singing "pass it on,
pass it on" comes to mind.) Mauss insists that gifts remain
powerfully gifts only as long as they are kept in passage, for
passage forestalls the promotion of any single "possessor"
(One might say any "individualistic creator") to a hierarchical
inequality. Gift passage, like Afro-American spirit work, assures the benefits of spirit only to a *community*.

A concern that poses itself here is the relationship between
considerations of space as habitable poetic territory and mythomania as performance. While I have used the general term
"mythomania" to denote the performance that defines the
classical in Afro-American culture, I have also suggested that
in mythomania, strategies are multiple, guises of the spirit

manifold, and genre, paradoxically, an almost noncategorical
denominator. Such flexibleness and permeability are functions
of the nonmateriality of classical space, which is always a *me-*
dium rather than a signally distinctive substance. The classical
space, one might insist, is a channel of passage and code of
transmission rather than a temporally bounded *message*. The
most intriguing way that Afro-American spirit has moved us
toward liberation has been through what we can term the *me-*
dium's transmission through the *medium* of fabrication, innovation, and improvisation. And definitions of "medium"
bring us appropriately to the principal poetic image—that of
the Afro-American hoodoo person or conjurer—which
emerges in a discussion of *Mules and Men.*

A "medium" is: "an agency, such as a person, object, or
quality, by means of which something is accomplished, conveyed, or transferred." A medium is also: "an intervening
channel through which something is transmitted or carried
on, such as an agency for transmitting energy." And, as we
know from what is frequently labeled "popular culture," a
medium is: "a person thought to have powers of communicating with the spirits of the dead." I believe the Afro-American
cultural sign that appropriately unites mythomania as classical
cultural performance, notions of the classical medium's space,
and useful notions of the poetic image is the sign "conjure."

〰〰〰

The conjurer in Afro-American culture is frequently referred to as a "two-headed doctor," a person of double wisdom who "carries power" as a result of his or her initiation
into the mysteries of the spirit. Such a person is a medium; she
works within the medium of a tradition called voodoo, or
hoodoo.

In Hurston's work we find the genealogy of the founders
of hoodoo, beginning with God and Jethro and moving on to
Moses, who in hoodoo's genesis story was the first to know
God's names, to learn the making words, to acquire the art of
writing, and to carry the signifying rod of power. God, in
hoodoo lineage,

> took Moses and crowned him and taught him. So
> Moses passed on beyond Jethro with his rod. He lifted
> it up and tore a nation out of Pharaoh's side, and Phar-
> aoh couldn't help himself. Moses talked with the snake
> that lives in a hole right under God's foot-rest. Moses
> had fire in his head and a cloud in his mouth. The

snake had told him God's making words. The words
of doing and the words of obedience. Many a man
thinks he is making something when he's only changing things around. But God let Moses make. And then
Moses had so much power he made the eight winged
angels split open a mountain to bury him in, and shut
up the hole behind him. (230)

But the (w)hole opens to allow the passage of the aboriginal
powers of hoodoo to the descendant and founder of the
"modern" line—Marie Leveau, quadroon child of a grandmother and mother who were hoodoo doctors.

Describing Marie Leveau's interactions with the spirit, one
of Hurston's informants, Luke Turner, tells how the greatest
of the two-headed healers (student of the powerful Alexander)
did her *work*:

> She go to her great Altar and seek until she become the
> same as the spirit, then she come into the room where
> she listens to them that come to ask. When they finish
> she answer them as a god. If a lady have a bad enemy
> and come to her she go into her altar room and when
> she come out and take her seat . . . Marie Leveau is not
> a woman. . . . No. She is a god, yes. Whatever she
> say, it will come so.

The merger of Leveau with the spirit at the great altar, her
ability to put to confusion enemies of those who seek her aid,
combined with her prophetic gift of articulating events that
must come to pass, provide a striking image of the Afro-
American cultural imagination. In Hurston's hands this poetic
image of the conjurer becomes more excitingly resonant than
the one in the work of the Afro-American writer Charles
Chesnutt, whose collected stories entitled *The Conjure Woman*
(1899) project the veritable control of a plantation by the conjure woman's ministrations.[15] Chesnutt, unlike Hurston,
never puts forward a truly scintillating image of the woman
prophet, magician, or healer herself as a figure irradiant in the
magnificence of her specific powers. In fact, the turn-of-the-
century black writer's Aunt Peggy is a function of a specifically male appropriation of the conjure woman's work. For
Uncle Julius McAdoo's telling of the "work" of Aunt Peggy
is, like the conjure woman's work itself, designed to influence
the economy of *his* situation. His telling of the work is meant
to gain, as it were, clearly male material benefits. His ultimate
aim is to alter the controlling interests of the white entrepre-
neur who has purchased the former plantation that Julius calls

home. Julius, however, does not "carry power" in the form signified by either Aunt Peggy or Marie Leveau.

In effect, the virtue of *Mules and Men* is that it amply defines the type of the conjure woman not only through stirring images like that of Marie Leveau but also (and with magnificent cleverness) through the writer's own initiation into the spiritual world of hoodoo. The last quarter of Hurston's collection chronicles her own initiations into the mysteries, first by Eulalia and then by a succession of male "doctors," culminating, at last, in her apprenticeship to Kitty Brown.

It seems to me that much of the positive cultural resonance accompanying Hurston's concluding relationship to *conjure* is a function of the importance conjure has historically possessed for an African diasporic community. Writing in opposition to one traditional, white historical thesis that claims enslaved blacks had no significant others to look to but members of the master class, the historian John Blassingame asserts:

> In addition to these activities [religious and recreational], several other customs prevented the slaves from identifying with the ideals of their masters. Because of their superstitions and beliefs in fortune tellers, witches, magic and conjurers, many of the slaves constructed a psychological defense against total dependence on and submission to their masters. Whatever his power, the master was a puny man compared to the supernatural. Often the most powerful and significant individual on the plantation was the conjurer.[16]

One reason the conjurer held such a powerful position in diasporic African communities was her direct descent from the African medicine man and her place in a religion that had definable African antecedents. There are various perspectives on the origin of conjure as an established practice in the United States, and some are far more gratifying to Afro-Americans than others. Less positive explanations tend to read like a 1951 *Encyclopaedia Britannica* entry that concludes: "Serpent-worship and obscene rites involving the use of human blood, preferably that of a white child, were considered features of this religion."[17] (254). One suspects that it was the high theatrics of those who sought to turn white credulity to profit that resulted in such a stupidly condescending description. These theatrics are captured in a report from the New Orleans *Times-Democrat* of 24 June 1896.[18] Describing a voodoo festival it reads as follows; "The rites consisted in building a large fire, in a dance on the part of the central personage, the destruction of a black cat and its devouring raw. The scene concluded with an orgie, in which the savage actors ended by tearing off their garments" (183). The participants in the festival were doubtless "actors" who must have been delighted with the newspaper's "savage" accounting since it probably increased the white patronage of future occasions. Chroniclers of voodoo, or conjure, who view it as a scene of primitivism usually define it as derivative—an aberration of certain orthodox and heretical practices of European Catholicism. For example, there is an etymology that considers the word *voodoo* an extension of the French *vaudois* meaning "witch." The next step in this etymology is to trace voodoo to the heretical Christian sect of the Waldenses which arose in the south of France in the Middle Ages. The reason for such a spurious French lineage, presumably, is the strength and the syncretic (combining Catholic and African elements) nature of voodoo in Haiti.

If there is a kind of "colonialist" history of conjure, however, there is also a more accurate and gratifying one. Michel Laguerre, in his 1980 study *Voodoo Heritage*, traces the origins of conjure to a set of religious practices of the Yoruba people of the West Coast of Africa.[19] The name *voodoo* derives from Vodun, the name of the principal deity of these Yoruba rites. Vodun rituals feature both a priest and a priestess, with the priestess (called the *Mambo* in Haiti) as the central figure—the person who is oracle to the spirit of Vodun carried in the sacred serpent. Combining with colonial French Catholicism, voodoo became the dominant religion of the masses in Haiti and a powerful and pervasive force among the African population of New Orleans (especially in Algiers, the city called "hoodoo town," across the river from New Orleans) and the southern Black Belt. The influence and effects of voodoo as a diasporic African religious practice can be traced to the early eighteenth century. And voodoo, or conjure, has been an affective presence among blacks from that time until the present.

Newbell Niles Puckett, writing of *Folk Beliefs of the Southern Negro*[20] in 1926, not only asserts that "perhaps a hundred old men and women" practiced voodooism as a profession in Atlanta in 1885 (196), but also cites instances of the effects and influences of conjure in places like Philadelphia and the Black Belt of his own day. The historian Charles Blockson calls attention to the twentieth-century conjure and healing work of Hannah Prosser of Lancaster County, Pennsylvania.[21] And Ralph Ellison's *Invisible Man* includes among its significant details of the Harlem environment the following shopwindow scene: "A flash of red and gold from a window filled with religious articles caught my eye. And behind the film of frost etching the glass I saw two brashly painted plaster images of Mary and Jesus surrounded by dream books, love pow- ders, God-Is-Love signs, money drawing oil and plastic dice" (228). The Afro-American comedian Richard Pryor has grafted the conjure woman onto the popular imagination with his magnificent rendition of the story of Miss Rudolph, who has a three-legged monkey and wears a monkey foot around her neck. The African American type of the hoodoo or con- jure woman, thus, has not only discernible African religious origins, but also perduring resonance.

While it is true that one receives less sense of conjure as a mass religion from accounts of United States practices than from accounts of Haitian voodoo, it is also true that mass be- lief in conjure among Afro-Americans is amply attested by the gigantic collecting work done by Harry M. Hyatt in his five-volume compendium of *Hoodoo, Conjuration, Witchcraft, Rootwork.*[22] Zora Hurston, as a scholarly compeer to Hyatt, offers one of the most profound pictures of Haitian voodoo in her 1938 book, *Tell My Horse.*[23] Voodoo, according to Hur- ston, "is the old, old mysticism of the world in African terms" (137). The strikingly womanist power of this African practice is captured in the opening anecdote to the voodoo section of *Tell My Horse.* Hurston reports:

> "What is the truth?" Dr. Holly asked me, and knowing
> that I could not answer him he answered himself
> through a Voodoo ceremony in which the Mambo,
> that is the priestess, richly dressed, is asked this ques-
> tion ritualistically. She replies by throwing back her
> veil and revealing her sex organs. The ceremony means
> that this is the infinite, the ultimate truth. There is no
> mystery beyond the mysterious sources of life. (137)

What draws together the voodoo of Haiti and the conjure of the United States—in addition to their common African origin and enduring mass appeal—is their relationship to what I have earlier called workings of the spirit, mythomania, or nonce fabrication. One informant from Mary A. Owen's 1881 account called *Among the Voodoos* asserted: "To be 'strong in de haid'—that is, of great strength of will—is the most im- portant characteristic of a 'conjurer' or 'voodoo.' Never mind what you mix—blood, bones, feathers, grave-dust, herbs, sa- liva, or hair—it will be powerful or feeble in proportion to the dauntless spirit infused by you, the priest or priestess, at the time you represent the god."[24] Puckett reports: "It is difficult to generalize upon the matter of hoodooing, since the charms

are seldom made twice in the same manner; the materials used
and the way of putting them together depending almost entirely upon the momentary whim of the individual conjurer"
(239). In *Tell My Horse*, the *houngan*, or priest of voodoo, is
the carrier of the powerful Ascon (a version of Moses's sacred
staff). He speaks the secret "language" dictated by the *loa*s,
abolishes evil spirits, initiates believers into the mysteries,
commands the *verver*s (or signatures) of the gods, and may
even have the transformative power to convert himself into a
Bocor, or dealer in zombies. He is, in short, a powerful spirit
worker who gives credence to the general character of voodoo
or conjure as it has functioned in diasporic African history.
That character is best stated in a phrase drawn from Hyatt's
monumental collection: "To catch a spirit, or to protect your
spirit against the catching, or to release your caught spirit—
this is the complete theory and practice of hoodoo."[25]

The fullest resonance of Hurston's habitation of conjure
can be seen in the role it plays in her corpus. Three of her
seven well-known volumes are directly dependent upon the
type of the *houngan*, hoodoo doctor, or conjurer. *Moses, Man
of the Mountain*, *Tell My Horse*, and of course, *Mules and Men*
are all conjure books of the first magnitude. And the 1935
Mules and Men, as I have suggested earlier, demonstrates the
efficacies of conjure as a cultural image in what might be conceived as a self-contained manner—that is to say, through the
writer's own self-recorded journey home, her theoretical return. The power of the narrative's final sections—the implications and resonances of their *conjure*—is contingent upon a
textual orchestration that commences with the first words of
the narrative. We understand the force of Hurston's specific
habitation of the image only by following the narrative's riffs
and improvisations, subtleties and significations from the
outset.

〰〰

The first voice encountered in *Mules and Men* is that of the
anthropologist Franz Boas, a German Jewish scholar referred
to by Hurston in her autobiography *Dust Tracks on a Road* as
"the king of kings" (170). Boas's preface to the narrative begins as follows: "Ever since the time of Uncle Remus, Negro
folk-lore has exerted a strong attraction upon the imagination
of the American public." The second voice presented is Hurston's, in the introduction to the narrative. She describes first
her gratitude when Boas told her "You may go and collect

Negro folk-lore." She continues by telling how anthropology as a discipline provided a uniquely objective perspective on a folklore that she had known since birth.

While Boas praises Hurston's access to the subjective "inner life of the Negro," Hurston pays tribute to the objective perspective of Boas's anthropology. She enhances her introduction with a story about a Jewish man who steals the entire "soul-piece"—who appropriates to himself the inner essence of humanity—that God meant to distribute to all people in equal measure. Unable to contain or carry the power of the "soul-piece," the thief scatters bits over the ground as he is lifted violently across the mountains. People are only able to obtain "chips and pieces" of soul. In time, says the narrator, God is going to "ketch dat Jew. . . . [and] He's going to 'vide things up more ekal'" (20).

The concluding paragraph of the introduction offers gratitude to Mrs. R. Osgood Mason of New York City, who is described as a "Great Soul" and the "world's most gallant woman." Mrs. Mason not only possesses more than her fair share of soul but also has the financial resources that allowed her to support and contour Hurston's collecting enterprise at the rate of two hundred dollars a month for two years. Mrs. Mason is, in Hurston's phrase from *Dust Tracks*, a queenly "Godmother." Hurston's introductory discursive gestures combine with the narrative action of *Mules and Men's* chapters 6 through 10 of part 1 to give point to the narrative's scenes of initiation and hoodoo work.

In the five chapters mentioned, we are introduced to a lively cast of characters who enact a drama of spiraling violence and intracultural conflict that implicitly seeks the ameliorating mythomanic healer found in *Mules and Men's* concluding part. First, we meet Jim Allen, husband of Mrs. Allen, who runs the boardinghouse for the Everglades Cypress Lumber Company in Loughman, Florida—the sawmill camp in Polk County where Hurston collected the bulk of her tales for *Mules and Men*. A *lying* session (continuously, the tales in the narrative are designated "lies") has been in furious and prolific progress when Mr. Allen intones:

> "Y'all sho must not b'long to no church de way y'all tells lies. Y'all done quit tellin' em. Y'all done gone to moldin' em. But y'all want to know how come snakes got poison in they mouth and nothin' else ain't got it?" (130)

One of the young men participating in the session responds: "Yeah, tell it, Jim." Mr. Allen angrily retorts:

"Don't you be callin' me by my first name. Ah'm old
enough for yo' grand paw! You respect my gray hairs.
Ah don't play wid chillun. Play wid a puppy and he'll
lick yo' mouf." (130)

The young man apologizes, then uses proper address, saying,
"Mr. Jim, please tell how come de snake got poison."

In this exchange between Mr. Allen and Arthur Hopkins,
cultural hierarchies and narrational proprieties are threatened
for a moment, but are quickly—and deferentially—restored.
Cultural discourse continues in harmonious fashion. But conditions of possibility for greater disruption have been foreshadowed by circumstances leading up to the lying session itself. The reason a moment exists for leisurely fishing by the
Everglade Cypress loggers is a personnel shortage. Two
weeks before their excursion, the camp's "watchman who
sleeps out in the swamp and gets up steam in the skitter every
morning before the men get to the cypress swamp, had been
killed by a panther" (92). Moreover, on the day of the fishing
trip, the swamp boss fails to appear and the logging train must
be deployed elsewhere.

An unusual series of events, thus, leads to leisure, and an
unusual party is formed for the exercise of leisure. A traditionally all-male fishing party is replaced by a group containing Lucy and Big Sweet—women more than capable of holding their own on "the job." (Zora is also present and by
narrative implication takes on the character of the other
women by association.) These unusual circumstances come to
a disruptive head shortly after Mr. Allen's injunction to Arthur Hopkins on age and respect.

The men have been telling stories of cats when Gene
Oliver changes topics. "Talking 'bout dogs," he says, "they
got plenty sense. Nobody can't fool dogs much" (161). But
what might be a transition within subject categories becomes
a disruption when Big Sweet says, "And speakin' 'bout hams,
if Joe Willard don't stay out of dat bunk he was in last night,
Ah'm gointer sprinkle some salt down his back and sugar-
cure *his* hams" (161). The low-grade (but always threatening)
competition for narrative authority between men and women
seen in *Mules and Men's* encounters between Gold and Gene
(42 ff.), Mathilda and B. Moseley (49 ff.), and Shug and Ben-
nie Lee (56–57) in chapter 2 breaks forth into a palpable ani-
mosity with Big Sweet's remark.

Joe responds by telling Sweet to "quit tryin' to signify,"
and he bemoans the impropriety that has allowed her to be

present. But Sweet is implacable. Jim Allen tries to smooth things over with a quip. "Well, you know what they say—a man can cackerlate his life till he get mixed up wid a woman or get straddle of a cow" (162). Big Sweet turns on him viciously and says, "Who you callin' a cow, fool? Ah know you ain't namin' *my* mama's daughter no cow" (162). Her challenge, unlike the earlier and unintentional slight of Arthur Hopkins, cannot be simply answered or transformed. Instead, it demands a detailing of the hermeneutics of Afro-American narration itself.

Mr. Allen defensively responds: "Now all y'all heard what Ah said. Ah ain't called nobody no cow. Dat's just an old time by-word 'bout no man kin tell what's gointer happen when he gits mixed up wid a woman or set straddle of a cow" (162). Larkins White, one of the younger men, verifies the ontology of "by-words": "There's a whole heap of them kinda by-words. They all got a hidden meanin', jus' like de Bible." The distinction that Larkins makes is between a primary or visible scripture and a condensed, poetic distillate that constitutes earned, improvisational cultural wisdom.

Interpretive ability is of the essence of poetic faith. Larkins explains such abilities through a fitting invocation from his own stock of bywords. He says, "Most people is thin-brained. They's born wid they feet under de moon. Some folks is born wid they feet on de sun and they can seek out de inside meanin' of words" (163). After Larkins speaks, the ground is once more clear—the conversational floor reestablished, as it were—for Mr. Allen to step forth as a speaker. He tells the story of a recent college graduate who recommends that his father be tied astraddle a cow to keep the cow from bucking and kicking over the pail during milking. The father, who trades his intuitive sense for a bookish recommendation, comes to distress.

The full text of the tale from which Mr. Allen's aphorism (byword) has come does more than provide an example of the elder man's restored, communally sanctioned narrative authority. It also focuses on cows and preposterous college boys, displacing one term of the byword's unflattering comparison. Woman as a source and cause of unpredictability is, in fact, altogether absent from the full *ur*-text as recounted by Mr. Allen. The center of the story as he tells it is a "thin-brained" interpretation and solution that lead to a father's incalculable fate. Tied to the runaway cow, his answer to an inquirer who seeks to know where he is headed is: "Only God and dis cow knows" (164). Big Sweet's interruption and threat to the continuance of cultural discourse is, thus, only momentarily displaced. The breach is cleverly, but only momentarily, bridged by the suppression of an unflattering comparison.

The latent violence and threatened disharmony between men and women that surface most patently in the Big Sweet/Joe Willard exchange seem to receive ominous reinforcement through a shift in folktale content that appears at the beginning of chapter 8. In this chapter, the Afro-American folk figure John, who serves as the humorous trickster of a well-known postbellum cycle, is transformed. Generally pictured as a clownish fellow who outwits Ole Massa with luck and cunning, he is the entertaining and roguish hero of stories the loggers tell as they wait for the swamp boss. In chapter 8, however, he appears uncharacteristically as a Bad Man hero. With razor and gun, he convinces the bear and the lion that he properly owns the title "King of the World" (171–174). "Yeah," says the transfigured John, "Ah'm de king. Don't you like it, don't you take it. Here's mah coller, come and shake it" (173). Big Sweet assumes a character similar to John's before the chapter concludes. "Well," she says, "if Joe Willard try to take these few fishes he done caught where he shackup last night, Ah'm gointer take my Tampa switch-blade knife, and Ah'm goin' round de hambone lookin' for meat" (178). Joe Willard, the wandering philanderer who needs to be cured of his roving ways, is under threat, and there is an absence of heterosexual bonding that seems to point to a more general cultural instability and absence of communal integrity. Lucy, for example, who is supposed to be Big Sweet's friend and ally is, in fact, in league with Ella Wall, the rival from Mulberry who has attracted Joe's attention. No general and trustworthy female alliance seems extant.

In chapters 9 and 10—the last sections of part 1—threatened violence forcefully erupts. Big Sweet and Ella Wall, who are bent on deadly confrontation, are only prevented from bloodshed by the intervention of the quarter boss. Lucy tries to stab Zora because she believes the folklorist has alienated the affections of her man, Slim. (As, indeed, Hurston has.) Hurston decides that it is time for her to depart the sawmill camp.

Only a momentary focus on her new collecting site "in the phosphate country around Mulberry" (201) forestalls part 1's concluding scene of disorder and chaos. The setting in Ella Wall's territory heightens rather than diminishes the threats of violence. The moment of delay is filled with hints of disharmony, conflict, and murder. The world evoked by Mulberry storytellers is populated by Raw Head, Big Sixteen, High

Walker, and the Devil. We witness a man and wife parted by a devil's accomplice, see an expectant woman hoping for marriage frozen to death, and learn of High Walker's decapitation.

When Zora returns to the Everglades Cypress camp (ironically, to attend a wedding that projects a sense of harmony), it is only a matter of *when* and not *whether* a scene of disorder will occur. Bringing early narrative foreshadowings to fullness is the appearance of Crip. He is the new skitter man who replaces the watchman killed by a panther. Lucy has become his lover in return for his promise to aid her in killing Zora. A fight breaks out at the Pine Mill jook joint in which Joe Willard and Big Sweet are pitted against Crip and Lucy. The description of a community in disorder—a world undone by philandering males and women in competition—reads as follows:

> Lucy was screaming. Crip had hold of Big Sweet's clothes in the back and Joe was slugging him loose. Curses, oaths, cries and the whole place was in motion. Blood was on the floor. I fell out of the door over a man lying on the steps, who either fell himself trying to run or got knocked down. (225)

No restorative is immediately available. Narrative, fabricating, or poetic authority—like all other ordering principles—is absent. Flight from, rather than a cure for, disharmony is the narrator's response: "I was in the car in a second and in high just too quick" (225).

What she leaves behind are men and women who claim to carry "the law" in their mouths, who are of titanic proportions and energies. It would seem that only a set of cultural doctrines that go deeper than the lore of everyday life issuing from culture bearers such as Mr. Allen can compel and regulate this gigantic, vernacular cultural force. Big Sweet, for example, not only backs down a two-gun bearing quarter boss, but also stands as the recipient of Joe Willard's high praise: "You wuz noble! You wuz uh whole woman and half a man. You made dat cracker stand offa you" (195). Ella Wall, too, is full of robust energy that sounds much like John's when she intones: "I'm raggedy, but right; patchey but tight; stringy but I *will* hang on" (192). A portrait of energetic men who require a strong cultural brew is presented when Hurston confides that many of the sawmill hands were fugitives from justice—outlaws on the job who

> not only . . . chop rhythmically, but . . . do a beautiful twirl above their heads with the ascending axe before it begins that accurate and bird-like descent. They can

hurl their axes great distances and behead moccasins or sink the blade into an alligator's skull. In fact, they seem to be able to do everything with their instrument that a blade can do. It is a magnificent sight to watch the marvelous co-ordination between the handsome black torsos and the twirling axes (92).

Though *Mules and Men*'s narrator, fearing her own death, refers to the sawmill camp as *sordid* (193), one can infer from scenes in chapters 6 through 10 that she is thoroughly absorbed by the rhythms of a full-muscled heroically womaned, fiercely articulate vernacular community represented by the Everglades camp. One also infers that she understands that only a powerful, indigenously constructed set of guidelines and procedures will suffice to order such a community. Perhaps only an "outlaw religion."

Part 2 of *Mules and Men* virtually begins with the statement "The city of New Orleans has a law against fotune tellers, hoodoo doctors and the like" (p. 239). *Conjure*, the poetic image of primary concern, is a sign for "a suppressed religion. . . . [that has] thousands of secret adherents . . . [and] adapts itself . . . to its locale" (229). "New Orleans is now and ever has been the hoodoo capital of America" (229). In the capital city of conjure Hurston takes up the mysterious and magical work that can harmonize and renew a disrupted community. Her journey begins in spring and has the flamelike intensity of the very conjure she strives to inhabit. When Mrs. Viney asks, "But looka here, Zora, whut you want wid a two-headed doctor? Is somebody done throwed a old shoe at *you*?" (233), the folklorist responds, "Not exactly neither one, Mrs. Viney. Just want to learn how to do things myself."

We come, therefore, to the successive initiations that Hurston undergoes before becoming a friend, apprentice, and co-worker to Kitty Brown. Behind her and behind the reader of *Mules and Men* is a vision of a ruptured, but productive, vernacular community, a world whose undoing seems the result of competition for narrative authority, an absence of female bonding, and a philandering propensity of axe-twirling, prolifically articulate males. What type of initiation into what manner of poetic or spiritual space enables Zora to occupy a role in *conjure*?

〜〜〜

Her initiations, like those of all doctors in the founding line of conjure, occur at the hands of those who have been

assured of their ability to carry power and to engage in activities akin to God's. For the initiation rites are designed to teach,
to pass on making words, and to ready initiates for the crown
of power. The Africanness of conjure's genealogy in Hurston's
account begins with Jethro the Ethiopian, whose daughter
married Moses. It is strengthened by the Ethiopian wisdom
transported by Sheba to Solomon by means of her talking
ring.

The poetry of *conjure* as an image resides in the secrecy and
mysteriousness of its sources of power, in its connection to
ancient African sources syncretized by a community of diasporic believers with Christian scriptures, and in the masterful improvisational skills of its most dramatic practitioners.
The notion of Marie Leveau captured by Luke Turner's description of her first appearance to him gives a sense of the
majesty of a poetic conjure in the folk imagination. Speaking
of the annual feast conducted by Leveau on the Eve of St.
John, Turner says:

> "But Nobody see Marie Leveau for nine days before
> the feast. But when the great crowd of people at the
> feast call upon her, she would rise out of the waters of
> the lake with a great communion candle burning upon
> her head and another in each one of her hands. She
> walked upon the waters to the shore. As a little boy I
> saw her myself. When the feast was over, she went
> back into the lake, and nobody saw her for nine days
> again." (241)

The description provides some idea why Leveau is called the
"Queen of Conjure" and why she represents one instance of a
general poetics associated with carrying power. She is the
grand worker, the closest *modern* (born 2 February 1827) figuration of a line of spirit workers that begins with the world's
creation.

In order to obtain even a modicum of the conjure resources possessed by Leveau, Hurston must apprentice herself
to those who carry power in New Orleans. She describes her
initiations in both mystical and educational terms. Learning
conjure requires one to pay "tuition," to assume the status of
"pupil," and to look upon conjures practitioners as members
of the "college of hoodoo doctors" (247). Of the initiation's
mystical character, she writes:

> [The] preparation period is akin to that of all mystics.
> Clean living, even to clean thoughts. A sort of going
> to the wilderness in the spirit. The details do not ma-
> ter. (247)

Elsewhere, she compares her initiation to a movement from a
novitiate to a sacred wedding with The Spirit.

I take her phrase "the details do not matter" as a caution
not to view any single set of procedures as the only access or
fit initiation to The Spirit. Union with what is variously called
"The Great One," "The Power-Giver," "The Man God,"and
"The Spirit" can only be effected in the first instance by those
capable of "carrying power"—presumably a genetic *and* culturally specific capability. Furthermore, even those who seem
gifted to carry power must await the Spirit's voice and accept
the Spirit's dictates before approaching the altar. "Spirit!" intones Luke Turner after Zora's hours of fasting and accompanying psychic experiences, "I ask you to take her. Do you hear
me, Spirit? Will you take her? Spirit, I want you to take her,
she is worthy" (249) Bestowing the sobriquet "Rain Bringer,"
the Spirit does indeed accept Zora as a conjurer.

The conjure work in which she engages can be classified as
retribution, redress, reward, and renewal. Enemies are repaid
with punishment; grievances are remedied; faith yields divi-
dends of good luck and found love; the ailing are renewed.
Successful work is contingent upon the doctor's skill, the
client's faith, and an adequate sum of money invested toward
change. While Zora does aid in rituals designed to bring death
to an enemy, to prevent the rise of a rival professional, and to
gain a favorable court decision for an accused felon, the primary petitioners for retribution and redress are women. Her
first teacher—Eulalia—"specialized in Man-and-woman
cases" (233), and as Zora moves through successive initiations, the principal cases that come before her teachers are
brought by women. Communal disharmony, malaise, and
sickness seem metonymically represented by the troubles
these various women bear. And the very efficacy of conjure
seems to be reflected in the retributive justice and restored
harmony effected by successful negotiations with two-headed
doctors. Conjure is restorative in the sense both of a cure and
of a renewal of diminished passions and compassion.

The various rites enacted—upon suitable payment ranging as high as $250—by the conjurer represent a combination
of sympathetic and homeopathic magic, bringing into the
conjurer's act both physical items (such as hair or fingernails)
and performative items (such as dolls and miniature coffins).
Hurston notes at a number of instances that the entire wisdom
of whatever doctor she is working with cannot be placed in
Mules and Men. Nonetheless, she provides enough details of
90 her own learning, of her successful communication with the

Spirit and confident manipulation of spells and rites to convince us that she does, indeed, carry power.

At the commencement of her sojourn in New Orleans, she discovers a certain body of women whom she describes as follows: "I found women reading cards and doing mail order business in names and insinuations of well known factors in conjure. Nothing worth putting on paper" (239). Unlike this company of spurious businesswomen, Hurston, when she makes her way to the house of Kitty Brown, has acquired much that is "worth putting on paper." The wisdom she is able to transmit, in fact, is that of an entire vernacular community and its conditions of both disharmony and possible cure. That such a community has faith in the conjure wisdom, the hoodoo power, the Spirit work that she carries is attested by the attention devoted to such an audience in *Mules and Men*'s penultimate chapter.

"Before telling of my experience with Kitty Brown," writes the narrator, "I want to relate the following conjure stories which illustrate the attitude of Negroes of the Deep South toward this subject" (287). Zora, who has assumed the role of collector throughout the narrative, takes on the function of vernacular storyteller in part 2's chapter 6. What she relates are stories that demonstrate the presence of conjure as a process in everyday African American life and the efficacy of conjure in overcoming arrogant power and outgoing violence—like that of the "wealthy planter of Middle Georgia" who is undone by a black man's hoodoo. Her third story shows that malevolent works are possible when conjure falls into the wrong hands. Each of the tales implicitly speaks of a religion of conjure in black life. Rather than demonstrating the poetics of conjure, chapter 6 captures the sociology of the poetic image. It illustrates the nature and function of conjure as an agency in Afro-American life. And we remember that the bearer of the spiritual legacy in "modern" African American—indeed, one might say, modern African diasporic—life was not a king like Solomon, but a queen, priestess, or Mambo like Marie Leveau.

Womanly spiritual agency is certainly what one infers from the description of Kitty Brown that opens the final chapter of *Mules and Men*:

> Kitty Brown is a well-known hoodoo doctor of New
> Orleans, and a Catholic. She liked to make marriages
> and put lovers together. She is squat, black and benign.
> Often when we had leisure, she told funny stories. Her

herb garden was pretty full and we often supplied
other doctors with plants. Very few raise things since
the supply houses carry about everything that is
needed. But sometimes a thing is wanted fresh from
the ground. That's where Kitty's garden came in. (297)

"Fresh from the ground" we find the productive *garden*, like
Walker's discovered place of our mothers. In *Mules and Men*,
the garden is equivalent to a pharmacy; it is a place from
which healing roots and magical herbs of conjure derive. And
Kitty—in her squat black benignity—has the character of a
deceptively droll African religious sculpture. Her tremendous
powers among a congregation of vernacular believers is
masked by her unremarkable posture. Surely, however, it is
because she, like Zora, is a carrier of the Black Cat Bone that
she traverses the earth with her powers unseen. A storyteller
and a uniter of lovers, a woman who has syncretized Western
religion and African cultural traditions to ensure powers of
retribution, redress, reward, and renewal, she provides a
model of conjuring that the entire text of *Mules and Men* prepares us for. She is the intimate *home*, the imagistic habitation
or poetic space of the spirit in which works of mythomanic
transmission can take place.

The fact that Zora takes on Kitty's function—dancing as
her substitute in a strenuous conjure ritual—while Kitty bears
the suffering of spiritual initiation for Zora, suggests a relationship of identity between the narrator and the New Orleans two-headed doctor. Zora, in effect, inhabits Kitty's *conjure woman* as spiritual space. Kitty, in turn, says, "In order for
you to reach the spirit somebody has got to suffer. I'll suffer
for you because I'm strong. It might be the death of you"
(297). What the final initiation into conjure seems to imply is
the narrator's arrival at a point of cultural intimacy, a spiritual
space that enables her body to be a mere vehicle for the spirit's
passage. Her being as a whole seems to be bonded in womanist ways to a root worker who likes "to make marriages and
put lovers together."

━━━〜〜〜━━━

The rituals that Zora conducts in partnership with Kitty
Brown include, first, a dance for the death of a treacherous
"John Doe" who has taken Rachel Roe's money and used it to
lure a young girl to his bed. Next, she assists in a set of procedures designed to fulfill Minnie Foster's desire to have,

keep, and rule her man. Five days after the dance calculated to end John Doe's life he deserts his young lover and returns to Rachel. And in the penultimate paragraph of *Mules and Men*, we overhear Kitty's recital to Minnie of a formula designed to change her man's mind "about going away" (303).

Hurston's camaraderie with the vernacular community represented by inhabitants of the Florida sawmill seems to come to fullness in her final hoodoo partnership. Having made her way in the first three-quarters of *Mules and Men* through various spaces of the Afro-American vernacular, she at last achieves the power of a two-headed doctor. Her final appearance as a hoodoo healer locates her within a *community of women* who have the powers on their side.

In her appropriation of a corner in the house of conjure, Zora becomes a source of renewal, perpetuation, and harmony for the strong-willed community represented in chapters 6 through 10. Issues of narrative authority and gender are decisively resolved in the image of the conjure woman. There is no room for debate where Kitty Brown's powers are concerned. When she conducts hoodoo rites designed to change the philandering ways of bodacious men, they have no choice but to return to a faithful domesticity. Furthermore, the bonding between Zora and Kitty that provides enabling conditions for curing philanderers testifies to an achieved and trustworthy alliance between women. The absence of such camaraderie is, of course, a primary reason for the disruptions in the concluding chapters of part 1. Finally, the rites of conjure allow a petitioner like Minnie Foster to achieve a hoodoo or conjure brew that is strong enough to control the axe-twirling energies of a Gabe Staggers. When Minnie expresses her fear that Gabe's migratory employment with a construction gang might take him away forever, Kitty reassures her with a conjuring formula:

> "Oh, alright Minnie, go do like I say and he'll sure be back. Write the name of the absent party six times on paper. Put the paper in a water glass with two tablespoons full of quicksilver on it. Write his or her name three times each on six candles and burn one on a window sill in the daytime for six days." (302)

The formula works. Gabe returns with love in his eyes.

The powers of conjure to provide guidelines, controls, motivation, and remedies for a black vernacular community grow out of the ancient, authentic African origins of its practices. These powers are mightily enhanced, however, by the poetic image of conjure in Afro-American culture. That image is most scintillating and liberating when it appears as the Mambo, priestess, or conjure woman rising—ascending like Marie Leveau with the light of wisdom glowing from her head and the brilliance of her works of hand illustrated by votive candles. Narrative authority is sonorously captured in the words of Luke Turner: "Whatever she say, it will come so."

By inference, one might suggest that whatever Zora Hurston projects in terms of the vernacular community that she has so creatively explored must "come so." The two separate domains of her subtitle for *Mules and Men—Negro Folktales and Voodoo Practices in the South*—come together in the concluding postures of her narrative. "Negro folktales," or harmonious cultural discourse that provides and seeks such tales as reference, are contingent upon "voodoo practices" as regulators of Afro-American communal life. Without the outlaw religion of conjure and its powers to cure and ensure bonding, there could be no tales. In a sense, the energies of Jim Allen and Big Sweet coalesce in the space of conjure. Zora Hurston—as storyteller of part 2's chapter 6 and as two-headed doctor of chapter 7—combines the roles of bearer of cultural wisdom and woman with the "law in her mouth." One might, in fact, invoke the praise song of Joe Willard and say that Hurston as conjurer is "noble"; she is "uh whole woman and half a man." For her strictly womanly conjuring authority enables her to displace the quotidian narrative energies of Jim Allen by the time we arrive at part 2. She not only tells stories in her own right, but also relates stories that have to do with the most profound spiritual practices of a vernacular community. Rather than an engaging lay narrator, she is a spiritual griot seeking her authority in doctrines and practices that have ancient spiritual roots. By inhabiting the image of *conjure*, one might say, the narrator assumes not merely a power to "change things around" through storytelling, but an ability to "make" an emergent nation of Africans in America. Rather than a "sordid" and "quaint"collection of fugitives, the towering figures of the Everglades Cypress company are inhabitants of a diasporic community whose history has not been invented. Hurston is their uncompromising historian, presenting an unromantic picture of their hard-pressed striving. She also demonstrates, in powerfully poetic terms, however, that their lore and lives, rather than helpless prey to random violence and disorderly rivalry, are subject to the severe codes of conjure. And the space of conjure—both historically and in the narrative frames of her corpus—is most fully defined by

women.

In *Folk Beliefs*, Puckett writes:

> One of the first things we conjure-doctors have to do is to diagnose the case, tell the person whether he is conjured or not . . . and to find out who "layed de trick." The "trick" (charm) must be found and destroyed and the patient cured. If the patient wishes we must also be able to turn the trick back upon the one who set it. (207)

What Hurston discovers in the Everglades Cypress sawmill camp is an image of American enterprise captured by the double-.45-carrying quarter boss who commands the labor and leisure of a group of "outlaw" laborers. The vision is not far removed from a picture of American slavery. The community of the mill has been enslaved, as it were, by the "trick bag" of a dominating society. They have been subjugated to exploitative conditions through the sorcery of white America. Their escape is only through the wisdom of words. When Big Sweet, Joe Willard, or Ella Wall claim to have the "law in their mouths," they are indicating the power of their healing and liberating words to change their status from passive victims to heroic molders of poetic wisdom, indeed, to the role of hoodoo historians of a nation whose history has not yet been invented. They are all possibility in their poetry. The introduction of "voodoo practices" among them means that they can "turn the trick back upon the one who set it."

In *Mules and Men*, the verbal or narrative turning of the trick can be seen in the final storytelling of the narrator. If we remember that she is a full-fledged inhabitant of the Afro-American space of conjure, we shall have no trouble coding the vernacular and radical dimensions of her tale. For in her concluding role Hurston demonstrates the intense and powerfully fine trickery that she realizes as a function of womanly communitas in the house and garden of Kitty Brown.

Mules and Men ends with the story of Sis Cat, who one day catches a rat and sits down at the table to eat her prey. The rat cunningly asks: "Hol' on dere, sis Cat! Ain't you got no manners atall? You going set up to de table and eat 'thout washing yo' face and hands?" When Sis Cat returns from her ablutions, the rat is of course gone. The next time she catches a rat, however, ole Sis is wiser. When asked about washing and manners, she responds: "Oh, Ah got plenty manners. But Ah eats mah dinner and washes mah face and uses mah manners afterward."

The last line of *Mules and Men* delivered by Zora is: "I'm sitting here like Sis Cat, washing my face and usin' my man-

ners." The sentence signifies the full performative or mythomanic possession by spirit of a person who knows she has undone the traditional manners (and means) of accomplishing a
classic. She knows at the close of her work that she has refused
to craft a compendium of "Negro Folktales and Voodoo Practices" that would satisfy dry, scholarly criteria of anthropology. Hence, she tacitly slips the yoke that even the eminent
Franz Boas seems to put on her efforts in a preface that invokes
Uncle Remus as the prototype of the Afro-American tale-
teller. (One witnesses in this preface, of course, a relationship
of similarity between Chesnutt's Julius and Boas's Remus.
Both are displaced by Zora's hoodoo woman appearing in
Zora's own person.) But Zora has not merely slipped the yoke
or "turned the trick" on a limited anthropology by the conclusion of *Mules and Men*,[26] for, surely, she has also reclaimed
the *whole* soul of the human enterprise for her conjure. She
has rectified the theft of the "soul-piece" and become her own
patron's superior through initiation into a world that practices
arts different from what she calls "the American pharmacopoeia."

At the end of the general text of *Mules and Men*, Zora may
be among the "unwashed," but she is also among the culturally well fed. She had dined on the spirit, on the manna of
black culture, and knows that she has power to manipulate
such manna in significant ways. The glossary and appendix of
Mules and Men, as a kind of initial demonstration of her power,
offer an alternative "pharmacopoeia" that ironically instan-
tiates the *work* and workings of the spirit rather than "gloss-
ing" them. The *gloss*, as it were, is the *work*, containing remedies and healing words for those who would transmit the
spirit of a *sui generis* Afro-American culture.

Hence, Hurston's work is both a chronicle of the journey
to roots, and a *pharmakon* of root work. In his essay "Plato's
Pharmacy," Jacques Derrida explicates Plato's *Phaedrus* in
terms of the controlling metaphor of the *pharmakon*.[27] He defines the *pharmakon* as a phenomenon that serves variously as
a drug, a poison, a medium, a technical innovation, a gift, a
supplement, an *aide-mémoire*, an occult and "illegitimate"
birth, writing, graphemic record, etc. Drawing on Egyptian
mythology, he designates Thoth (the presenter of the *pharmakon* to a disapproving Pharoah who seeks to reject and sup-
press it) as a "god-doctor-pharmacist-magician . . . [who]
sews up . . . wounds and heals . . . mutilation" (90).

With *Mules and Men*, Zora Hurston has astutely defied
King Boas and Queen R. Osgood Mason in the invention of
a *pharmakon* conceived as the script or spirit work of black

creativity. She has also, of course, achieved the healing status—the ability to sew up wounds and correct old mutila-
tions—that accompanies a proper knowledge of the pharmacy's resources. The *pharmakon*, as poison, may well be deemed
Hurston's contamination of the formal discourse and terms of
the anthropology of her own era—an era in which womanist
concerns such as those of Ruth Benedict, Margaret Mead, and
Elsie Clews Parsons were proliferating. *Mules and Men* in a
sense kills the kingly script of a mentor's and a patron's power,
undoing the official mode of fieldwork through a kind of cultural autobiographical pharmaceutics. Aware of and capable
of employing an official disciplinary language and perspective, *Mules and Men* also speaks (or writes) a radically alternative, vernacular, and black autobiographical set of polluting
formulas that enable the conjured passage of spirit. Hurston's
Thoth is a root worker of extraordinary linguistic ability and
multiple names whose legacy for Afro-American intellectual
history is, at least, a type of double writing that effectively
negotiates both formal and vernacular worlds.[28]

〰〰

Having set a classic model of creative black woman as hoodoo worker or conjurer—"rain bringer," "candle lighter,"
"striker of straight licks with a crooked stick"—Zora can well
afford to sit back like Ole Sis Cat. She not only has come with
Mules and Men to inhabit the space of an Afro-American classic, but also has provided our present era's point of reference
for an African woman's creativity in America. (What Eliot
would have termed the "presence" of the past for black
women writers.) *Mules and Men* is the space in which we must
judge and comprehend such appearances in recent black
women's writing as Sister Madelaine of Alice Walker's *The
Third Life of Grange Copeland* (1970).[29] Sister Madelaine is a
businesswoman, fortune-teller, and two-headed doctor rolled
into one. She is a woman whose son enrolled at Morehouse
College tells her that "witch-riding" and "witches" have been
displaced by Freudian dream theory and modern sleep research. But it is the dollars earned by Sister Madelaine that
produce a college-bred son who becomes a leader of the cam-
paign for civil rights. The impulse of the spirit toward liberation, as I have suggested, works in myriad ways. Toward the
conclusion of *The Third Life*, we learn that Madelaine's son
"had spent much of his childhood ashamed that his mother
was a fortuneteller, but by the time he left Morehouse and

joined the [Civil Rights] Movement he was as proud of how she earned her living as his best friend was that his father was a surgeon. His mother had faced life with a certain inventiveness, he thought, and for this he greatly respected her" (237). A filial respect akin to that expressed by Madelaine's son is accorded by Toni Morrison's Ajax to his mother in the novel *Sula* (1973).[30] Ajax's mother—who sits "in her shack with six younger sons working roots" (126)—is the most interesting woman Ajax has ever met. She inspires thoughtfulness and generosity in all her sons. The narrator of *Sula*, with the understated irony of one who admires fully what she seems to condemn, says of Ajax's mother: "She was an evil conjure woman . . . [who] . . . knew about the weather, omens, the living, the dead, dreams and all illnesses and made a modest living with her skills" (126). With her teeth restored and a straightened back, the woman would have been "the most gorgeous thing alive." She has paid, however, for the weight of her vast pharmacy of "hoary knowledge."

From his mother, Ajax gains a love of airplanes. I shall provide an extended discussion of *Sula* in the next chapter, but for the moment I want simply to emphasize that in the novel the conjure woman and flying are coextensive. And in Morrison's *oeuvre*, Ajax's love of airplanes seems to give birth to Solomon, the Flying African, and his skyward aspiring clan in *Song of Solomon* (1977). The cultural connection between Milkman Dead and Ajax's conjuring mother is, of course, mediated through Pilate, who is *Song of Solomon's* true medium. She is the person who has the power of communicating with spirits of the dead, and who is (in apt lexical play) a most excellent spirit of the Deads. In one of the eerier thanatotic moments in the narrative, she manifests a long knowledge of the Bible (chapter and verse), a furious reverence for the sanctity of dead men's bones, and a transformative ability (akin to Papa Legba of hoodoo provenance or Leibert Joseph of Paule Marshall's *Praisesong for the Widow*)[32] that bring her into harmony with the best of a two-headed sorority.

When we witness the forceful expressive cultural succession of Zora's conjure woman found in works like those of Walker and Morrison, we know that the creator of *Mules and Men* did, indeed, accomplish the foremost task of the authentic Afro-American cultural worker. To seek a habitation beyond alienation and ancient disharmonies in a land where Africans have been scarred and battered, shackled in long rows on toilsome levees, is the motion of such cultural work. The home that marks the journey's end or theoretical return is the poetic image conceived as a classical space in which one institutes the type of locational pause that Bachelard might have called *eulogized place*—a revered site of culturally specific interests and values. *Conjure* is, to borrow a title adopted for his nationalistic work by Amiri Baraka, the *Spirit House* of black women's creativity. Its efficacy does not consist in its material presence nor in its genteel reconciliation of opposites such as form and content, context and meaning. Rather, it is an improvisational pause, a riff in a mighty orchestration, a nonce solo in which notes or objects at hand are combined to turn the trick on identifiable adversaries.

Red flannel, lodestone, anvil filings, roots, bones, rocks, dust tracks, snake skins, rabbit's feet, photographs, hairpins, brimstone—anything at hand can serve the conjurer as *bricoleur*, enabling her to escape oppressively overdetermined meanings or the agonies of alienated affection. We listen as a conjure woman of Algiers speaks of her improvisation: "Sometimes I take a small piece of lodestone, or at other times a little dirt corked up in a bottle [explained to be "graveyard dirt"], at other times the foot of a rabbit, at times a wishbone of a chicken, or, if I have time, I just make up a package sewed neatly in a red flannel covering."[33]

The secret of the conjurer's trade is imagination, which can turn almost anything into a freeing mojo, a dynamic "jack," or a cunning conjure bag. Quoting from a recent popular song, one might say the trick of spirit work is to "move in space with minimum waste–maximum joy."

The work to be accomplished is not only classically literary or expressive, but also generally healing in a manner captured by the conflation of conjure with the witch as image. In a suggestive study entitled *Witches, Midwives, and Nurses*,[34] Barbara Ehrenreich and Deirdre English write:

> Women have always been healers. They were the unlicensed doctors and anatomists of western history.
> They were pharmacists, cultivating healing herbs and exchanging secrets of their uses. They were midwives, travelling from home to home and village to village.
> For centuries women were doctors without degrees
> . . . They were called "wise women" by the people, witches or charlatans by the authorities. (3)

In Afro-America, the richest cultural wisdom resides in what Derrida calls the resources of a pharmacy—a space in which mythomania works. African women in America have been wise workers of this space. Embroidering, improvising, troping on a standard pharmacopoeia, they have transmitted the soul or spirit of a culture with rainbringing energy. If their work has sometimes been labeled "women's work" as an act of condescension, we know such a label is no more than the gesture of thievish, envious kings seeking control. For the labors of black women have always been coextensive with those of Thoth. Like all classical spaces, their *conjure* has possessed the merits of a gift—the powers of a culturally specific pharmacopoeia. One must not conclude a discussion of *conjure* as poetic image, however, with anything approaching the static or the material. The trick, it would seem in light of what has been said so far, is to end not with a pharmacy but with pharmacokinetics—the healing spirit in motion.

Commenting in his autobiography, *The Big Sea*, on a college classmate's insistence that the only way to get material rewards from whites in order to build material buildings for blacks is to compromise black dignity, Langston Hughes says, "I began to think back to Nat Turner, Harriet Tubman, Sojourner Truth, John Brown, Fred Douglass—folks who left no buildings behind them—only a wind of words fanning the bright flame of the spirit down the dark lanes of time" (310). The force of conjure's image is not caught, nor is black dignity preserved, in material buildings secured by compromise. Its spirit is caught, instead, in bright words such as those that Zora (reverberating with the vernacular energies of Big Sweet and Ella Wall) uses to describe her stature toward the end of *Dust Tracks on a Road*.[36] Her words are pharmacokinetics par excellence; they provide a fitting space in which to conclude the present chapter.

I have given myself the pleasure of sunrises blooming out of oceans, and sunset drenching heaped-up clouds. I have walked in storms with a crown of clouds about my head and the zigzag lightning playing through my fingers. The gods of the upper air have uncovered their faces to my eyes. I have found out that my real home is in the water, that the earth is only my stepmother. My old man, the Sun, sired me out of the sea. Like all mortals, I have been shaped by the chisel in the hand of Chance, bulged out here by a sense of victory, shrunk there by the press of failure and the knowledge of unworthiness. But it has been given to me to strive with life, and to conquer the fear of death. I have been correlated to the world so that I know the indifference of the sun to human emotions. I know that destruction and construction are but two faces of Dame Nature, and that it is nothing to her if I choose to make personal tragedy out of her unbreakable laws. (347–48)

We live in *conjure* when we are warmed by such words. Combining the various meanings of "conjure," black women creators have thrust oppressive kings from state, exercised potently magical and occult influence, and performed liberating "tricks" with words. Their acts, surely, have fanned a quintessentially African spirit down dark lanes of time.

And their reverberant pauses—their sonorous moments of locational value in this transport—have left us unique places of esteem as well as conjuring spaces. If these *places* are not physical buildings, they are, nonetheless, building places: places that imagistically give consciousness to place in Afro-American women's expressive traditions. It is the task of the following chapter to extend our poetics to Afro-American women's place.

CHAPTER THREE

On Knowing Our Place

If woman has always functioned "within" the discourse of
man, a signifier that has always referred back to the opposite
signifier, which annihilates its specific energy and diminishes
or stifles its very different sounds, it is time for her to dislo-
cate this "within," to explode it, turn it around, and seize it;
to make it hers, containing it, taking it in her own mouth,
biting that tongue with her very own teeth to invent for herself a language to get inside of.

> *Hélène Cixous, "The Laugh of the Medusa"*

Lord, how can I bear it, lord what will the harvest bring?
Putting up all my money and I isn't got a doggone thing.
I'm a weary traveler, roaming around from place to place.
If I don't find something, this will end me in disgrace.

> *Mississippi John Hurt, "Blue Harvest Blues"*

ONE WAY OF commencing an investigation of place is to
proceed by distinctions, examining first the standard inscriptions of place in classic Afro-American male texts and turning
next to place as a sign in Afro-American women's expressivity. Ralph Ellison's *Invisible Man* and Richard Wright's *Native
Son* provide indisputedly classic male models.[1] In *Invisible
Man,* we encounter a scene in which the protagonist, who is
still a neophyte in the Brotherhood, and his colleague Tod
Clifton are forced to fight with the nationalist Ras the Ex-

horter. Ras gets the better of Clifton and raises his knife to slash the boy's throat when suddenly he is overcome by a sobbing surge of feeling. Releasing Clifton, he delivers a hortatory condemnation of the Brotherhood and its black membership. His harsh message is matched in effect only by the power of his style:

> "You [Clifton, are] young, don't play you'self cheap, mahn. Don't deny you'self! It took a billion gallons of black blood to make you. Recognize you'self inside and you wan the kings among men . . . You black and beautiful. . . . So why don't you recognize your black duty, mahn, and come jine us?"
>
> His chest was heaving and a note of pleading had come into the harsh voice. He was an exhorter, all right, and I [the protagonist] was caught in the crude, insane eloquence of his plea. He stood there, awaiting an answer. And suddenly a big transport plane came low over the buildings and I looked up to see the firing of its engine, and we were all three silent, watching.
>
> Suddenly the Exhorter shook his fist toward the plane and yelled, "Hell with him, some day we have them too! Hell with him!" (364–65)

The scene powerfully revises a moment in Richard Wright's *Native Son* when Bigger and his friend Gus meet on a South Side Chicago street. Leaning against a building, comforting themselves in a sunshine warmer than their kitchenette apartments, their attention is suddenly drawn upward. An acrobatic skywriter is spelling out the bold, commercial message: USE SPEED GASOLINE. Bigger gazes in childlike wonder and says, "Looks like a little bird" (19). Gus responds, "Them white boys sure can fly." Bigger continues, "I *could* fly a plane if I had a chance." Gus promptly responds, "If you wasn't black and if you had some money and if they'd let you go to that aviation school, you *could* fly a plane."

The appearance of an airplane in both *Invisible Man* and *Native Son* signifies what might be called a "traditional" dynamics of Afro-American place. Its appearance, one hastens to note, does not mark a dichotomy signaled by Leo Marx's topos of "the machine in the garden." [2] Neither Ellison nor Wright is concerned to juxtapose Anglo-American aviation and a state of black, prelapsarian innocence and plenitude. Flight does not disrupt a harmonious, fruitful, pre-industrial state of Afro-American affairs. Rather, the transport and the skywriter in the two novels suggest an enormous confinement of black life; they are not disruptions of place but industrial/

technological signifiers implying black placelessness. They have the effect of making traditional Afro-American geographies into placeless places. Why "placeless"? Because Ras's Harlem, like Bigger's South Side, lacks the quality of *place* as it is traditionally defined.

For place to be recognized by one as actually PLACE, as a personally valued locale, one must set and maintain the boundaries. If one, however, is constituted and maintained by and within boundaries set by a dominating authority, then one is not a setter of place but a prisoner of another's desire. Under the displacing impress of authority even what one calls and, perhaps, feels is one's *own place* is, from the perspective of human agency, *placeless*. Bereft of determinative control of boundaries, the occupant of authorized boundaries would not be secure in his or her own eulogized world but maximally secured by another, a prisoner of interlocking, institutional arrangements of power.

What the appearance of the skywriter and the transport reinforce are messages or warnings implicit in those border signs that have greeted Ellison's and Wright's protagonists prior to the planes' arrival. The invisible man, for example, has found himself from the beginning of his odyssey encircled by whites who give every sign of their social and technological authority. Not only is Ellison's antihero shocked by the actual electricity of white invention, but also by the stinging, crackling challenge thrown at him by white men when he inadvertently utters the phrase "social equality." Indeed, the essential sign (that insistence of the "letter in the unconscious")[3] is in place when his dream after the first battle royal brings a mocking return of that which the invisible man tries always to repress. The fundamentals of white intention lie in the letter that the boy finds at the end of a series of interlocking boxes that his grandfather calls "years." This primary letter reads: KEEP THIS NIGGER–BOY RUNNING.

If Bigger needs signs of his confinement other than the cramped, rat-infested quarters to which he shiveringly awakens, he surely receives at least one prior to his sighting of the plane. He watches as workmen mount a looming portrait of the incumbent state's attorney, Buckley. The poster is a parodic sign invented for black territories. Its broad countenance and pointing finger do not say: Uncle Sam Wants You! Instead it reads: IF YOU BREAK THE LAW, YOU CAN'T WIN! Bigger understands that it is bucks from the tenement owners that keep the state's attorney BUCKLEY. He thinks: "You crook. . . . You let whoever pays *you* off win!" The contract between owners and intrusive legal countenances is signed

some pages later when Bigger gazes at a South Side board that reads: THIS PROPERTY IS MANAGED BY THE SOUTH SIDE
REAL ESTATE COMPANY.

> He had heard that Mr. Dalton [Bigger's employer and
> the man whose daughter Mary he has murdered]
> owned the South Side Real Estate Company, and the
> South Side Real Estate Company owned the house in
> which he lived. He paid eight dollars a week for one
> rat-infested room. He had never seen Mr. Dalton until
> he had come to work for him; his mother always took
> the rent to the real estate office. Mr. Dalton was some-
> where far away, high up, distant, like a god. He owned
> property all over the Black Belt, and he owned prop-
> erty where white folks lived, too. But Bigger could
> not live in a building across the "line." (164)

A corner of the city tumbling down in rot, a territory
overseen by Buckley's law, a rat-infested cell behind the "line"
above which Mr. Dalton, the owner, soars like a distant god,
or a sleek skywriter—this is Bigger's assigned and placeless
place.

Given the signs, there is every reason for Bigger to want
to fly, and there is scant wonder that Ras refuses to reject the
machine in Harlem, shouting passionately, "Hell with him,
some day we have them too!" For it is, in effect, flying machines that connote the abilities of their owners, their pilots,
and their lawgivers to control all boundaries and invest even
what seems one's own locality with the radical instability of
the sign: KEEP THIS NIGGER-BOY RUNNING.

~~~~~

The first cause and longer history that comprise the genesis of such arrangements are not unknown to either Wright or
Ellison. It is Wright, though, who most cogently captures this
history in locational, or place, terms. His depiction occurs in
*12 Million Black Voices: A Folk History of the Negro in the United
States* (1941).[4] Published the year after *Native Son* had created
a veritable storm of criticism and catapulted its author to the
forefront of literary celebrity, *12 Million Black Voices* was created in collaboration with the photographer Edwin Rosskam.
It stands as one of Wright's most striking creations.

12 Million Black Voices adopts for its narration a polyphony
of sound, voices, and tones that have their source in an Afro-
American, vernacular "us" or "we." There is an intensity of
narrative identification in *12 Million Black Voices* that testifies

better to Wright's engagement with the folk than do some of his fictions. And at the outset of the history, he attempts to portray the enabling conditions of Afro-American PLACE in their unimaginable violence, terror, and materialism, as well as in their dialectically empowering status in relationship to Western progress. Michel Fabre notes that for Wright the folk history of the Negro was "emblematic of that of . . . the Third World *and of modern man at large.*" [5] (My emphasis.)

The first section of *12 Million Black Voices,* "Our Strange Birth," details the beginnings of this emblematic history, offering the *ur*-placement, as it were, of the *Negro:*

> We millions of black folk who live in this land were born into Western civilization of a weird and paradoxical birth. The lean, tall, blond men of England, Holland, and Denmark, the dark, short, nervous men of France, Spain, and Portugal, men whose blue and gray and brown eyes glinted with the light of the future, denied our human personalities, tore us from our native soil, weighted our legs with chains, stacked us like cord-wood in the foul holes of clipper ships, dragged us across thousands of miles of ocean, and hurled us into another land, strange and hostile, where for a second time we felt the slow, painful process of a new birth amid conditions harsh and raw. (12)

I shall return to the notion of a "second" birth. For the moment it is sufficient to note that for Wright's narrator a semantics of Afro-American existence crushes together two, perhaps competing, definitions of "confine." Definitions of the term as childbirth and as imprisonment converge in the *hole,* that place of knotted pain and scant hope that is the first, imprisoning birth of the Afro-American. The question of generative space bounded into sui generis Afro-American PLACE is answered by *12 Million Black Voices* in the following way:

> Laid out spoon-fashion on the narrow decks of sailing ships, we were transported to this New World so closely packed that the back of the head of one of us nestled between the legs of another. Sometimes 720 of us were jammed into a space 20 feet wide, 120 feet long, and 5 feet high. Week after week we would lie there, tortured and gasping, as the ship heaved and tossed over the waves. In the summer, down in the suffocating depths of those ships, on an eight- or ten-week voyage, we would go crazed for lack of air and water, and in the morning the crew of the ship would

discover many of us dead, clutching in rigor mortis at the throats of our friends, wives, or children. (14)

If the space of Wright's quoted dimensions is measured, one realizes that it represents darkness unabounding and fever-pitch of noise, crushing weight of compressed bodies rolling, in unimaginable stench, a blackout of all signs of a human world—space narrowed to the sensations of all that was left: the body in pain.[6] The boundaries set for Africans left them—as Ralph Ellison and Richard Wright suggest in *Invisible Man* and *The Man Who Lived Underground* respectively—in the hole.

The British abolitionist Thomas Clarkson, in his account of the nineteenth-century slave trade from Bristol, reported that "the space allotted to each slave on the Atlantic crossing measured five and a half feet in length by sixteen inches in breadth . . . chained two by two, right leg and left leg, right hand and left hand, each slave had less room than a man in a coffin."[7] In Clarkson's testimony, as in *12 Million Black Voices,* we find a conflation. A "strange" Afro-American birth implicitly converges with African death in the fetid hole ("less room than a man in a coffin"). The hole, thus, stands as an ironic indictment of the commercial birth of modern man. We hear the complex resonances of this admixture of genesis and death in the following description from *12 Million Black Voices:*

> Against the feudal background of denials of love and happiness, the trade in our bodies bred god-like men who exalted honor, enthroned impulse, glorified aspiration, celebrated individuality, and fortified the human heart to strive against the tyrannical forms of nature and to bend obstreperous materials closer to a mold that would slake human desire. As time elapsed, these new men seized upon the unfolding discoveries of science and invention, and figuratively, their fingers became hot as fire and hard as steel. Literature, art, music, and philosophy set their souls aflame with a desire for the new mode of living that had come into the world. Exploration opened wide the entire surface of the earth as a domain of adventure. (16)

The dialectic implicit in this description recalls the dialectic that George Kent,[8] a fine critic of Wright, discerned in the life and writings of the author of *12 Million Black Voices*. The dialectic is described by Kent as a determinative tension between "blackness and the adventure of Western culture." In

terms of a dynamics of Afro-American PLACE, we find this
dialectic inscribed as a below (*blackness*) and an above (*the Western adventure*) deck. The "glint of the future" in the eyes of the
captors, their exaltation as "god-like" and "new men" indi-
cate that what Wright deems the productive actions of modernity are unequivocally situated above. Below, there resides
an anguishing katabasis captured by Robert Hayden as
follows:

> *Deep in the festering hole thy father lies,*
> *the corpse of mercy rots with him,*
> *rats eat love's rotten gelid eyes.*[9]

Wright's description of "above" is not, however, exhausted
in encomium. For there are, perhaps, no more significant
words in his praise song than "the trade in our bodies."
Though technological adventure seems to carry the energy of
the passage cited, a prior economic inscription is, in fact, determinative.

The diorama of inventive progress, one might say, is
turned by the motor of commercial capitalism. Trade, and in
particular and most expressly, the European slave trade moves
the drama. The West Indian scholar Eric Williams is one of the
most decisive advocates of the theory that African slavery had
economic origins. "Here, then, is the origin of Negro Slavery.
the reason was economic, not racial; it had to do not with
color of the laborer, but the cheapness of the labor. As compared with Indian and white labor, Negro slavery was eminently superior."[10]

One might say that the hole, as the PLACE of Afro-
American beginnings, is a function, *not* of an absence of hu-
manitarianism, a declension of mercy, a racialistic decrease of
love, but of "trade" pure and simple. Williams insists that
slave trading was distinguishable from other forms of British
commerce in a single respect only: its principal commodity—
human bodies.

PLACE as an Afro-American portion of the world begins
in a European DISPLACEMENT of bodies for commercial purposes. Commodification of human beings meant that relationships of property, and not free, human, personal relations,
marked the spaces between Europeans and Africans. *Ownership* was the watchword over the hole. And within its suffocating spaces occurred a brutal purgation, a violent acclimatiza-
tion and reaction formation that left a black vessel to be filled.

I promised earlier to return to the "second birth." This second birth is the generational moment that marks the closure
of the hole experience, of the first floating instability and suf-

focation below deck. The narrator makes clear that at the end of a first displacing voyage there was yet another "slow, pain- ful process of a new birth amid conditions harsh and raw" (12). Like the lower regions of the transporting ship, the new land for Afro-Americans was not a space of limitless possibil- ity. It was but an extension of the hole experience whose black masses might justly have said: "We are the children of the Af- rican captives reduced to slavery." Their relationship to the land under conditions of ownership, under conditions of an- other possessing all rights in their bodies *durante vita,* under destabilizing conditions of constant commerce, made Amer- ica not a home for them, but a hole. Afro-America was a PLACE *assigned* rather than discovered. The "second" birth, in short, was just another deep hole of temporary placelessness from which one had to extract empowering reasons for en- during until the next sunrise.

The nature of American plantation agriculture brought the life of this "second" generation into accord with that of their African predecessors in respect to PLACE. The hole was a "place in motion," a floating signifier of commodified labor. Similarly, the millions bound in Afro-American slavery for the sake of agricultural capital became a floating, ceaselessly moving body of predominantly male, commodified labor. Eric Williams writes:

> The slave planter, in the picturesque nomenclature of
> the South, is a "land-killer." This serious defect of slav-
> ery can be counter-balanced and postponed for a time
> if fertile soil is practically unlimited. Expansion is a ne-
> cessity of slave societies; the slave power requires ever
> fresh conquests.[11]

And following and providing the force for such "con- quests" in the plantation South was the great majority of the black population in America. The displacement of the slave trade that produced a placeless ship's hole was complemented after landfall by a southern agriculture that moved, prodded, drove "gangs" of men ceaselessly south and westward, away from exhausted land valued in a way defined by Thomas Jef- ferson when he wrote: "We can buy an acre of new land cheaper than we can manure an old one."[12] What, then, could be the meaning of Afro-American PLACE within the (w)hole of plantation, slave agriculture?

The semantics of place as they are depicted in *12 Million Black Voices* are captured in a threefold depiction that we can extrapolate from sections 1 and 2. First, "[O]ur black backs continued to give design and order to the fertile plantations" (24). The place of the black person is that of a tool, of personal property (*chattel personal*). Next, "[W]e sit in cabins that have no windowpanes; the floors are made of thin planks of pine. Out in the backyard, over a hole dug in the clay, stands a horizontal slab of oak with an oval opening in it; when it rains, a slow stink drifts over the wet fields" (57–58). The cabin is the locational, objective correlative for the laborer's enforced, restricted, confined space. Once instituted in *12 Million Black Voices,* this one-room arrangement of things (for slave cabins, like the later shacks of black sharecroppers, possessed but a single room) signifies not a room of one's own, but, instead, a room in which one is owned. Its controlled space is mirrored by the one-room school into which crowd, *12 Million Black Voices* tells, "sometimes seventy children, ranging in age from six to twenty." It is also reflected on a northern cityscape by the kitchenette which "creates thousands of one-room homes where our black mothers sit, deserted, with their children about their knees" (109). The one-room space is a function of bent backs that give design to plantation economies; it is precisely not a proud sign of home ownership. Third, there is the motion in which bent backs and dingy shacks combine:

> Black and white alike . . . go to the pea, celery,
> orange, grapefruit, cabbage, and lemon crops. Some-
> times we walk and sometimes the bosses of the farm
> factories send their trucks for us. We go from the red
> land to the brown land, from the brown land to the
> black land, working our way eastward until we reach
> the blue Atlantic. . . . We sleep in woods, in barns, in
> wooden barracks, on sidewalks, and sometimes in jail.
> Our dog-trot, dog-run, shotgun, and gingerbread
> shacks fill with ghosts and tumble down from rot.
> (79).

The motion described is a ritual of "owned" labor—the bent back moved from place to place with sheltering structures that are only temporary. Like ceremonial huts erected by some pre-industrial cultures, the rotting dwellings are testimony to motion seen, to rituals enacted for human use, signifying structures energized for a moment by human presence and then abandoned to the elements. They are ghostly, tumbling emblems of ceaseless motion rather than emblems of PLACE. Registering the combination of visions of the hole in their past and the kitchenette in the future, we won't find it difficult to see why the narrator of *12 Million Black Voices* characterizes black PLACE as follows:

There are millions of us and we are moving in all directions. All our lives we have been catapulted into arenas where, had we thought consciously of invading them, we would have hung back. A sense of constant change has stolen silently into our lives and has become operative in our personalities as a law of living (143).

Displacement and denial of the African personality is compensated—within the very spaces of the holes of ownership and commodification—by a new, operational law of personality. That law is one of placeless PLACE; it transforms a commercial dispossession into a mirroring alternative to Western economic arrangements. What emerges from the confined, imprisoning, one-room hole, in a word, is an instability that gives rise to a distinctive folk culture.

This folk culture's very labor in motion and sui generis conceptualization of PLACE transform "confinement" into new birth. *12 Million Black Voices* chronicles this birth as the welding of "a separate unity with common characteristics of our own" (41). The subtitle of Wright's narrative—*A Folk History*—comes to imply, then, a subversive place in historiography. For *12 Million Black Voices* is, finally, the voicing of a collective countermotion to Western material acquisitiveness and its desire for stable authority and dominion.

Keepers of the historical discipline in the United States such as U. B. Phillips and Stanley Elkins have traditionally assumed that what was coextensive with keeping the "nigger" on the run, or in "his place," was an extrahistorical position for the folk. Wright's voicing of the story of the twelve million, however, reveals a space within this running, as it were, an area marked by self-generated folk boundaries:

> We who have followed the plow . . . have developed a secret life and language of our own. . . . We stole words from the grudging lips of the Lords of the Land . . . And we charged this meager horde of stolen sounds with all the emotions and longing we had; we proceeded to build our language in inflections of voice, through tonal variety, by hurried speech, in honeyed drawls, by rolling our eyes, by flourishing our hands, by assigning to common, simple words new meanings, meanings which enabled us to speak of revolt in the actual presence of the Lords of the Land without their being aware! Our secret language extended our understanding of what slavery meant and gave us the freedom to speak to our brothers in captivity; we pol-

ished our new words, caressed them, gave them new
shape and color, a new order and tempo, until, though
they were the words of the Lords of the Land, they became *our* words, *our* language. (40)

The described process of transforming the lexicon of ownership into unique signifiers is self-reflexive because it mirrors
Wright's own historical wresting of essential lineaments of
an extra-ordinary history from a bleak hole. The self-
consciousness of the narrator about the nature of his historiographical task is suggested a short space before the above quotation when he writes:

> To paint the picture of how we live on the tobacco,
> cane, rice, and cotton plantations is to compete with
> mighty artists: the movies, the radio, the newspapers,
> the magazines, and even the Church. They have
> painted one picture: charming, idyllic, romantic; but
> we live another: full of the fear of the Lords of the
> Land, bowing and grinning when we meet white faces,
> toiling from sun to sun, living in unpainted wooden
> shacks that sit casually and insecurely upon the red
> clay. (35)

The narrator, thus, sets himself in opposition to what is
known to traditional, southern history as the "pro-slavery argument," the one ironically reinforced even by an abolitionist
author like Harriet Beecher Stowe when she provides a view
of Uncle Tom's cabin as a "small log building, close adjoining
to 'the house'" with "a neat garden-patch, where every summer, strawberries, raspberries, and a variety of fruits and veg-
etables flourished under careful tending."[13] Stowe's earthly
garden, like *Gone with the Wind*'s happy portraiture of slavery,
hardly seems akin to the one-room history of *12 Million Black
Voices*.

What finally emerges from Wright's folk history, I think,
is a PLACE where there exists a "fragile" black family possessed of a kinship system of its own and sustained by institutions (patterns of behavior) that include codes of conduct vis-
à-vis whites and standards of love, hope, and value that find
objective correlatives in the Afro-American church and in
Afro-American sacred and secular song. At the structural center of *12 Million Black Voices*,[14] after Wright has described the
emergence of an Afro-American family based not on "property ownership" but on "love, sympathy, pity, and the goad-
ing knowledge that we must work together to make a crop"
(60), the folk history moves to Sunday and the dressing, prep-

aration, and departure of this "fragile" black family for church. The type font of the narrative shifts to italics as the narrative voice assumes the office of a black preacher, situating at the center of a black folk history a story of rebellion in heaven, hard trials in earthly life, a redemptive coming of Christ, and a foreshadowing of the Day of Judgment. The photographs illustrating this section are of collective Afro-American assembly, rapt attention, prayerful enthrallment, and shouted ecstasy.

Returning to regular type, the narrative reads, "The preacher begins to punctuate his words with sharp rhythms, and we are lifted far beyond the boundaries of our daily lives, upward and outward, until, drunk with our enchanted vision, our senses lifted to the burning skies, we do not know who we are, what we are, or where we are . . ." (73). A black folk collective in church takes flight; its consciousness is raised to human heights of genuine "personality." In the third section of *12 Million Black Voices,* the narrator—describing Sunday storefront, black assemblies in the North—asserts: "Our churches are centers of social and community life, for we have virtually no other mode of communion and we are usually forbidden to worship God in the temples of the Bosses of the Buildings. The church is the door through which we first walked into Western civilization; religion is the form in which America first allowed our personalities to be expressed" (131). The centrality of the black church for *12 Million Black Voices* reinforces an interpretation of Wright's denotation of PLACE as an in-motion, spiritual domain crafted in a sui generis language (i.e., Black English Vernacular).

Black, folk PLACE, though, is scarcely an exclusively religious domain according to *12 Million Black Voices.* For immediately following the worship service found at the center of the narrative and preceding the discussion of storefront churches in section 3 are energetic characterizations of Afro-American secular rhythms. The roadside jook of blues harmonicas and shaking hips is the salvific place of the South; frenzied ballrooms, blues, and jazz are the inscriptions of secular energies and personal style in the North. What both the sacred and the secular occasions of sermons, dance, blues, jazz, and generally energetic collectivity imply is suggested by the following reflection:

> Day after day we labor in the gigantic factories and
> mills of Western civilization, but we have never been
> allowed to become an organic part of this civilization;
> we have yet to share its ultimate hopes and expecta-

tions. Its incentives and perspectives, which form the core of meaning for so many millions, have yet to lift our personalities to levels of purpose. Instead, after working all day in one civilization, we go home to our Black Belts of the South, our naive, casual, verbal, fluid folk life. (127)

A sophisticated, formal, literate, stable Western "civilization" remains the bounding agency for "Negro" existence. Within the confines of that *existence,* however, the human spirit gives birth to a "brittle" (128) collective life which produces expressive alternatives to Western tradition:

> [O]ur hunger for expression finds its form in our wild, raw music, in our invention of slang that winds its way all over America. Our adoration of color goes not into murals, but into dress, into green, red, yellow, blue clothes. When we have some money in our pockets on payday, our laughter and songs make the principal streets of our Black Belts—Lenox Avenue, Beale Street, State Street, South Street, Second Street, Auburn Avenue—famous the earth over. (129)

It would be erroneous to overemphasize a valued folk PLACE in *12 Million Black Voices.* For even the engaging descriptions of style at the center of the narrative and the fully orchestrated descriptions of collective style in part 3 cannot forestall our realization that Wright's history is as much an elegy as a discovery. Section 3 is entitled "Death on the City Pavements," and it concludes as follows:

> The sands of our simple folk lives run out on the cold city pavements. Winter winds blow, and we feel that our time is nearing its end. Our final days are full of apprehension, for our children grapple with the city. We cannot bear to look at them; they struggle against great odds. Our tired eyes turn away as we hear the tumult of battle. (136)

Section 4, "Men in the Making," begins not with the voice of the "folk," but with the voice of the children of the folk: "We are the children of the black sharecroppers, the first-born of the city tenements" (142). If, as one person has suggested, city tenements honeycombed with kitchenettes are "vertical slaveships,"[15] then out of their hole have come—in a "third birth"—a new Afro-American generation.

The valued coalition for this new generation is not the brittle, fragile, tenuous folk family of black America, but the "disciplined, class-conscious groups" of collective (read: COMMUNIST) social activism. The narrator tells us that the Great Depression of the 1930s found some blacks mired in the old folkways, longing for Africa, or motivated by an "inarticulate . . . naive, peasant anger" which manifested itself in the 1935 Harlem riot. Class-conscious black industrial laborers, however, were "for the first time in our lives [encountering] the full effect of those forces that tended to reshape our folk consciousness, and a few of us stepped forth and accepted within the confines of our personalities the death of our old folk lives, an acceptance of a death that enabled us to cross class and racial lines, a death that made us free" (144). The crucifying death of a folk culture gives birth to Afro-American Communist Man as sharer in the Western mechanical dream. One thinks of the concluding dream of *Invisible Man* in which the bridge as emblem of Western technology is humanized and incorporated into humane existence by the dissemination of bloody blackmale seed upon the waters.[16]

Similarly, *12 Million Black Voices*'s conclusion is not only utopian, but also aggressively masculine. The very title of its final section—"*Men* in the Making"—provides a specific gender coding. The reasons are not far to seek.

The occupations of the two million blacks who migrated from the South to the North between 1890 and 1920 are labeled by *12 Million Black Voices* as twofold: "In the main, we black folk earn our living in two ways in the northern cities: we work as domestics or as laborers" (117). Here we have the material reason for Wright's gender coding. In the North, the Afro-American world of work splits into "[black women] domestics" and "[black men] laborers." What is the result?

The result is an essentially Afro-American male vision of the world. That vision projects a merger of Afro-American males and the progressive forces of Western industrial technology, a merger that, by its very nature, excludes black women and their domestic consciousness and calling. Industrial labor's effects on black men are described as follows:

> [I]t is in industry that we [black men] encounter experiences that tend to break down the structure of our folk characters and project us toward the vortex of modern urban life. It is when we are handling picks rather than mops, it is when we are swinging hammers rather than brooms, it is when we are pushing levers rather than dust-cloths that we are gripped and influenced by the world-wide forces that shape and mold the life of Western civilization. (117)

By contrast: the "orbit of life is narrow [for black, women
domestics]—from their kitchenette to the white folks' kitchen
and back home again—they love the church more than do our
men, who find a large measure of the expression of their lives
in the mills and factories" (131).

While the narrator's characterization is obviously a rendition of Marxian notions of a determinative connection
between relations of production and states of human consciousness, it is also a somewhat ruthless portrayal of Afro-
American women. And it foreshadows the almost scandalous
characterization that follows when *12 Million Black Voices*
claims "more than even that of the American Indian, the consciousness of vast sections of our black women lies beyond the
boundaries of the modern world, though they live and work
in that world daily" (135). I want to suggest that this scandal-
izing of the name of Afro-American women (and American
Indians!) is a function of a desperately felt necessity for the
blackmale narrative voice to come into "conscious history"
(147).

At the close of *12 Million Black Voices,* black men are industrial workers of the world; they are "in the making" because they have become making men. By contrast, black
women are sitting in kitchenettes "deserted, with children
about their knees." Rather than workers in the public world of
Western progress, they are "domestics." Their situation remains essentially unchanged from their role during the flour-
ishing days of plantation agriculture in the South when they
worked the "Big House" (36) as "Mammy" (37). There is this
difference, though, according to Wright's folk history: In the
South they seemed to fare better than black men and to have
a relationship to the Lords of the Land that gave them stability
and enabled them to be the effective heads of black families.
"Because of their enforced intimacy with the Lords of the
Land, many of our women, after they were too old to work,
were allowed to remain in the slave cabins to tend generations
of black children . . . through the years they became symbols
of motherhood, retaining in their withered bodies the burden of our folk wisdom, reigning as arbiters in our domestic
affairs until we men were freed and had moved to cities where
cash-paying jobs enabled us to become the heads of our own
families" (37). (Of course, the fate that Frederick Douglass
portrays where his grandmother is concerned hardly accords
with Wright's description.) Juxtaposed against the implicit
stability of black women in Wright's quotation is the phrase
"when a gang of us [black men] was sold from one plantation
to another" (37). This blackmale labor in motion contrasts

sharply with black women's static retention of the cabin's space.

The interiority of the cabin becomes conflated with the words "intimacy," "motherhood," "folk wisdom," and "domestic," suggesting a different set of markers and boundaries for woman's PLACE in folk history. What *12 Million Black Voices* does, in effect, is narrow the geographies of black women in the same measure that is implied by a familiar white southern quip used to justify the exclusion of blacks from educational opportunities: "All the geography a nigger needs to know is how to get from his shack to the plow" (64). The tight rounds of black women's lives would seem to run from intimacy, to childbearing, to domestic servitude in endless white kitchens. It is almost predictable that the narrator would invest such women—in their dotage—with a mystifying folk wisdom. There is little doubt, however, that the strongest accents of black women's characterization fall on what might be called their essential inessentiality in the progress of black males. They are, in fact, inessentiality *in potentia*. "Until"—"until we men were freed"—in the passage describing the southern black woman marks a moment of radical conflation. It renders "her" as the always already displaced. Early on in *12 Million Black Voices,* it summons a future in which black men *will* enter conscious history.

Certainly the goal of a close analysis of Wright's characterization of black women is not to bring him shamefully before the bar of feminist opinion. *12 Million Black Voices* has its moments of exoneration, or, better, amelioration, for its implied exclusions of black women. The work, to cite but one instance, wrests a poetry of childbirth, children, and black motherhood from dim confines of holed spaces:

> Our black children are born to us in our one-room shacks, before crackling log fires, with rusty scissors boiling in tin pans, with black plantation midwives hovering near, with pine-knot flames casting shadows upon the wooden walls, with the sound of kettles of water singing over the fires in the hearths . . . (62).

How different (even with the cringe that attends "rusty") this scene is from the "alienated childbirth" described by Adrienne Rich in *Of Woman Born*.[17] In a scathingly detailed portrayal, Rich depicts the Western manner of transforming childbirth into a "medical emergency" dominated by males, hospital hierarchization, analgesia, forceps, and a general abandonment of the woman (175). Further, Rich suggests that children, out of such alienating beginnings, are at best considered cursed blessings. By contrast, *12 Million Black Voices* tells us: "A child is a glad thing in the bleak stretches of the cotton country, and our gold is in the hearts of the people we love, in the veins that carry our blood, upon those faces where we catch furtive glimpses of the shape of our humble souls" (59). Wright's lyricism further extends to a definition of the relationship between a black folk woman and her children: "[N]o matter what the world may think of them, that [black] mother always welcomes them back with an irreducibly human feeling that stands above the claims of law or property. Our scale of values differs from that of the world from which we have been excluded; our shame is not its shame, and our love is not its love" (61). In this inscription of folk motherhood, Wright suggests a valorized space set by the folk themselves. MOTHER does seem a black-determined PLACE.

In section 3, however, as I have already noted, black mothers' productions comprise a type of orphan-life characterized by abandonment (135). The fathers' desertion is the norm. "Courts and morgues," therefore, "become crowded with our lost children" (136).

While she is valued in one instance of Wright's narrative, the folk mother is scarcely a reliable place of refuge. The eulogized place (conscious history) of black men "in the making" has no complement, finally, among domestic black women. Even the procreative function, which in traditional Western bourgeois mystifications is considered a sacred women's enterprise, is ultimately discounted by Wright's history as an exercise in abandonment. How black men "in the making" are made and nurtured is never made manifest. For woman remains an ahistorical remnant of folk culture. She is decisively not a productive force of Western modernism. With her storefront ecstasy and limited geography from kitchenette to kitchen, she represents a backwash of conscious history.

〜〜〜〜

But, of course, the negative account of black women in *12 Million Black Voices* is not simply a function of a simplistic assignment of occupational roles. No effective analytical end for this book would be achieved, I think, by suggesting a complementary or corrective historical account depicting and praising the virtues and victories of black professional women such as Mary McLeod Bethune, Charlotte Hawkins Brown, and others, or the trade-union initiatives of women such as Connie Smith and Moranda Smith (no relation), or the tales of black women escaping domestic drudgery and entering colleges or industry in increasing numbers with the advent of World War II. It was not that Wright lacked knowledge of black women's roles in the labor movement or the Communist Party. A voracious reader and ardent autodidact, Wright did not lack knowledge. What he lacked, it seems to me, was immunity to the lure of a peculiarly materialist historiography.

It is fair to say, I think, that the implied subject of *12 Million Black Voices,* as of all histories, is history itself. The historian of Wright's history, like all historians, must persistently entertain an awareness of the import of each of his discursive gestures in relationship to a general domain called "history." The past and the events and ascriptions of causality are not simply *historical,* or past, but functions of the present relation of their writer to a discourse of containment, i.e., "history." There is a more elaborate and extended argument about the self-reflexivity and "reality effect" of the historian's enterprise, but it needn't detain us here. [18] For all I mean to suggest by the claim that history is the subject of *12 Million Black Voices* is that Wright did not receive a revealed vision of the past, but, rather, consciously constructed a "folk" past in harmony with a particular notion and under the guidance of a particular conception of "history." And insofar as his specific "historical" past is his own discursive construction, we can comfortably say that he did not simply miss the continent of black women during an innocent and objective voyage of discovery. No, in fact, he sighted the continent, then refigured it in accordance with his preferred historiographical strategies of scientific socialism. The determinants of *12 Million Black Voices* are simply to be found in the important critical essay "Blueprint for Negro Writing," which appeared four years prior to the publication of the folk history. [19]

In the section of "Blueprint" entitled "The Problem of Perspective," we find the following claim: "[A]nyone destitute of a theory about the meaning, structure and direction of modern society is a lost victim in a world he cannot understand or control" (341). While discouraging a facile adoption of "isms," Wright is clear about the necessity for perspective, defined as a governing theory of the world's operations:

> Perspective is that part of a poem, novel, or play which a writer never puts directly upon paper. It is that *fixed point in intellectual space* where a writer stands to view the struggles, hopes, and sufferings of his people. (My emphasis; 341)

He continues:

> Of all the problems faced by writers who as a whole
> have never allied themselves with world movements,
> perspective is the most difficult of achievement. At its
> best, perspective is a preconscious assumption, some-
> thing which a writer takes for granted, something
> which he wins through his living (341–42).

Though the mystifying word "preconscious" appears, Wright
brackets it with "living," or *experience*. Hence, perspective
seems to be the equivalent in consciousness of a specific, individual relation to relations of production: i.e., "living." A
Marxian problematic carries the day.

"Preconscious" continues, however, to haunt perspective,
giving it the ambiguous status of both a state of reflection derived from *individualized* experience and a scientifically deriv-
able *donnée* of relations of production. First, Wright says that
perspective means for the Negro writer a reflective consciousness that recognizes the magnitude of the world's working
class and understands the connection between the interests
(ironically, given his own dismissal of such women) of a "Negro woman hoeing cotton in the South and the men who loll
in swivel chairs in Wall Street and take the fruits of her toil"
(342). This definition, though, competes with the one that
concludes "Blueprint"'s section on "Perspective":

> Perspective for Negro writers will come when they
> have looked and brooded so hard and long upon the
> harsh lot of their race and compared it with the hopes
> and struggles of minority peoples everywhere that the
> cold facts have begun to tell them something. (342)

"The Problem of Perspective," it seems to me, represents
the METAPLACE of Wright's construction of historical and fictive PLACE. And contrary to specifications of his own blueprint, this place is not *fixed*. It is a floor, or platform, that vi-
brates with competing motions of race and class as Wright
strives to reconcile the formerly alienated interests of black
masses (or Nation) with the (Marxian) aims and ends of the
Negro writer.

There is no call for an extant or tangible reality where a
blueprint is concerned. It is always an idealistic projection of
what will be—a metaplace. Hence, Wright can deem the space
of his own intellectual occupancy as the place where competing interests converge. The space of a Marxian socialism that
privileges the consciousness and interests of the proletariat—
of the working, industrial classes—becomes, for Wright, a

ground on which a racialistically determined Negro separa-
tism or "nationalism" (a folk history, in fact) will transmute
itself, through dialectical logic, into black working-class consciousness.

The mind that provides the blueprint is, in effect, already
in PLACE. It occupies a constructive theory as its META-
PLACE. Wright explicitly offers himself in "Blueprint," then,
as the architect of both a social and an artistic Afro-American
revolution. He is, implicitly, the writer who has made himself
over, who has *placed* himself in terms of his own design.

The rub, of course, is that the design is not an original
creation, but, in the way of all hermeneutical spaces, a reading, or interpretation. And as with all interpretations, there is
an unexplained remainder. While class interests and consciousness are supposed to subsume all before them, they are,
in fact, hard-pressed to account for the persistence of a felt
nationalism and the tangible activities of the domestic black
woman with a hoe. And it is the remainder that keeps things
in motion.

Wright's Marxian situation as a writer and his designation
of Marxism as the fitting perspective or metaplace for the
Afro-American writer have curious results in *12 Million Black
Voices*. Negro nationalism, for example, is *not* transmuted,
leaving behind valued relics of a former arrangement of black
life. And domestic black women are *not* read in terms of the
combined comprehension of Negro nationalism and Marxian
economics suggested by "Blueprint." Instead, they are murdered; they are left to die on city pavements. They are *remain-
dered,* as my earlier discussion of kitchenettes implies, in deserted spaces of an outworn history. I shall return to this
image of murdered victims in a moment.

For the present, I want to suggest that Wright's META-
PLACE is less a place of achieved metamorphosis than one of
"metagenesis." The earlier question of this essay about the beginning and nurturing of "men in the making" returns in the
definition of the word "metagenesis": *n. Biology. The occur-
rence in certain organisms of alternating sexual and asexual reproductive cycles. Also called "alternation of generations."* What we
would traditionally describe as (1) man-dependent and (2) independent woman's modes of productivity are implied by the
term "metagenesis." Wright's metaplace is marked by an alternation of generations. He chooses, however, to invest male
initiatives with the greatest value. His choice is a function of
his essentially male prospect or perspective. One severe limitation of his choice, however, is that a Marxian orientation,
per force, constricts the role of women.

Bettina Aptheker writes as follows about the erasure of
revolutionary woman effected by a Marxian critique:

> First, the majority of industrial workers [the proletar-
> iat] have been and are men. Women are concentrated
> precisely in service, clerical, and sales work [nonrevo-
> lutionary classes] so that our political subordination is
> built into even the theoretical concepts of the working
> class. Second, domestic labor—which occupies a sub-
> stantial portion of most women's time and energy—is
> designated as "unproductive" and apparently "nonex-
> ploitative." It remains, at least theoretically (if not
> practically), invisible, within the political economy of
> capitalism. Third, in Marxist theory, the masses of
> women almost always derive their class status from the
> men to whom they are attached . . . Women are con-
> tinually placed on the periphery of the "real" [revolu-
> tionary] drama of history.[20]

In sum, we see that Wright's reliance on Marxism as a
METAPLACE left him in the hole. His choice of a historiographical "fixed place" forced him to eliminate women from
Afro-American "conscious history." Like his successor, Ralph
Ellison, he allowed the astonishing technological power of the
West represented by factories and machines to blind him to
the woman's (and by implication, "folk") power of a black nation within.[21] Both Ellison and Wright endorse machines as
signs of a redemptive modernism. Both are correct about the
redemptive *potential* of machines. Their vision fails, however,
when it reads the machine as *the text itself* rather than as a hol-
ographic displacement, a condensation and distortion, as it
were, of a dream of power and authority.

We can return now, perhaps, to Wright's plane urging the
use of speed gasoline and Ellison's transport high above Harlem disorder. Both can be seen as modern inscriptions of the
ship on which a FOLK arrived from Africa. The planes are a
return of the repressed content of slavery, requiring an immense act of willed belief to be read as hopeful signs of Afro-
American modernism.

This Afro-American male will to believe produces a cognitive dissonance in *12 Million Black Voices:*

> On top of this [erosion and rape of the land by timber
> interests] there come, with a tread as of doom, more
> and more of the thundering tractors and cotton-
> picking machines that more and more render our labor
> useless. Year by year these machines grow from one

odd and curious object to be gaped at to thousands that
become so deadly in their impersonal labor that we
grow to hate them. They do our work better and faster
than we can, driving us from plantation to plantation. (79)

A shorthand for this observation reads: Machines, by their
very conditions of existence (i.e., profit), put us in the hole.
But, in a passage cited earlier, we find the following joyous
claim: "[I]n industry," black men encounter "experiences that
tend to break down the structure of our folk characters and
project us toward the vortex of modern urban life" (117). I
want to suggest that both Wright and Ellison mistook the hole
of industrial wage slavery for the matrix of a potentially productive black urban modernism. Both mistake machines as
productive (if numbing) interiors—wombs—from which a
modern, certainly a revised and redemptive, Afro-American
consciousness will be born. Ellison's invisible man, as a case
in point, steps from the numbing shocks of a womblike machine in the factory hospital episode and finds that the last
thing to be removed from his body is the "cord which was
attached to the stomach node" (238). He is birthed by a machine. Wright similarly translates the PLACE of an emergent,
modern, industrial Afro-American man as a machine's interior: "It seems as though we are now living inside of a machine; days and events move with a hard reasoning of their
own" (100).

The crucial mistake, of course, is in the reading of the machine as a type of generative Western woman. If the daughters'
ironic desire is for the signs and signatures of the white fathers, then the sons welcome the interiors of machines projected, as it were, from the fathers' ribs. The missilic, flying
form of planes clearly indicates, however, that they are, at
best, male-centered wombs. For what, in fact, are dreams of
flying? Freud writes

> The close connection of flying with the idea of birds
> explains how it is that in men flying dreams usually
> have a grossly sensual meaning; and we shall not be
> surprised when we hear that some dreamer or other is
> very proud of his powers of flight.[22]

The consequences of Wright's and Ellison's cases of mistaken
identity reveal themselves at the conclusions of *Native Son* and
Invisible Man. The protagonists of the novels are in states of
confinement; neither is coming out. Bigger will be electro-
cuted; preliminary and threatening shocks offered by an array

of signs will be translated into extermination. The invisible
man will go on thinking that his withdrawal of power from
Monopolated Light and Power is an act of subversion. In
truth, the only thing the West has always in abundance is
power. What Ellison's protagonist may never secure is a responsible authority, or control of power. These endings surely
warrant a fear of flying.

〜〜〜〜

The fear is justifiable. For sexuality is charged with a complex history in black folk history. When considering a dynamics of PLACE, for example, one must note that while slave
ships across the Atlantic carried black men in their holes,
black women were elsewhere.

The Afro-American historian Deborah Gray White cor-
rects one traditional view of the slave trade when she writes

> There was . . . a problem with [Stanley] Elkins' dis-
> cussion of the Middle Passage [in his study entitled
> *Slavery*]. Blacks, he insisted, traveled the Atlantic in
> the holds of slave ships. Elkins was right in his asser-
> tion that holds were "packed with suffocating human-
> ity." However, both sexes did not travel the passage the
> same way. Women made the journey on the quarter
> and half decks.[23]

White continues:

> Male and female slavery were different from the very
> beginning. As noted previously, women did not gener-
> ally travel the middle passage in the holds of slave ships
> but took the dreaded journey on the quarter deck. Ac-
> cording to the 1789 Report of the Committee of the
> Privy Council, the female passage was further distin-
> guished from that of males in that women and girls
> were not shackled. The slave trader William Snelgrave
> mentioned the same policy: "We couple the sturdy
> Men together with Irons; but we suffer the Women and
> children to go freely about." (63)

The most accurate description of general transactions
above deck is "access." "Access" translates as "rape"—a violent, terrorizing abuse of African women sanctioned by ownership and enslavement. If the African man in coffinlike holes
felt the chafing of "iron" and the nauseating ship's roll as
domination by powerful men who could produce "iron mon-

sters," then African women must have experienced a quite different and unmediated relationship to the slave trader's technology. Hard, physical evidence that the traders were not
incomprehensible spirits of power would have come immediately to African women in the form of rape.[24] Their relationship to white traders was not, of course, a sexual one. It was
one of terrorizing power—of missilic horror. Angela Davis
writes as follows in "The Legacy of Slavery: Standards for a
New Womanhood":[25]

> It would be a mistake to regard the institutionalized
> pattern of rape during slavery as an expression of white
> men's sexual urges, otherwise stifled by the specter of
> white womanhood's chastity. Rape was a weapon of
> domination, a weapon of repression, whose covert goal
> was to extinguish slave women's will to resist, and in
> the process, to demoralize their men. (23–24)

If in the shackled space below deck, deep groans betokened
the death of mercy and love, then on the open and unshackled
decks screams signified the brutal demise of inviolate sexuality.

Black women's restriction to plantations while black men
were on the move, then, hardly implied "intimacy" in any traditional sense. It was, rather, an extension of the ship's terror
tactics of "access."

We return to "Blueprint" now with an enlarged historiographical perspective. The ambivalence of Marxian class consciousness and nationalistic concern with race—of "precons-
ciousness" and material relations of production—clarifies
itself as sexual ambivalence, or metagenesis. For if the way of
class consciousness implied by a Marxian critique is pursued,
then the future will produce an Afro-American modern man
birthed in mechanical glory from the womb of the machine.
If, however, a nationalist history is privileged, black men of
the future, like those of the folk past, will continue to be men
"of [accessible] woman born."[26]

Asexual birth from the machine displaces a painful history
of rape and relegates the victims of Euramerican rape to a historical void. And valorization of the machine as a sign of the
possibilities of a new, male proletarian bonding across racial
lines necessitates a violent repudiation of the domestic black
woman. Ironically, the accessed black woman becomes, out
of her very victimization, a hated symbol to be eradicated by
aspiring black male consciousness. A Marxian problematic
forces the writer to devalue women, therefore, in both folk
culture *and* "conscious history." This black male, Marxian

blind spot, or silence, conditions the fictive texts and traditions of Wright and Ellison.

If, for example, Bigger Thomas believes the entire
world—and especially the white Mrs. Dalton—is blind as a
result of its allegiance to an archaic folk, racial perception, Ellison's invisible man is equally contemptuous of those who
cannot see. Disguised merely in sunglasses, the invisible man,
like Bigger the murderer, deceives an entire "folk" community. But surely it is rather Wright and Ellison who have
blinded themselves with transcendent optimism, an aggressively male optimism that discounts woman's history (or her
story) in order to project an alliance between black and white
male industrial workers as the oversoul of modernism. It takes
far more than dark glasses in America, however, to dissolve
the old, folk category of race. And race's inescapable and
omnipresent signifier is, in fact, the accessible body of domestic black woman—whether as victim of rape or sufferer, in
our times, of teenage pregnancy. In truth, the only escape
from such an indisputable and grounding historical signifier is
a brutally internecine one. What has first to be effected by the
black male of Wright's historiography is not transcendence,
but murder.

The corollary image for the black man in flight is the image of black (domestic) woman murdered—left, as I have
said, to die in the deserted spaces of outworn history. If Bigger's text is skyward, Bessie Mears's story in *Native Son* has
clearly to do with deaths on city pavements. Bessie's story is
one that even Ellison, in all his Oedipal subtlety and anxious
revisions, merely repeats without a difference.

The prefiguration of the kitchenette women of *12 Million
Black Voices* represented by *Native Son*'s domestic black
woman occurs immediately after Bigger has lured Bessie into
sexual intercourse with money stolen from the murdered
body of Mary Dalton:

> The same deep realization he [Bigger] had had that
> morning at home at the breakfast table, while watch-
> ing Vera [his sister] and Buddy [his brother] and his
> mother came back to him; only it was Bessie he was
> looking at now and seeing how blind she was. He felt
> the narrow orbit of her life: from her room to the
> kitchen of the white folks was the farthest she ever
> moved. (131)

Bessie, however, is scarcely blind. She knows Bigger and the
situation of both his and her life—*intimately*. The dialogue of

a scene between Bigger and her that takes place a short time later in the novel reads

> "If you killed *her* [Mary] you'll kill *me*," she said. "I ain't in this."
> "Don't be a fool. I love you."
> "You told me you *never* was going to kill."
> "All right. They white folks. They done killed plenty of us." (168)

To which Bessie responds, "That don't make it right." She is, of course, right—on all counts.

Avatar of the violence of traders above deck, undeceived about the exploitative intent of their "tools," victim of a denigrating Western will to domination—Bessie is accessible, domestic, and unprotected. She possesses the most lucid vision in *Native Son*. She is the *only* character in the novel (and one among the few critics of Bigger Thomas) who realizes that Bigger's murderous course is a mistaken redaction of Western tactics of terror. Bigger, for example, reflects with calm and cunning self-satisfaction that his relationship to Bessie has been one of commercial trade: "[H]e would give her . . . liquor and she would give him herself. . . . He knew why she liked him; he gave her money for drinks" (132). It is not black love (or industrial workers' wages) that secures the relationship between Bigger and Bessie as far as the former is concerned; it is stolen capital. He is a murderer and petty thief who uses Bessie as a means of passage.

The operative word, of course, is "uses," for the entire megalomaniacal scheme of ransom that Bigger concocts relies on Bessie's forced complicity. To gain her compliance, he browbeats, bribes, bullies, and beats her. His greatest anxiety vis-à-vis the black domestic, though, is captured not so much by his early actions as by the phrase he rehearses: "He could not take her with him and he could not leave her behind" (220). The suppressed term in this statement of anxiety is "alive": "[H]e could not leave her behind [alive]." Variously described as a "dangerous burden" (135) and a weak, accusing, demanding liability (221), Bessie is coded by *Native Son* in exactly the same terms that *12 Million Black Voices* uses for kitchenette domestics. Bessie is the accessible woman who operationalizes folk history as opposed to conscious modernism. What, then, is to be done with/to her by "men in the making?" The scene in *Native Son* reads as follows:

> He was rigid; not moving. This was the way it *had* to be. Then he took a deep breath and his hand gripped

the brick and shot upward and paused a second and then plunged downward through the darkness to the accompaniment of a deep short grunt from his chest and landed with a thud. *Yes!* (222)

How terrifyingly different *Native Son*'s affirmative is from the "yes" of James Joyce's Molly Bloom. For Wright's scene is the murder of Bessie Mears after Bigger has raped her in the deserted spaces of a rotting South Side tenement—a structure which stands as the very emblem of what *12 Million Black Voices* calls "death on the city pavements." Bigger carries the fatally battered body of Bessie to a window and drops it into an air shaft:

> The body hit and bumped against the narrow sides of the air-shaft as it went down into *blackness*. He heard it strike the bottom. (My emphasis; 224)

Significantly, Bigger discovers immediately after this act that he has forgotten to retrieve from Bessie's pocket the remainder of the money stolen from Mary Dalton. Hence, not only the accessible body but also the currency of accession hits bottom. The old folk order (of "blackness") is dead. Long live the bigger man (of Western culture) in the making!

Without a sustaining folk presence, however, as James Baldwin so astutely realized in his critique, Bigger is doomed.[27] He is destined, in fact, not to a new birth from the machine, but to death in the throes of the machine's numbing power. And it is bitterly appropriate that the raped and murdered body of Bessie Mears should return as witness to Bigger's mistaken interpretations of the skywriter's text. Her body, wheeled into a coroner's inquest, startles him:

> He had completely forgotten Bessie . . . [but] understood what was being done. To offer the dead body of Bessie as evidence and proof that he had murdered Mary would make him appear a monster; it would stir up more hate against him. (306)

Wright describes his protagonist's additional responses as sympathy and shame. But the overall import of Bessie's witness is Bigger's indictment.

If Bigger is a product born of mechanistic Western technology, he is scarcely a maker. He has made nothing; he has forgotten much. His pride in rejecting even a Communist vi-

sion of the world as set forth by his attorney, Boris Max
("What I killed for must've been good! . . . I feel all right
when I look at it that way," 392), should not be conceived in
Marxian terms. It should be read, instead, in terms of the
Freudian description of flying cited earlier: "In men flying
dreams usually have a grossly sensual meaning, and we shall
not be surprised when we hear that some dreamer or other is
very proud of his powers of flight."

In codifying the dynamics of Afro-American PLACE, it
seems necessary, then, to draw a distinction between the locational positions of black men and black women. This necessity is made abundantly clear by Bigger's reflection after Bessie tells him that whites who discover his murder will, surely,
accuse him of rape. Bigger reflects:

> Had he raped her [Mary]? Yes, he had raped her . . .
> But rape was not what one did to women. Rape was
> what one felt when one's back was against a wall and
> one had to strike out, whether one wanted to or not,
> to keep the pack from killing one. (213–14)

Rape, of course, is *precisely* something done to women. It is
not an act of rebellious and heroic self-defense like Claude
McKay's posture in his bellicose "If We Must Die." Its signal
presence in Afro-American history is an archi-sign for whitemale authority and domination.

What Wright's historiographical revisionism amounts to,
then, is history repeating itself as parody—coming around for
a second time, like *The Eighteenth Brumaire of Louis Bonaparte*.[28] Marx begins *The Eighteenth Brumaire* with the observation "Hegel remarks somewhere that all facts and person-
ages of great importance in world history occur, as it were,
twice. He forgot to add: the first time as tragedy, the second
as farce" (320). Marx goes on to discuss how the ascendancy
of Louis Bonaparte in France represented a parodic return of
the revolutionary guise and rhetoric of 1789. "Parodic" because both the dress and slogans were in the service of the
most ineptly conservative, totalitarian principles imagin-
able—the "*idée napoléonienne*" that fostered imperialism of the
grossest order. Marx's historiography is instructive in this instance because it enables us to view Bigger Thomas as a farcical representation—within Afro-American discourse—of the
white slave trader. Bigger becomes readable as a parodic,
black repetition of the male principle of Western ascendancy
that Wright celebrates as the genesis of modernism. Like
Louis Bonaparte, both Bigger and his creator are betrayed by
slogans and disguises that cover brutal aspects (access?) of

Afro-American folk history. Refusing to acknowledge the full
woman's dimensions of that history, both creator and protagonist are destined to farcical repetition.

In a word, the METAPLACE of flight, machines, technology, and, in particular, Marxism in a blackmale writing of
place is a parodic space where black women are concerned.
Generating its own asexual fantasies and violent chauvinisms,
it mandates, finally, a brutalized corpse of Bessie Mears as the
sacrificial token of its value.

Bessie's witness, though, is not merely a parodying
corpse. The vision of Wright's domestic is ironically and resonantly expressive in *Native Son*. For she does, in fact, sing
the workingwoman blues, and the uncanny ambivalence of
Wright's METAPLACE reveals its generative force in his novel's
actual recording of her blues. What but the black domestic
blues is Bessie's lyrical lament that

> "All my life's been full of hard trouble. If I wasn't hun-
> gry, I was sick. And if I wasn't sick, I was in trouble
> . . . I just worked hard every day as long as I can re-
> member . . . then I had to get drunk to forget it . . .
> All you ever caused me was trouble, just plain black
> trouble. All you ever did since we have been knowing
> each other is to get me drunk, so's you could have me.
> That was all! I see it now. I ain't drunk now. I see
> everything you ever did to me." (215)

If Bessie had ever been blind, her blues reveal clearly that now
she sees all. Wright, who once projected a book on black domestics, was aware of Bessie's blues knowledge. His motion-
picture version of *Native Son* has a moment in which a blues
song that he himself wrote is sung by none other than Bessie
Mears.

~~~~~

Afro-American PLACE, in blues terms, is both a folk location and a matter in which Afro-American women are
deeply implicated. For the blues are capable of absorbing and
transmuting both a "low-down" black exploiter like Bigger
and the horrors of domestic intimacy. In *12 Million Black
Voices,* Wright defines such song as the expression that keeps
"alive deep down in us a hope of what life could be, so now,
with death ever hard at our heels, we pour forth in song and
dance, without stint or shame, a sense of what our bodies

Essentially placed as reproductive and spiritual space, woman is
supposed to see nothing but moving shadows in the mirror—never
a quintessential self producing the moving cry—I am that
(p. 165).

want, a hint of our hope of a full life lived without fear, a whisper of the natural dignity we feel life can have, a cry of hunger for something new to fill our souls, to reconcile the ecstasy of living with the terror of dying" (126).

The blues are, indeed, a PLACE that houses the "ecstasy" of human living and the terror of death. In their classic manifestation, they are a black woman's PLACE.

In *12 Million Black Voices,* the words of the text may move teleologically and eschatologically to the death of the Afro-American folk, but in the structural and visual center of the history are two photographs. One shows a black woman clad in Sunday white with arms extended to heaven, eyes closed, and mouth open in a praise song to the Lord. The other shows a black woman clad in a tight skirt, surrounded by an admiring community of black men and women who observe her blues dance. The text reads:

> *Shake it to the east*
> *Shake it to the west*
> *Shake it to the one*
> *You love the best.* (74)

Though Bessie's raped and murdered body is witness at the conclusion of *Native Son* to black men's mistaken notions about flight, her blues remain. Furthermore, the photographs of Wright's folk history testify to the expressive singularity that is coextensive with her *domestic* status in Afro-American history. Her hard and troubled place finds expressive resonance, not in paeans to the Western machine, but in the communal hermeneutics of Afro-American song. If the necessary reaction of Afro-American males to machines and flying is an endless wandering and transcendental optimism, then the Afro-American woman's response is a domestic blues.

By song here, I do not mean only actual blues stanzas, of course, but, rather, an alternative expressive impulse in Afro-American life and culture that provides a notion of PLACE quite different from the flying inscriptions of Ellison and Wright. The blues stand as the sign of a domestic writing of the dynamics of Afro-American PLACE that looks not upward, but to the hard earth beneath black feet. Such expressivity does not look individualistically and optimistically to the top of Western civilization. Instead, it turns a critical gaze on the communal bedrock of Afro-American domestic life.

Its locus, as Toni Morrison's novel *Sula*[30] stunningly demonstrates, is *the Bottom.* What emerges from a writing of the dynamics of the Bottom is a vision of black women in the making, a vision that restores value to a woman's folk history devalued by Wright.

~~~~~~

In an interview conducted by Robert Stepto,[31] Toni Morrison describes her relationship to space and place as follows:

> I felt a very strong sense of place, not in terms of the country or the state, but in terms of the details, the feeling, the mood of the community. . . . I think some of it is just a woman's strong sense of being in a room, a place, or in a house. Sometimes my relationship to things in a house would be a little different from, say, my brother's or my father's or my sons'. I clean them and I move them and I do very intimate things "in place." I am sort of rooted in it, so that writing about being in a room looking out, or being in a world looking out, or living in a small definite place, is probably very common among most women anyway. (213)

Insofar as black domestic labor makes a narrow circuit from kitchenettes to white folk's kitchens, it may be considered beyond the reaches of conscious history by Wright and others.[32] But insofar as it becomes—in the inscription of Morrison's writing of "intimacy"—a production of order, it is at the ritual foundation of the black community's systematic definitions of itself. In fact, as avatars of those who were accessible and unshackled between the above-deck worlds of white sailing machines and their suffocating holes, the domestic marks the boundaries of communal space.[33]

Interiority and the frontier of violation coalesce in the accessible body of the African woman. The question of propriety, a "normal" place query, is conflated or confused with one of "intimacy." The body's male owner and violator (the European slave trader) is in an altogether different relationship to it than its intimate occupant. And the nature of the intimacy achieved by the occupant as domesticator is quintessential to definitions of Afro-American community. The occupant marks the "boundary case" of ownership.

In Morrison's description this marking, or systemization, of interiority is a function of *cleaning*. And it is the anthropologist Mary Douglas who most persuasively coalesces ideas of order and danger, cleaning and violation in her discussions of dirt in *Purity and Danger*.[34] She writes:

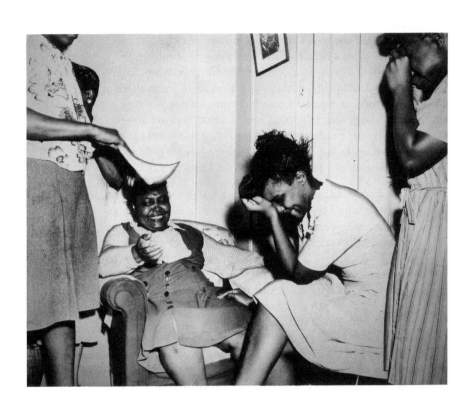

The fiddle be callin' our gods what left us/ be givin back
                                                    some
devilment and hope in our bodies worn down and lonely over
these fields and kitchen.

                    —Ntozake Shange

Dirt is the by-product of a systematic ordering and
classification of matter, in so far as ordering involves
rejecting inappropriate elements . . . We can recognise
in our own notions of dirt that we are using a kind of
omnibus compendium which includes all the rejected
elements of ordered systems. It is a relative idea. Shoes
are not dirty in themselves, but it is dirty to place them
on the dining-table. (35)

Douglas's definition of dirt as "matter out of place" is suggestive for the purifying negotiation of matters mandated by the
above-deck world of the slave ship. A rejection of the assumptions, if not the conditions, of violation—an obstinate insistence on a deeper intimacy, as it were, provided conditions of
possibility for the very existence of Afro-American system.
The unmediated, above-deck world reduces the scope of concern from a desire for possession of the Western machine to a
psychic quest for an achieved and ordering intimacy of wom-
en's *self*-consciousness. The shift is something like that between world historic forces and embedded ancestral energies
of survival and even poetic consciousness as defined by phenomenology.

Continuing her conversation with Stepto, Morrison notes
that when she wrote her novel *Sula,* she

was interested in making the town, the community,
the neighborhood, as strong as a character as I could
. . . My tendency is to focus on neighborhoods and
communities. And the community, the black community . . . it had seemed to me . . . was always there,
only we called it the "neighborhood." (214)

What Morrison ultimately seeks in her coding of Afro-
American PLACE is a writing of intimate, systematizing, ordering black village values out of a woman's consciousness, a
writing conscious always of black woman's self-possession.
For in "City Limits, Village Values," [35] she suggests that black
writers retain always a respect for "community values," for
"village values" (38). And chief among these values, in her
view, is the "advising, benevolent, protective, wise black
ancestor . . . imagined as surviving in the village but not in
the city" (39). Such ancestors in the works of black women
are almost always venerable women such as Kitty Brown or
Toni Cade Bambara's Minnie Ransom.

Morrison, thus, pulls away from what has been considered the standard Afro-American story of a willed and unvar-
ying progress of black men from rural hamlets to passionate

endorsement of modern, urban technological arrangements of life. Her notions of Afro-American making as they are told in *Sula* seem almost to emanate from an altogether different expressive tradition. *Sula* begins not in the manner of *Native Son* with airplanes over the city, but with a definition of an "intimate" black neighborhood at the moment of its negation: "In that place, where they tore the nightshade and blackberry patches from their roots to make room for the Medallion City Golf Course, there was once a neighborhood . . . It is called the suburbs now, but when black people lived there it was called the Bottom" (3). Morrison's narrative is, thus, marked by the motion of return, of reclamation. Her place or setting is the "village" or "community" or "ancestral" home of the folk in their ritual confrontation with stark daily and yearly necessities occasioned by what the narrator of *Sula* calls "A joke. A nigger joke" (4).

The "nigger joke" of the novel is offered as an explanation for the name of "that place." It is called "the Bottom" because it originated in the tricky economics of Afro-American slavery. Having promised a slave both freedom and a piece of "bottom land" if he performed some very difficult chores, a white master reneges, granting freedom easily enough but constructing a ruse to convince the slave that barren hill land buffeted by wind and eroded by rain is "rich and fertile" *bottom land* (5). Explaining to the skeptical slave that from God's perspective, the barren hill is the very bottom of heaven, the white master succeeds in his deception.

This etiological tale of place naming inscribes the fact and fantasy of capitalism. It is the writing of an American betrayal that can be read as follows in the words of W. E. B. DuBois: "But the vision of 'forty acres and a mule'—the righteous and reasonable ambition to become a landholder, which the nation had all but categorically promised the freedmen—was destined in most cases to bitter disappointment" [36] (233–34). The joke within the Bottom's economics is the deprivation of the "means of production" that characterized America's relationship to former slaves.

This betrayal, broken promise, and sublation are determinative in the world of *Sula*. For life in the Bottom is exalted neither through agricultural production nor productive industrial labor associated with construction and running of a "modern" world. Instead, the Bottom's character is a redaction of the folk's innovative survival of a "joke."

The joke, in fact, represents the signifying difference within the whole of the novel's discourse. It mocks the Bottom's rocky autonomy like the repressed content of preconscious thought.[37] Drawn down into a collective white and black unconscious, the denial of black advantage reemerges as an acceptable discursive form (a joke) whose displacements and distortions allow its content to escape censure. Blacks and whites alike tell the joke to secure meager comforts of self-esteem and self-justification. The "nigger joke," then, not only names "that place," but also provides the unconscious of Medallion and the Bottom with a slightly pleasurable rationale for powerlessness in the face of an exclusive, capitalistic control of the world. Working–class white men tell the joke when they are out of work. Immigrant men and boys tell it in order to bond with racist whites. Blacks tell it to achieve self-exoneration. All who tell it laugh to keep from crying at their powerlessness.

A community veritably created as the function of a "joke" requires special rituals for survival. The return of the repressed signaled by the "nigger joke" represents a general absence of control, an antecedent and exterior determination of, at least, the space in which a community can set life in motion. Since the denial represented is general, or global, as I have suggested by noting the variety of groups that it subsumes, it seems fitting that capitalism's most indisputable moment of global-technological 'modernism" should produce the preeminent ritualist of *Sula.*

Who can deny that the most awesome mobilization of capitalism's prowess the world had ever witnessed until 1914 was World War I? And who, after reading *Sula,* fails to apprehend Shadrack, the handsome young black man bathed in the terrifying fires of that global disaster, as a sign of capitalism's control of man's fate?

Upon his discharge from a veterans' facility, Shadrack makes his way back to the Bottom and institutes an annual ritual—National Suicide Day, scheduled for the third of January. He is the first character we encounter in *Sula,* and the chapter in which his story is recounted is entitled "1919." The format of the narrator's differentiating tale is, thus, a chronicle.

Shadrack has seen a fellow private destroyed by war. The boy's face is blown off in the very first moment of the very first battle in which Shadrack participates; this carnage drives Shad insane. The picture of brains sliding down the back of the private's body, which ". . . ran on, with energy and grace, ignoring the drip and slide of brains" (8), is an image of dismembered humanity, of the absurd horror produced by exploitative workings of power. Upon his return to the Bottom,

Shadrack says "No," in madness and in thunder, to such terri-

fying and unstable conditions of existence. His National Suicide Day is intended as a prophylaxis against disorder.
Through a manipulation of images and instruments of death
it is meant affectively to reduce death to a "residual" category.[38] As the guardian of spaces of sudden and unpredictable
death, Shadrack becomes a latter-day Charon, an antinomian
figure of matted hair, obscene language, and exposed genitals
who provides reassuring grounds of "abnormality" for the
Bottom's traditional rites of birth, harvest, and matrimony.
Shadrack, one might say, is an unequivocal *public wrong*
against which the Bottom defines its right. "Once the people
understood the boundaries and nature of his madness, they
could fit him, so to speak, into the scheme of things" (p. 15).
He is scarcely a mere eccentric. He appears, in fact, as a gigantic Blakean inscription on the landscape of *Sula*. His most distinctive signature is that of the existentialist. Reversing the
Bible's characterization of Shadrack[39] as a man whose faith enabled him to escape the commandments of authority and the
furnace of the State, Morrison's mad ritualist is a consciousness blasted and terrified into non-sense by the awesome
workings of State power. God is decisively dead in Shadrack's
universe; the initiative belongs to madmen alone. Like the
Bottom community itself, Morrison sets this wrongman in
distinctive contrast to Mrs. Helene Wright, the second character, encountered as the chronicle moves to "1920."

Helene Wright (née Sabat) has evolved in a way that directly counterpoints Shadrack's emergence. From the outlawed dominion of the Sundown House of prostitution in
New Orleans, where she was born, and an association with
witches marked by her surname, "Sabat," she has moved to
the sheltering Ohio matrimony that makes her "Wright." The
Bottom unwittingly cooperates in the woman's obsessive
flight from her mother's sexuality by domesticating her name;
they call her, simply, Helen. Without sketching her history in
detail, one can surely read Helene as a descendant of the
women described in Morrison's *The Bluest Eye,*[40] black
women who have tamed both their hair and their passions in
order to be rid of "the funkiness . . . The dreadful funkiness
of passion, the funkiness of nature, the funkiness of the wide
range of human emotions" (p. 68). Helene is, likewise, a precursor of that community of Dead women in *Song of Solomon*
who spend their days inside the house, making artificial
roses.[41] Her privileged project in *Sula* is the thinning of both
her daughter's nose and her imagination.

She succeeds mightily in dimming Nel's imagination until
it is but a faint remnant of the luminescent energy displayed

on the daughter's return from her great-grandmother Cecile's funeral in New Orleans. On the night of her return, having glimpsed possibilities of life beyond the Bottom and having witnessed her mother's sad reversion to a coquette under the "mate eyes" of a white train conductor, Nel declares her difference. Her mirror-stage reverie reads, "I'm me. I'm not their daughter. I'm not Nel. I'm me" (28). But the "me" dreamed by the daughter is effectively erased by her church-going, compulsively orderly, and communally respected mother. For Helene's house is one of oppressive neatness, providing a marked contrast to the *Peace* residence at Number Seven Carpenter Road.

Again, Morrison's subtle delight in nominalism, a delight that competes in *Sula* with an ironic essentialism, surfaces in the name "Peace." For surely a more cacophonous household than Eva Peace's would be difficult to discover outside of Morrison's own corpus, excepting the provinces of Latin American fiction. Eva, the one-legged grandmother of Sula, lives in her house with assorted boarders, a white hillbilly whom she derisively calls "Tar Baby," her daughter Hannah who will "fuck practically anything" and requires "some touching every day," her son Ralph (called "Plum") for a brief time, and three four-foot-tall grotesques collectively named by Eva "the Deweys."

The very construction of her dwelling, described in a subtle rephrasing of Christian scripture as "a house of many rooms," testifies to a kind of antinomian disorder (30). Eva's place has

> been built over a period of five years to the specifica-
> tions of its owner, who kept on adding things: more
> stairways—there were three sets to the second floor—
> more rooms, doors and stoops. There were rooms that
> had three doors, others that opened out on the porch
> only and were inaccessible from any other part of the
> house; others that you could get to only by going
> through somebody's bedroom. (30)

The depiction reminds one of those surreal constructions in the paintings of Escher. The house's ceaseless increase is a testimony to its owner's desire for expanded dominion. In a curious way, in fact, it attests the very "manlove" that we are told is the ruling creed of the Peaces. The endless stairways, for example, are a delight for the Freudian dream analyst.[42]

The multiplication of structure at Eva's, however, is finally closer to the antinomian increase of Shadrack's inversive inventories[43] than to conspicuous capitalistic display. The ceaseless expansion is a compensatory gesture by a woman who has suffered dismemberment in the office of survival. When her husband, BoyBoy (who is not unlike "the Deweys" in either his name or his infantile and abusive behavior), deserts her in the dead of winter, Eva is hard-pressed to find means of survival. After her infant son "Plum" almost dies of constipation and she is forced literally to extract the rocklike waste from his anus in a bitterly cold outhouse, she resolves to take action. She leaves her children with a neighbor and disappears for eighteen months, returning with her left leg severed and enough money in hand to depart her one-room cabin and build Number Seven Carpenter Road as a boarding-house.

What one might say is that Eva, in Morrison's rewriting of the biblical first woman Eve, is scarcely a chaste, whole help-meet for Patriarchy. She is a dismembered black woman who refuses to expire in the backwash of any man's history. Like Shadrack, she says "Uh uh. Nooo" to the given arrangement of things (34). In order to defeat the dreadful course of capitalism's "joke," she subjects herself to dismemberment, sacrificing a leg for the sake of insurance premiums, or so the myth of her loss is told.

She converts her very body into a dismembered instrument of defiance—and finance. Her act is as much an utterance of the *non serviam* as that of her slave precursor described by a Works Project Administration interviewee as follows: "I knew a woman who could not be conquered by her mistress, and so her master threatened to sell her to New Orleans Negro traders. She took her right hand, laid it down on a meat block and cut off three fingers, and thus made the sale impossible." [44]

Similarly, Eva refuses to become a will-less object of exchange left to die in barren one-room arrangements of the Bottom. She becomes, instead, one in the Party of Shadrack, advocating an inversive "manlove" that makes both her and her daughter "sooty" in the estimation of Helene Wright. In addition, she absolutely refuses to be bound by traditional, middle-class definitions of motherhood and responds to her daughter Hannah's query "Mamma, did you ever love us?" with the following tirade:

> "No time [to play or engage in affectionate gestures].
> They wasn't no time. Not none. Soon as I got one day
> done here come a night. With you all coughin' and me
> watchin' so TB wouldn't take you off and if you was
> sleepin' quiet I thought, O Lord, they dead and put my

hand over your mouth to feel if the breath was comin'
what you talkin' 'bout did I love you girl I stayed alive
for you can't you get that through your thick head or
what is that between your ears, heifer?" (69)

In the bleak world of 1895 (the year of Booker T. Washington's Atlanta Compromise Speech and the one before the infamous *Plessy* v. *Ferguson* decision that made "separate but equal" the Jim Crow law of the land), there was *no* time for black women to engage in playful nonsense. There was but one incumbency: a dismembering sacrifice of the body to ensure survival and life for the children. The refusal of maternal nonsense is displayed, however, not in Eva's mere tirades against traditional behaviors, but in her fiery execution of her own son.

When Plum finally returns to the Bottom after his service in World War I, he is a heroin addict. Refusing to allow him to regress to infancy and, as she graphically states it, "crawl back in my womb" (71), Eva pours kerosene over him and sets him on fire. She is pictured in her homicidal scene as a giant heron or eagle swooping down in dreadful judgment on her own child. (This scene of conflagratory motherhood, surely, qualifies Richard Wright's claims and reinforces Adrienne Rich's notions of the "cursed blessing." Moreover it is certainly antiphonal to Shange's portrayal of a mother who is always "there," as we shall see in the next chapter.) It has been suggested that Eva in her fiery manifestation displays the protean character of the Indian goddess Shiva; her first relation to Plum is as a benevolent lifegiver. Burning him for heroin addiction, she becomes the avenging face of the goddess.

Her act, whether godlike or more secularly murderous, places her on a plane with Bigger Thomas, who rationalizes his murders in the name of an achievement of "personal" space. Eva tells Hannah, "He was a man, girl, a big old growed-up man. I didn't have that much room. . . . I done everything I could to make him leave me and go on and live and be a man but he wouldn't and I had to keep him out so I just thought of a way he could die like a man not all scrunched up inside my womb, but a man" (72). One imagines a more intelligent Bigger talking of Bessie Mears's "solace in death," of his having helpfully removed her from the "scrunched up" confines of a narrow existence. Eva, in her thronelike chair in a child's wagon, is an imperious and arrogant agent of death, just as she is the willful namer of man's fate, labeling and constricting the Deweys to an unindividuated, libidinal existence and mocking the mountain boy of beautiful voice with the disagreeable name "Tar Baby."

She is, finally, a mythic character, not quite allegorical, and not fully developed as an avatar of some non-Christian pantheon. She is, nonetheless, a positer of a creed that defines her daughter and granddaughter. She is also, as we have seen, the absolute controller of more than one fate in the novel. Ironically, with all of her self-defining hatred of BoyBoy ("[I]t was hating him that kept her alive and happy," 37), she is the chief advocate for monogamous marriage, telling her newly married women boarders just what they should do for their husbands and counseling her granddaughter Sula to settle down into marriage and a family. The admixture of advocacy and hatred, inversive survival energy and arrogant murder, makes Eva the type of morally ambiguous character that Morrison seems so adept at creating and so astute in evaluating. Of Eva, she says:

> "[She] plays god, names people and, you know, puts her hand on a child. . . . She decided that her son was living a life that was not worth his time. She meant it was too painful for her; you know the way you kill a dog when he breaks his leg because you can't stand the pain. He may very well be able to stand it, but you can't, so that's why you get rid of him." [45]

Aware of Eva's godlike response to the incumbencies of survival in 1895, Morrison draws us to her as Milton leads us to his early majestic Satan, only to show us, in time, the morally culpable will to power that has conditioned our own sympathy with evil. For Morrison, Eva is not, finally, an empowering model of Afro-American liberation but a self-absorbed and imperious survivor of disaster.

~~~~~~

When we arrive at the year 1922, we are aware that Morrison, like her most readily identifiable male precursor, Jean Toomer, has presented characters and details of a setting that is meant to suggest an ancestral village. [46] Polarities have been established, rituals described, and village origins and occurrences subjected to subtle scrutiny. The emergent world of the Bottom is not unlike the Dixie Pike village in Toomer's *Cane* (1923). For, as in *Cane*, there is from the outset of *Sula* a strong sense that an era and its kinship and expressive structures are in decline. Toomer's narrator speaks of a "plaintive soul, leaving, soon gone" (12), and Morrison's narrator opens her story with word of deracination—nightshade and black-berry bushes being torn up along with the rambling commercial structures of an erstwhile neighborhood. Further implicating the tone and texture of *Cane* in *Sula* are the similar appearances in the two works of grotesques—symbolic characters who carry a burden of significance and who are, even when most lyrically described, bereft of wholeness. Toomer's Becky is an isolated white woman who violates traditional southern sexual taboos. His Fern is a sexually liberated hysteric who combines the landscape's beauty with the resonances of a Jewish cantor's singing. The men and women of *Cane*'s three sections share the qualities of beauty, strangeness, incompletion, hysteria. All tremble, at points, on the verge of the outrageous, whether in their passivity, their obsessive search for rootedness, or their distraught determination to make something—anything—happen.

What Toomer implies is that "village values" may produce an exceedingly resonant folk harmony when there are no competing sounds. At evening fall, after the sawmill has blown its final whistle, the supper-getting-ready songs of black women are perfect correlatives for a sensual landscape. But in the glaring light and blaring dissonance of southern day and northern noon, village values and their expression may stand, with all their haunting nostalgia, merely as a promise— "a promise of a soil-soaked beauty; uprooted, thinning out. Suspended a few feet above the soil whose touch would resurrect" (96).

In truth, Toomer's Georgia hamlet and his Washington world of the black bourgeoisie are not chosen places controlled by blacks. Rather, they are, like *Sula*'s Bottom, functions of slavery and a "nigger joke." Their apparently tranquil intimacy and autonomy remain romantic mystifications if they are not read as reaction formations of Western confinements. It is all too easy, for example, to blink the denial that is always coimplicated in definitions of "village values." The "joke" is as much a factor, finally, in *Cane* as in *Sula*.

What is compelling about comparison of the two works is that Morrison would, indeed, seem to emanate from a tradition different from that of Wright and Ellison. Henry Louis Gates, Jr., describes *Cane*'s lineage as a lyrical or "speakerly" tradition in black letters, distinguishing writers such as Toomer and Zora Neale Hurston from realist writers such as Sterling Brown and Richard Wright.[47] And nowhere is *Sula*'s situation as lyrical and symbolic narrative better observed than in the chapter entitled "1922," which begins with the statement "It was too cool for ice cream."

~~~~~

It is "too cool for ice cream" because Nel and Sula, as twelve-year-old black girls "wishbone thin and easy-assed" (52), are not yet mature enough to participate physically in the sensual, sexual mysteries signified by ice cream. The location of Edna Finch's Mellow House (the ice-cream parlor) in the community is at the end of a gauntlet of young and old black men who stare with "panther eyes" at the young girls. All of the men are thinking of images summoned by the phrase "pig meat," but one twenty-one-year-old black "pool haunt of sinister beauty" named Ajax actually utters the phrase, stirring the budding sexuality of the two girls like confectionary ice on warm and eager tongues.

The opening scene of "1922" is, thus, rife with sexuality. And while the surname "Finch" carries connotations of a delicate flight and extends the bird imagery of *Sula* (We recall Eva's "heron" or "eagle"), "mellow" indicates "ripe," or "mature." The oxymoron marked by "sinister beauty" for Ajax is complemented by the innocent lust of adolescent girls and the almost blues innuendo of Morrison's handling of "ice cream." Surely, Edna's mellow confections appear more like the male equivalent of the blues' "jelly roll" than Baskin-Robbins's multiple flavors. Vanilla and lemon come together as follows:

> The cream-colored trousers marking with a mere seam the place where the mystery curled. Those smooth vanilla crotches invited them; those lemon-yellow gabardines beckoned to them. They moved toward the ice-cream parlor like tightrope walkers, as thrilled by the possibility of a slip as by the maintenance of tension and balance. The least sideways glance, the merest toe stub, could pitch them into those creamy haunches spread wide with welcome. Somewhere beneath all of that daintiness, chambered in all that neatness, lay the thing that clotted their dreams. (51)

This mutual dream of Sula and Nel is scarcely one of real "ice cream." What brings the two girls together, in a word, is the Phallus, the Law of the Fathers, whose "mystery" makes it a creamy veil for their adolescent dreams.[48] The PHALLUS is, of course, to be distinguished from the penis. The PHALLUS is not a material object but a signifier of the Father, or, better, of the Father's LAW.

In the writing of Freud, infantile drives institute a tripartite pattern of lack-absence-differentiation. Originally "at one" with the breast of the Mother, the child experiences hunger (lack) as an absence of the breast. Eventually, he or she discovers in the Mother's absence his or her *difference* or differentiation from the Mother. A twofold relationship results. The child makes demands; the Mother has desires. The child wishes to become the desired of the Mother. (A simple instance is alimentary—the child demands food; the mother desires toilet training.) In order for CULTURE to occur, this dyad of desire must be interrupted by a third term. That term is the Father as PHALLUS, as the LAW.

Here we come to the Oedipal stage in which those children possessed of a penis want to be the absent PHALLUS *for* the Mother but find the Father always already there. Hence, they tremble before the thought of death (castration/lack) and subjugate themselves to the master, the LAW of the PHALLUS. They know they will accede to Fatherhood in due course.

Children without a penis substitute a baby—as a sign of presence and satisfaction, and a possible fulfillment of desire—for the absent PHALLUS. What Jacques Lacan makes of the traditional corpus of Freud is a signifying drama in which the PHALLUS represents the condition of possibility of socio-sexual differentiation and cultural production by *standing for* the third term, or Father. It is the marker, as it were, of male power and familiarly patriarchal discourse. It is both precultural and culture-founding.

The PHALLUS, in a word, is the signifier that institutes male-dominant cultural discourse and mandates a division of physiologically differentiated children into two, unequal sexes. To create a habitable space beyond the LAW of the PHALLUS, symbolic manipulation—an unveiling—is *necessary.*

In fact, what causes the discourse of "1922" to coalesce (or clot) is the triple repetition of Sula's and Nel's exorcising ritual of the Phallus. It is important to say at the outset, however, that Sula and Nel, for all their apparent bonding, do not share a single perspective. While the Phallus may be an object common to their dreams, how very different are their dreams! Nel lapses easily into a "picture of herself lying on a flowered bed, tangled in her own hair, waiting for some fiery prince. He approached but never quite arrived" (51). Sula, by contrast, "spent hours in the attic behind a roll of linoleum galloping through her own mind on a gray-and-white horse tasting sugar and smelling roses" (52). Different fantasies, to be sure. Sula is a rider and a taster of confections; Nel awaits a fire that never quite kindles. The visions of both girls, however, include not only an implied relationship to the Phallus, but also the presence of some further person, a dream companion of the same gender.

This third party signals a triangulation described by Nancy Chodorow in *The Reproduction of Mothering:*

> Girls cannot and do not "reject" their mother and women in favor of their father and men, but remain in a bisexual triangle throughout childhood and into puberty. They usually make a sexual resolution in favor of men and their father, but retain an internal emotional triangle.[49]

Discussing the work of the psychologist Hélène Deutsch, Chodorow explains that when women are involved in heterosexual erotic relationships with men, relational triangles represent a reproduction of the type of mother-daughter bonding described in the foregoing quotation (200). There can be little doubt about both Nel's and Sula's erotic attraction to "the thing that clotted their dreams." Similarly, there can be little doubt about the "nontraditional" character of that signifier in their lives. For both girls are "daughters of distant mothers and incomprehensible fathers (Sula's because he was dead; Nel's because he wasn't)" (52). In a sense—and as a consequence, at least in part, of a "nigger joke"—Nel and Sula are *not* members of a traditional "family," and, hence, cannot play out the usual family romance.

For example, Sula cannot maintain any affectional pre-Oedipal bonding with a mother who, pressed by the exigencies of her need for touching, admits to not liking her daughter, to seeing Sula (quite justifiably in the male-bereft economies of the Bottom) as a burden and a cross to bear. Hence, a rejected Sula watches her mother burn to death without so much as stirring a muscle. Similarly, Nel, as the diminished product of a mother bent on eradicating sexuality along with her daughter's distinguishing physical identity, is incapable of finding a maternal perch for her affections. The two girls, therefore, come to stand to each other as more MOTHER than their actual mothers. They enact their supportive displacement as a function of the incumbencies of a black "village" existence.

Similarly, Sula and Nel are required to construct the role of the FATHER from that assembly that marks the male gauntlet from the Time-and-a-Half Pool Hall to Edna Finch's Mellow House. This further displacement mystifies the Phallus even further in their mutual imaginings. And it is, ultimately, the displacements occasioned by the "nigger joke" that necessitate a threefold enactment of Phallic rites in "1922."

First, there is a ludic enactment in which "the beautiful, beautiful boys . . . [whose] footsteps left a smell of smoke behind" (56) are metaphorically appropriated as "thick" twigs peeled "to a smooth, creamy innocence," like ice cream (58). Sula's first act is an artist's response; she "traced intricate patterns . . . with her twig" (58). But soon both Nel and Sula are hollowing out holes in earth. Their separate holes join, and Nel's twig snaps. Both girls, then, throw their twigs into the hole and collect all the debris from the clearing around them and bury it, with the twigs, in the earth. The first rite is completed. The Phallus has been metaphorically exposed and exorcised; its mystery has been appropriated by the absorptive (earth) womb, which seems capable of serving as the whole (as opposed to the broken or fragmented twig) ground of bonding between the girls. It is as though a "creamy" pleasure can be shared by a common hole. Demystification and burial (a purgative burial and "cleaning") are engaged as common ritual acts.

In the second instance of the Phallic rites, however, the girls' responses dramatically differentiate them. Chicken Little comes into the clearing, and while Nel badgers him about his polluting behavior (i.e., picking his nose), Sula accepts him as he is. In an adolescent figuration of her mother's relationship to male lovers, Sula suggests that Chicken "didn't need fixing" (43). And it is Sula alone who climbs the tree with the little boy, showing him a world beyond the river. Nel remains on the ground and, hence, is not party to a Freudian reading of tree climbing.

In the section of the *Interpretation of Dreams* entitled "Representation by Symbols," Freud observes, "I added [in explanation of one of his patient's dreams] from my own knowledge derived elsewhere that climbing down, like climbing up in other cases, described sexual intercourse in the vagina" (401). Nel is further excluded from the scene when she takes no active part in burial. Sula alone responds in mocking revelry to Chicken's infantile boast of (sexual) achievement: "I'm a tell my brovver" (60).

> She picked . . . [Chicken Little] up by his hands and
> swung him outward then around and around. His
> knickers ballooned and his shrieks of frightened joy
> startled the birds and the fat grasshoppers. When he
> slipped from her hands and sailed away out over the

water they could still hear his bubbly laughter. The water darkened and closed quickly over the place where Chicken Little sank. (60–61)

Morrison's own mocking designation of the Phallus, in all of its mystery, as a false harbinger of apocalypse—"Chicken Little"—begins the demystification that is completed in the little boy's burial by water. Immediately after he sinks below the surface, Sula rushes across the footbridge to Shadrack's shack. Overwhelmed by the neatness of its interior, she forgets to ask the mad ritualist if he has seen her throw Chicken Little in the river. He, thinking she seeks reassurance about the permanence of human life, speaks the single word "Always."

Sula has just discovered the absence of benevolent design and the limits of conscious control in the universe. Hence, Shadrack's reassurance is absurdly comic. And in the absurdity of what is (given Shadrack's fiery history) a common knowledge of disorder, the two characters are bonded. Sula becomes one in the party of Shadrackian antinomianism.

The final enactment of Phallic rites in "1922" expands the categorization of "the mystery" from false herald of apocalypse to Christian sign of the Transcendental Signifier—the Law Itself. In its burial rites for Chicken Little, the community of the Bottom summons Jesus Christ as the metonym for the son—the son, who, as Eva tells Hannah in reference to Plum, is "hard to bear." "You wouldn't know that," she explains to her daughter, "but they is" (71).

The women of Greater Saint Matthews take Jesus "as both son and lover," and in his "downy face they could see the sugar-and-butter sandwiches and feel the oldest and most devastating pain there is: not the pain of childhood, but the remembrance of it" (65). Phallic mystery, even in its most transcendental form as the Law, has its woman's redaction: loss, pain, absence. The actual fathers are disappeared by a "nigger joke" in *Sula* that emasculates them and denies them any legitimate means of production. They desert children, who, thus, become reminders of dismemberment, dispossession. The joke's consequences demand a compensating ritual, and in *Sula,* it is a funereal exertion of religious frenzy: "They [the women of Greater Saint Matthews] danced and screamed, not to protest God's will but to acknowledge it and confirm once more their conviction that the only way to avoid the Hand of God is to get in it" (66).

And so "in the colored part of the cemetery, they sank Chicken Little in between his grandfather and aunt" (66). Butterflies mark the scene of this third burial—butterflies that signify graceful flight and sexual delight and unite, once more, at a higher level of abstraction and joke-compensation, the dreams of Sula and Nel: "Two young girlfriends trotting up the road on a summer day wondering what happened to butterflies in the winter" 966).

The butterflies return as "lemon yellow" delight when Ajax releases a jar of them in Sula's bedroom on one occasion when they make passionate love. And how, with his lemon yellow as sign, could we mistake Ajax as other than one of the party of New Orleans, Sundown House conjurations? Rochelle Sabat, in an early instance of *Sula*'s bird imagery, appears as "the woman in the canary-yellow dress" wafting an odor of gardenias (25).

～～～

Morrison is such a careful artist and her prose is so richly nuanced that her work begs attention to every detail. It would be a mistake, however, to obscure the importance of "1922" by pushing on immediately with further readings. For, it seems to me, the genealogical and thematic lines of the novel are practically all in place with the close of the third enactment of the Phallic rites. Nel, who passively and quite conventionally by the bourgeois gender standards of her heritage awaits the fiery prince, is a natural for the role into which Helene Wright has "scrunched" her. She will be wife and mother, not an artistic tracer of innovative designs.

Sula, by contrast, will be the daring heir of her grandmother and mother's easy sexuality, an ally of Shadrack's in an absurdly boring world where a little "touching every day" may provide the only relief—and release. Nel will shout cautions while Sula climbs trees.

It is important, however, in marking out the dynamics of Afro-American PLACE, not to reinscribe uncritically the Law of the Father, to remystify the Phallus by insisting too strenuously on the significance of "1922." There is, in fact, a reading of *Sula* that claims that heterosexuality in general is under erasure in the novel. In "Toward a Black Feminist Criticism,"[50] a fine essay to which I have already alluded, Barbara Smith writes:

> Despite the apparent heterosexuality of the female
> characters I discovered in re-reading *Sula* that it works
> as a lesbian novel not only because of the passionate
> friendship between Sula and Nel, but because of Mor-
> rison's consistently critical stance toward the heterosex-

ual institutions of male/female relationships, marriage, and the family. Consciously or not, Morrison's work poses both lesbian and feminist questions about Black women's autonomy and their impact upon each other's lives. (165)

Smith is surely correct about *Sula*'s unflagging critique—in the strictest philosophical sense—of traditional heterosexual arrangements. If BoyBoy and Jude (Nel's whiny husband) are signs of the Father and Husband in *Sula,* then neither finds positive signification. Further, if Eva, Helene, Hannah, and Nel are taken as signs of Mother and Wife, a similar absence results. Marriage does not work in *Sula* in the manner of, say, the implicit valorizations of that institution suggested by the Dick-and-Jane primer of white family life that appears in *The Bluest Eye.*[51] And it is surely true that Nel's and Sula's relationship is the signal, foregrounded instance in the novel of productive, symbiotic human allegiance. The girls begin by loving each other with the uncritical acceptance and shared curiosity of adolescent adoration. They remain, as well, emotionally dependent even when they are physically separated or distanced by seeming betrayal. As a representation of women's bonding, then, *Sula* works toward Smith's specifications.

One question to be posed, however, is: How adequately does a lesbian reading, which foregrounds and privileges a loving and compatible relationship between Sula and Nel, explain the PLACE and dynamics of Morrison's village as a whole? I want to suggest that a lesbian reading, while persuasive in its description of the best aspects of the relationship between Nel and Sula, requires expansion and complement in order to capture the novel's exquisitely detailed and richly imaged concern for the values of the Bottom.

For example, though it is true that *Sula* does not contain a marriage that works like the Dick-and-Jane postulates of *The Bluest Eye,* it is also true that such postulates are subjected—in the very portrayal of black life in *The Bluest Eye* and in the omniscient narrator's reduction of such postulates to gibberish-like epigraphs—to almost comic inversion. The mystifying ideality of Dick-and-Jane postulates becomes absurd in the face of lived black existence. Moreover, if heterosexual arrangements that lead to a mindless and deserted reproduction of mothering are the only heterosexual arrangements considered by a critical reading of *Sula,* then it is fair to say that Morrison is unabashedly critical of them.

However, there is a heterosexual relationship in *Sula* between the protagonist and Ajax that possesses—in Morrison's and her narrator's view—all of the skyward possibilities and potentially resonant camaraderie that would result if "Lindbergh . . . [were to sleep] with Bessie Smith" (145). The following quotation from *Sula* can scarcely be read as a condemnation of heterosexuality:

> He [Ajax] liked for her to mount him so he could see her towering above him and call soft obscenities up into her face . . . She looked down, down from what seemed an awful height at the head of the man whose lemon-yellow gabardines had been the first sexual excitement she'd known. . . .
>
> *If I take a chamois and rub real hard on the bone, right on the ledge of your cheek bone, some of the black will disappear. It will flake away into the chamois and underneath there will be gold leaf. I can see it shining through the black. I know it is there*
> How high she was over his wand-lean body, how slippery was his sliding smile.
>
> *And if I take a nail file or even Eva's old paring knife— that will do—and scrape away at the gold, it will fall away and there will be alabaster. The alabaster is what gives your face its planes, its curves. That is why your mouth smiling does not reach your eyes. Alabaster is giving it a gravity that resists a total smile.*
>
> · · · · ·
>
> *Then I can take a chisel and small tap hammer and tap away at the alabaster. It will crack then like ice under the pick, and through the breaks I will see the loam, fertile, free of pebbles and twigs. For it is the loam that is giving you that smell.*
> She slipped her hands under his armpits, for it seemed as though she would not be able to dam the spread of weakness she felt under her skin without holding on to something. (130)

"Weakness" translates in this scene as complementarity, the protagonist's realization that she is the indispensable "water" for the man of sinister beauty's loam. The ritual of earth and twigs in "1922" rewrites itself as heterosexual pleasure and fulfillment. Woman is on top.

It is as though a woman blues singer like Bessie Smith flies, while a male pilot takes delight in sexual pleasure rather than achieving gratification from an aggressively asserted power of the Phallus. Morrison's poetical and sensual writing of this heterosexuality suggests a bonding that might possibly

bring a Bottom community down from its "suspension"—
that might re-root it in fertile loam. "He swallowed her mouth just as her thighs had swallowed his genitals, and the house was very, very quiet" (131).

The swallowing of the actual penis, rather than the burial of the Phallus, might produce a resounding quiet and genuine Peace. In her engaging essay "Sorceress and Hysteric,"[52] Catherine Clément writes as follows about accommodative strategies for the anomalous delineated by Lévi-Strauss:

> The anthropoemic mode . . . consists in vomiting the abnormal one into protected spaces—hospitals, asylums, prisons. The other, the anthropophagic mode, examples of which are found especially in ahistorical societies, consists in finding a place for anomaly, delinquency, and deviancy—a place in the sun at the heart of cultural activity. (8)

To "swallow" is to incorporate anomaly into the community as "place in the sun," not to confine it as burial. In Sula and Ajax's heterosexuality, we discover a model that rewrites the "joke" of a capitalism that emasculates the blackmale penis in the office of the Law of the Fathers.

Reclamation, thus, takes the form in *Sula* of an artistic, mystical, and inverted totemic feast that erases rather than reinscribes the Phallus. Sula, in the role of a male Pygmalion's deconstructor rather than in that of a female statue in passive transformation, goes through layers and layers of suppression in order to arrive at the soul of community. Her swallowing is beneficently anthropophagic. Is, then, Ellison correct in his claim that blackmale genitals offer salvation for technological society?[53] Scarcely. Genital display in *Invisible Man* is a homosexual occasion; only men are present. In *Sula* woman is on top as the domestic flier, the ritual blues purifier and cleaner of congestive layers whose excavation leads, finally, to fertile and reclaimed "dirt."

An interested reading of the Sula/Ajax relationship—one that led, say, to the assertion that the resonant combination of flight and blues signaled by their merger is a heroic writing of Afro-American PLACE—might well be accused of overprivileging the male principle. But such an accusation would be justified only if Ajax's real majesty was ascribed, exclusively and quite mistakenly, to some self-generating source.

A right reading of Ajax does not cast him in the role of a romantic, autonomous street-corner male. He is properly understood, in a very cogent sense, not as "his own man," but as the offspring of his mother's magic:

[Ajax's] kindness to . . . [black women] in general was
not due to a ritual of seduction (he had no need for it)
but rather to the habit he acquired in dealing with his
mother, who inspired thoughtfulness and generosity in
all her sons.

She [Ajax's mother] was an evil conjure woman,
blessed with seven adoring children whose joy it was
to bring her the plants, hair, underclothing, fingernail
parings, white hens, blood, camphor, pictures, kerosene, and footstep dust that she needed, as well as to
order Van Van, High John the Conqueror, Little John
to Chew, Devil's Shoe String, Chinese Wash, Mustard
Seed and the Nine Herbs from Cincinnati. She knew
about weather, omens, the living, the dead, dreams
and all illnesses and made a modest living with her
skills. Had she any teeth or ever straightened her back,
she would have been the most gorgeous thing alive,
worthy of her sons' worship for her beauty alone, if
not for the absolute freedom she allowed them (known
in some quarters as neglect) and the weight of her
hoary knowledge.

This woman Ajax loved, and after her—airplanes.
There was nothing in between. And when he was not
sitting enchanted listening to his mother's words, he
thought of airplanes, and pilots, and the deep sky that
held them both. (126)

The magical black Conjure woman as source of knowledge, as teacher of respect for women, as hoary sage whose
attraction is *not* physical beauty, progenitor of seven sons who
may yet seed the earth with possibilities of camaraderie for
black women—this is the village value, or locational pause,
the PLACE, as it were, that provides conditions of possibility
for successful heterosexual bonding in *Sula*. Of Ajax's perception of Sula, we learn:

Her elusiveness and indifference to established habits of
behavior reminded him of his mother, who was as
stubborn in her pursuits of the occult as the women of
Greater Saint Matthew's were in the search for redeeming grace. . . . [He suspected] that this was perhaps the
only other woman he knew whose life was her own,
who could deal with life efficiently, and who was not
interested in nailing him. (127)

But as pleasantly sanguine for a vernacular reading of *Sula*
as Ajax's conjure associations may sound, we know that the
heterosexual bliss of the novel comes only after Nel has dis-

covered Sula naked and alone with Nel's husband, Jude. This
discovery blasts Nel and creates a rift in the friendship between the two women. Further, we know that the same ma-
terially possessive drive that makes Nel unable to forgive Sula
forces Sula herself to transmute egalitarian flights of pleasure
into a plan to "nail" Ajax. When the conjure woman's son
senses her intention, he returns to a male dominant position
in intercourse and heads for a Dayton, Ohio, air show: "He
dragged her under him and made love to her with the steadi-
ness and the intensity of a man about to leave for Dayton"
(134).

Finally, then, both Nel and Sula are victims of village values that define a "pure" woman as an adoring and possessive
holder of her man, a glad bearer of sons, even though the labor required to produce a boy child is exceedingly difficult.
Noting the number of children she has borne, a French
woman says to Adrienne Rich: "*Vous travaillez pour l'armée,
madame?*"[54]

And the sons—so difficult to bear—are always leaving for
wars, leaving to encounter Shadrack's and Plum's fates. In
their wake lies only the "remembrance" of innocence. It
seems apt with this description of the sons to note Morrison's
dedication to *Sula:* "It is sheer good fortune to miss somebody long before they leave you. This book is for Ford and
Slade [the author's sons], whom I miss although they have
not left me." From a psychobiographical perspective, the
author plays a series of dramatic maternal roles—from arch-
destroyer, through dismembered single parent, to magically
artistic conjure woman bequeathing a love of flight. It is not,
however, the biographical that forms the crux of the novel.

What *Sula* ultimately writes is the failure of a potentially
redemptive heterosexuality—a relationship in which flight is
a function of black woman's conjure and not blackmale industrial initiative. When this failure becomes apparent, Sula has
already been branded pariah by the Bottom and has assumed
her role as a "witch" or sorceress who, in effect, defines
boundaries of the domestic.

Women become stolidly traditional mothers and loving
wives under the threat of Sula's pollution:

> Once the source [defined as Sula] of their personal mis-
> fortune was identified, they had leave to protect and
> love one another. They began to cherish their husbands
> and wives, protect their children, repair their homes
> and in general band together against the devil in their
> midst. (117–18).

We return with this quotation to the purity and danger of Mary Douglas. Sula is a domestic; she is an ironic agent of systemization and purity. Her force lies, finally, in a heritage and allegiance that enable her to serve as a defining anomaly, a marginal check on the system of community. As heir to the *manlove* of the Peaces and self-possessed arrester of conjure's sinisterly beautiful offspring, she is a natural cohort for the thunderingly obscene Shadrack. Her hermeneutical richness is signified by the mark above her eye which is variously read as a rose, a serpent, a tadpole, and funeral ash from the seared Hannah. When she dies in a closed room, not unlike a suffocating hole, she assumes the fetal position of one who, like the riddled subject of Sophocles' Sphinx, has come almost full circle. She slides back into the watery womb.

It is Shadrack, the mad ritualist, then, who carries the day. The most energetic defender against dismemberments and absurdities of a "nigger joke," he all but erases the joke by leading a rebellious group of Bottom inhabitants on a winter suicide parade. Like inversive Luddites, or kamikaze pilots of another war, they march against the very signs of their denial, attacking the construction from whose labor they have been barred, moving like banshees through the very center of Medallion. Many of them are killed when the ground shifts and the incomplete tunnel fills with water. Like Sula, they expire in the womb of their genesis—they are doomed victims of a joke-work that kept them "running."

Shadrack remains above the cacophony, ringing his bell, saddened by the death of Sula, whom he believed would endure "always." And, perhaps, Sula does fully endure in Nel's vomiting forth of the bolus of mud and leaves, the terrible loneliness for a friend that emerges as the circling cry and penultimate sound of the novel: "O Lord, Sula, . . . girl, girl, girlgirlgirl" (174). The cry's repetitions, like other repetitions and eternal returns in the novel, is a bare human talisman against life's signal and absurd arrangements.

But this is not the end.

～～～～

It is important to note that Nel's final appearance is appropriated to a narrative "present." *Sula*'s final chapter is entitled "1965," and we become aware that the very chronicle of *Sula* is the difference within *a larger history.* The Bottom's story is the always already remainder constructed by an interested narrator's voice from selected and residual categories, signifi-

cant details, actively foregrounded heroisms. There is, to be
sure, an inexorable history ruled by the "joke" inscribed in
Sula. It runs from *present* (the opening pages of the book as
"prologue") destruction and reversal of value to *present* (the
final chapter, "1965," as epilogue) destruction and reversal of
value. Just as the master has duped the black slave into accept-
ing barren hill land only by manipulating language, so the
narratively present-day white citizens of Medallion linguistically reverse the acceptable scale of material values and declare
the hills a desirable locale. Nigger heaven, one might say—a
segregated point of conjure, community, and conspicuous ritual—becomes the "imminent domain" of white leisure:
"room for the Medallion City Golf Course."

The internal or domestic chronicle of *Sula,* however, effects a resonant refiguration of discursive priorities. For the
chronicle employs language in a way that foregrounds, not the
historical "joke," but the selective years and images of Afro-
American communal PLACE. The Bottom, thus, becomes the
difference—an objectified differentiation in productive expressive display—that raises Sula's name above the very historical
medal and commemoration of whiteness marked by the
place-name "Medallion." The novel is titled *Sula,* not *Medallion*. It is "Sula" and "the Bottom" that offer figurative commemoration for consciousness. Not a material medal, but
spiritual images, one might say, are Morrison's medium. As
with the town in Toomer's fascinating short sketch entitled
"Esther," "the town [of Medallion] has completely disappeared" during most of the text of *Sula*'s symbolic chronicling
of village values of its "Bottom." The Bottom's existence and
signifying difference are notable because they are marked and
remarked at the moment of their demise by a narrator who
appreciates their ancestral resonances and domestic codifications of "purified" black experience.

Sula, in its brilliant employment of language, becomes,
then, representative of the signifying difference within Afro-
American discourse as a whole—a *chronicled* outlet from history. Reversing a traditional iconography of airplanes and
flying, it suggests that "Negro" folk history contains domestic conjurations that unite Lindbergh and Bessie Smith.
Rather than a cadaverous remainder, the folk history carried
by black women's rituals in *Sula* signifies a symbolic and
chronicled *difference*. Finally, PLACE becomes not a matter of
matter—material production and planes—but a question of
symbolic manipulation.

Rather than adopt an extant historiography, Morrison
plays over, beyond, behind, and below history, symbolically

chronicling domestic rituals of black life. *Sula,* as a result, bears little resemblance to a male standard story and its psychology of material dispossession and possessiveness. When Morrison describes Sula as an artist without a medium, and hence a dangerous figure (121), what she seems to imply is the problematic of, say, the French psychologist Jacques Lacan.[55] Rather than simply the Conjure Woman as symbolic medium or symbolic alternative, I think she means to suggest the expressivity of language in general. For language is never univocally "standard" or fixedly "historical." It is always, instead, the very site of the split subject.

Briefly, Lacan claims that when the child (between six and eighteen months of age) sees his image in a mirror, he responds with a "flutter of jubilant activity" at the discovery of what he believes to be "myself," or "me."[56] Ironically, the "self" captured by saying "I am *that*" is already alienated, a secondary identification in which the subject is subjugated to the mirror. There is only that secondary identification. Entrance into language and the symbolic order reaffirms this split. The "I" speaking is the "I" already spoken by language. The sign, to recur to an earlier discussion, is the site of *différance*. In *Heterologies,*[57] Michel de Certeau captures this Lacanian problematic as follows: "The lie [represented by literature or myth or iconography] is the element in which the truth can emerge, the truth that the Other always institutes the subject by alienating it" (56).

In terms of the dynamics of Afro-American PLACE, these formulations translate as follows: language, myth, iconography constructed by Afro-American expressive traditions are locational mirrors to which we point in our intellectual and affective assertion "I am *that*." Such "secondary identification" is alienating only when we stubbornly cling to notions that an identical self and an empirically derived (*à la* scientific socialism or Black Studies history) version of Afro-American PLACE is possible. But if we accept the incumbency of "otherness" as the condition of locational, expressive being, then we realize that the mirror of domestics is the otherness of industrial men in the making. This mirror—presented to consciousness by the chronicled imagistic field of *Sula's* village values—is the mirror paradoxically affixed to the tain of Afro-American male reflections on urban, technological arrangements of power.

The village is the PLACE where the great American joke of denial has always held sway, but where more than one black woman has inversively, symbolically, linguistically, lyrically decided, like Bessie Smith, or Rosa Parks: "Mm: I can't move

no moe/ There ain't no place/ for a poor old girl to go." [58] For
black women, this "taking place" has been not only effectively
reflective but also politically liberating.

～～～

Refusing to give way to historiographical myths of an erasure of race by the mechanistic glories of technological flight,
black women have settled down to business. Either they have
appropriated flight to gainful ends like Willa B. Brown,
whose Chicago flying school was one of the first of its kind in
the United States;[59] or they have transformed the joke of Western capitalism in the manner of Sarah Breedlove, whose lineage includes the millionaire cosmetologist A'Lelia Walker.[60]

At the heart of *Sula*'s Bottom stood, among other busi-
nesses, Irene's Palace of Cosmetology, a woman's place where
they "used to lean their heads back on sink trays and doze
while Irene lathered Nu Nile into their hair" (3). A'Lelia
Walker's "business" was to remake herself, to stop her hair
from falling out, and to get away from the scarred domestic
knees and reddened hands that had marked her mother as
maid, as laundress. What she did was energetically to take care
of business by taking the result of her dream life (An old man
from Africa conveyed a formula for hair renewal to her in a
dream) and doing something about her own, and all black
women's, hair. The dream as an inversive mirror of consciousness produced a "flutter of jubilant activity"—"I am *that!*"

Similarly, Morrison takes care of business by constructing
the very mirror that brings us to a new sense of our multiply
gendered self through her own inversive mirrorings. She offers us not a univocal place of flight, but a complexly communal PLACE where we can come to see ourselves. Her work
metaphorizes the energies of the persona framed by the Washington, D.C., poet, Ethelbert Miller, in words with which we
move toward a conclusion of these reflections on Afro-
American PLACE. Miller's poem "Only Language Can Hold
Us Together" reads as follows:

> only language
> can hold us together
>
> i watch the women
> bead their hair
> each bead a word
> braids becoming
> sentences

she would
never comb her hair
it was always wild

like new poetry
it was difficult
to understand

she would enter
rooms where old women
would stare & mumble
 bold ones would say

"where's her mother"

she never understood why
no one ever understood the
beauty of her hair

like free verse
so natural as conversation
so flowing like the french
or spanish she heard or
overheard she thought she knew

"i want to go to
mozambique she said one day

combing her hair
finding the proper beads
after so long

"I want to go to
mozambique" she said

twisting her hair
into shape the way her
grandmother made quilts
each part separated &
plaited

"i want to go to
mozambique or zimbabwe
or someplace like luanda

i need to do something
about my hair

if only i could
remember
the words
to the language

that keeps
breaking in my
hands"

Morrison "re-members" our alienation from ourselves
and enables us to know our PLACE and to be less despairing
about our hair and heritage. For, in truth, it has often seemed
that in blackmale writings of a putatively asexual Western
technological world as our proper PLACE, the dominant expressive impulse has been toward an escape from "bad hair"
rather than from "bad air." Morrison allows the alienating
"badness" of the other's gaze to be refigured as.village values,
a mirroring linguistic construction—a springy "lying" down
if you will—in which we can find ourselves, and where especially black men may yet make a jubilant response, saying,
"We are *that!*" Or, in more vernacular terms:

> I will pack your water: from the boggy bayou
> Hey now tell me sweet baby, who may your
>   manager be
> Before many more questions, won't you *please* make
>   arrangements for me,
> Your hair so doggone curly and your eyes ain't blue.
> That's why baby, I'm making a fool about you.[62]

Morrison has enabled us to know an Afro-American woman's
PLACE by showing us just what must be done with the words,
the values, the language that a "nigger joke" has too often
caused to break in our hands. Her manipulations of the symbolic, thus, bring her into fine accord with Sula, of whom we
are told: "Sula never competed; she simply helped others define themselves" (95). Afro-American women's PLACE is both
our alienation from univocal male placements and our resonant (re)presentation and mirroring to consciousness of a
fuller and more objectively valid picture of where we stand.
Claiming from conjure and its "tricks" with words a *locational
value* that forms an essential part of our being, *Sula's* chronicled PLACE of the symbolic order and split subject offers a site
for further transformations. Morrison's signal poetic image
(the domestic Village) offers possibilities for a (re)presentation
of the world.

This (re)presentation—while it captures *PLACE*—occurs
in time. Time in Afro-American women's expressivity is, in
fact, the very possibility of expressivity. For it is the "changing" instant that makes possible the invention of "a language
to get inside of." And it is time that constitutes the subject of
the concluding chapter of these poetics.

Time is not displayed as simple chronological order, but rather as an instant created and occupied by and susceptible to aesthetic practices (p. 181).

Time is neutral until it is marked by an event (p. 199).

CHAPTER FOUR

The Changing Instant

In fact the only time that can be called present is an instant.
   St. Augustine

   . . . the reason i'm so peculiar's
cuz i been studyin up on my daddy's technique
& everythin i do is magic these days
& it's very colored
very now you see it/now you
dont mess wit me

                    i come from a family of retired
sorcerers/active houngans & pennyante fortune tellers
wit 41 million spirits critturs & celestial bodies
on our side
   Ntozake Shange

WITHIN A POETICS of Afro-American women's expressivity, space and place are more easily analyzed than time.
This is scarcely surprising, given the perspective of a Western
symbolic order in which "woman" is either locative—placed
and kept in her place—or spatially generative in the manner
described by Julia Kristeva in "Women's Time":[1]

> When evoking the name and destiny of women, one
> thinks more of the *space* generating and forming the
> human species than of *time,* becoming, or history . . .
> the problematic of space, which innumerable religions

of matriarchal (re)appearance attribute to "woman,"
and which Plato, recapitulating in his own system the
atomists of antiquity, designated by the aporia of the
chora, matrix space, nourishing, unnameable anterior
to the one, to God and, consequently, defying metaphysics. (33–34)

Essentially placed as reproductive and spiritual space, woman
is supposed to see nothing but moving shadows in the mirror;
never is she envisioned as producer of the very mirror in
which we come to a new consciousness.[2] The problematic of
male mirrorings and mirrored males once again presents itself.

Time for Tennyson's Lady of Shalott is unreachable motion. Not as young or energetic as Alice, she accepts her
cursed place by plying a woman's craft, weaving—or is it
static desire?—until the reflector cracks, sending her and her
craft to an untimely death. Alice, by contrast, refuses to wait.
Stepping through the mirror, she rejects the shadow for the
act. Like Alice, Janie Crawford, in Hurston's *Their Eyes Were
Watching God,* finds a self for *jouissance*[3] through the looking
glass. Janie's uncovered and still lustrous hair converges with
gleaming territories through the glass to produce an image of
a distinctively Afro-American woman's developmental time:

> Years ago, she had told her girl self to wait for her in
> the looking glass. It had been a long time since she had
> remembered. Perhaps she'd better look. She went over
> to the dresser and looked hard at her skin and features.
> The young girl was gone, but a handsome woman had
> taken her place. She tore off the kerchief from her head
> and let down her plentiful hair. The weight, the length,
> the glory was there.[4]

Unlike the Lady of Shalott's, Janie's mirror is unbroken; it is
available for use. Further, the curse that motivates the mirror's
appearance in Hurston's novel is cast *by* Janie on the male
knight-errant of Etonville, Joe Starks. It is Joe's death, in fact,
that promotes the possible glories of a new and active existence for Janie.

What we witness in the quite distinctive instances of Tennyson's Victorian medievalism and Hurston's Afro-American
modernism is the difference that time makes in the life and
poetics of women.

In one classical philosophical reading of the world, time is
defined as the measure of motion with respect to before and

after.[5] As a "measure," time might be conceived only as dura-
tion. But "before" and "after" presuppose questions of order
and change. One commentator writes, "It is, in fact, by rec-
ognizing before and after in change that time is apprehended."[6] He continues, "So although without time change
could not take place, without change time could not be recognized." "Time," an "event," "change," "motion"—all are
dependent variables phenomenologically conjoined. In order
to actually be *before,* "before" must be marked and remarked
by a consciousness present throughout the instant transforming "before" to "after." "Change" requires a change of mind;
a measure of motion is the mind in an instant (without extension).

The difference between Tennyson's lady and Hurston's
woman resides in what Shelley designates as "the mind in creation."[7] While Tennyson's Lady is cursed by the man in the
mirror, the black woman bestows the curse. She moves
through the vagaries of the symbolic order with her mind as a
mirror of production. Janie's rejoinder to the symbolic order's
conceptualization of her role as dutiful and merely reflected
wife of the Mayor might well take the form of Sula's words:
"I don't want to make somebody else. I want to make myself."[8]

"Making" contains suffixal energies that allow it to mark
time's significance in a poetics of Afro-American women's expressivity. "Ing" represents both praxis and afterthought. It
implies *motion* that moves a state of affairs through the instant
to a new *now.* At the same time, it suggests a superaddition—
a refiguration. "Ing" opens *make's* field of signification in a
manner that allows suffixion to become supplement. The active afterthought is imaged as a timed process, or *making.* The
seemingly suffixal difference is, in effect, the making of make
as well as the quiddity of what is made. The recapitulation
here is like Hurston's gloss becoming the work itself or Morrison's village becoming the ironic tain for male mirrorings.

In a subversively womanist way Janie makes herself up in
the mirror rather than allowing herself to be passively reflective. Her mind controls horizons by bracketing all that is inessential to her makeup. She remembers everything that she
does not want to forget, and her forget-me-nots are radically
different from the mementos of the Lady of Shalott.

Janie's mirror is Afro-American woman's demystification
of what Kristeva calls the "problematic of space." By extrapolating from her image, we can, at least, ameliorate the difficulty of situating time in a poetics of Afro-American women's
expressivity. Hurston leads us to conclude, in fact, that time

is the motion of Afro-American woman's self-making with respect to before and after.

The generality of this formulation needs, however, additional features that are inferable from *Their Eyes Were Watching God*. These features include: the phenomenological necessity for the Afro-American woman's controlling mind, a dedication to a suffixal energy that disrupts the stasis of an existing symbolic order, and, finally, the death of inanition of traditional blackmale signifiers.

What energizes space and fosters change of place in the poetics of Afro-American women's time is woman as mind in the making. Such specifications move us beyond Aristotle's "the measure of motion with respect to before and after," and carry us to a definition of time not as a philosophically idealized entity but as a logical space.

A logical space is a "mathematical construct used to represent certain conceptual interconnections. By representing real things (instances of those concepts) by means of elements of the mathematical construct (their 'locations') we also represent relations among those things."[9] The logical space stands in opposition to the philosophical attempt (*pace* Kant) to construct a theory of time on the basis of the human understanding's ability to specify an adequate theory of both actual and possible appearances of time. Logical space is a postulated construct like the spectrum in which all colors and color relations can be embedded for the sake of theoretical explanation.

As a logical space, time is a representational line, a conceptual domain where measures of a real number line and theories of the physical sciences converge. It constitutes, in this formulation, a framework that embeds the totality of relations among things with respect to both time and world history. Time, as a logical space, may be thought of—like the spectrum—as a construct designed to mirror our conceptual framework of time insofar as it concerns properties and relations that are held to be temporal.

From the perspective of time as a logical space, Hurston's mirror is more than a temporal image of her protagonist's change from a girlhood "before" to a womanly "after." It is also a representation of our conceptual scheme of Afro-American woman's time in general. It mirrors various relations of production, gender, and language. As such, its power is sufficient for both Janie's making and for possible worlds of black women's productivity. It is a temporal image, both structured and structuring.

The representational capacity and productivity of Afro-American women's time are synonymous with what Kristeva terms "aesthetic practices" (52). Having discussed how two feminist generations situate themselves vis-à-vis a Freudian reading of the world, Kristeva suggests that the task of a third generation is neither to identify with the history and power derived from such a male patriarchal reading, nor to counter-invest in utopian communities of women. A third generation, according to Kristeva, must further a postmodernist project that places under suspicion the very notion *identity* that is the teleology of the Freudian project. Such furtherance involves, first, an "interiorization" into *every* identity of the "founding separation [castration] of the sociosymbolic contract" (52).

I take Kristeva's injunction to mean that socially constructed gender relations can be revised. Such a revision would not be a new gender identity or a specifiable bisexualism, but an analytical siting of the potentialities of *"victim/ executioner* which characterize each identity, each subject, each sex" (52). Such a revision and its analytical possibilities are defined by Kristeva as "aesthetic practices."

Aesthetic practices present a mirror of *différance;* they serve, as well, to frame a new ethics for a postmodern world dominated by "mass media, data-bank systems, and modern communications technology" (52–53).

Janie—in her own figuration of aesthetic practices—undoes the exclusions and sacrificial logic of the symbolic order of the male dozens.[10] As revisionistly un-Freudian as Kristeva, she unveils the Phallus. And Hurston herself undoes exclusions of a traditional Afro-American male novel by constructing the autobiographical narrative of Janie, a narrative that unfolds, as I have already suggested, as a poetics of black women's everyday life.

The acts of Janie and her creator constitute a shifting of horizons. Insofar as they revise a traditional symbolic order, they are *afterthoughts.* Insofar as they replay themselves through a reader's or an audience's participation, they are events—(re)presentations of aesthetic practices.

The temporal image is both an imagined event and an event energized through the reading, performance, or participation demanded by its intersubjectivity. The generic form assumed by such images varies. They may be represented by slave narrative instants such as Linda Brent's, southern representations in which the self is drawn as a literate manipulator of the master's symbolic and psychosexual orders. Or they may appear in the form of a choreopoem such as Ntozake

Shange's *for colored girls who have considered suicide/when the
rainbow is enuf.*

Whatever their form, temporal images describe an instant,
or a *now,* that is transitional. And this transitional import of
the image renders it—in the words of "layla," the protagonist
of Shange's choreopoem *boogie woogie landscapes*—"a hazard
to definitions." [11] Any symbolic order's taxonomy of expressive forms will be surprised, or perhaps undone, by the image
as an instant exploding into new form. Layla's image in
Shange's production reads as follows:

> inside the cave i imagine i can
> cook something to eat/but my hands dont work
> the skillet burns up/my mother's smoke
> scars my arms/my mouth blurts some phrase
> i wd have a fierce yellow
> but i dont know what that means
>
> . . . . .
>
> smudges/i'm soft graphite
> i'm clumsy & reckless/i'm a hazard to
> definitions.

The conflation between the cave and a mother's oven is as remarkable as the conjunction between inept, colorless expression and "soft graphite." The portrait is one of stammering
frustration.

Yet, layla's night life companion #5 says: "she created
ebony blurs/that she cdnt reach less she leave a furrow/of slate
fingerprints/she made things black." And layla herself says: "i
feel like an oven." An initial clumsiness and hazard reveal
themselves—in the expressive instant—as capable both of
writing (graphite's markings) and nurturing (an oven's cooking). From soft graphite layla creates living color. From smol-
dering ash, she evolves into a "marine intrusion":

> dontcha wanna be music/dontcha wanna be music/
>   dontcha wanna
> be daybreak & ease into fog/a cosmic event like
>   sound/& rain
> yah/like rain
> like when a woman can walk down gold street
> feeling like she's moved to atlantis
> when the mine's been closed a hundred years
> & the only gold is music seepin thru fog
> it's what we call a marine intrusion

interlopin visions & lost deities findin the way
home
cuz we don't recognize what's sacred anymore. (113)

From hazard to sacred intrusion marks an aesthetic trajectory. The instant signals the possibility of a new ethics—"lost deities findin the way home."

~~~~~

In *The Confessions,* St. Augustine reflects that "if nobody asks me, I know [what time is]; but if I wish to explain it to someone who asks me, I do not know." [12] To suggest that time's image in a poetics of Afro-American women's expressivity is a hazardous instant of self-making is to know what time is. But a demand for specification or fitting illustration can produce anxiety.

The broadness of the field covered by such a definition gives it the character of an omnibus category. Why, for example, couldn't "aesthetic practices" serve equally well for a poetics of space or place? Furthermore, shouldn't we have reservations about the philosophical complexity of the definition? Can we adduce a text that illustrates the benefits of such complexity? Shange's own *Sassafrass, Cypress and Indigo* [13] is, I believe, a work that illustrates the determinately temporal character of the image of Afro-American women as makers and reveals, as well, the virtues of a philosophically informed model of time.

The convergence of a work like *Sassafrass, Cypress and Indigo* and a poetics of the temporal image carries as one of its entailments the specification of a category of Afro-American women's writing that might be called the *Timed Book.*

Without projecting too far ahead of my critical analysis, let me suggest that what I call the Timed Book is, in effect, not a book at all, but a boogie-woogie landscape. Where the traditional novel is concerned—even in its postmodernist or magical realist moments—the Timed Book is sheer witchery. I shall have more to say about the genre after an analysis of *Sassafrass, Cypress and Indigo.*

~~~~~

In her essay "Program Note," Shange writes:

i cant count the number of times i have vicerally
wanted to attack deform n maim the language that i

waz taught to hate myself in/the language that perpetu-
ates the notions that cause pain to every black child as
he/she learns to speak of the world & the "self." yes/
being an afro-american writer is something to be self-
conscious abt/& yes/in order to think n communicate
the thoughts n feelings i want to think n communicate/
i haveta fix my tool to my needs/i have to take it apart
to the bone/so that the malignancies/fall away/leaving
us space to literally create our own image.[14]

The statement describes and portrays linguistic revolt.
Virgules, which are traditionally employed to separate alternatives such as *either/or,* are deployed to *summon* alternatives
and to avoid closure. Rather than duality, Shange creates a
plenitude of options. She produces a fluidity akin to a jazz
solo. Her statement riffs on (without disconnecting itself
from) the orchestrations of a standard grammar.

To take apart the symbolic order "to the bone," is to riff
within it and signify on it until it yields a signal image, creating aesthetic space. This space is temporal. Shange occupies it:

> my dreams draw blood from ol sores
>   these stains and scars are mine
> this is my space
>   i am not movin.[15]

A timed space of revisionary writing is, thus, filled by and
yields a peculiar sound.

> until we [Afro-American writers] believe in the singu-
> larity of our persons/our spaces, language & therefore
> craft, will not be nurtured consciously/our writers will
> come across it/if they want. but we wont recognize it
>
>   .   .   .   .   .
>
> we assume a musical solo is a personal statement/we
> think the poet is speakin for the world/there's some-
> thing wrong there, a writer's first commitment is to
> the piece itself. how the words fall & leap/or if they
> dawdle & sit down fannin themselves. writers are deal-
> ing with language, not politics. that comes later. so
> much later. to think about the politics of a poem before
> we think about the poem is to put what is correct be-
> fore the moment.[16]

Shange's own nurturing of the "moment" yields an image of
the black woman writer as both healer and the creator of a jazz

of her own. *Sassafrass, Cypress and Indigo* is a product of such nurturing.

~~~~~~

Set during the flammable days of the Black Arts and Black Power movements, Shange's polytextual narrative opens on a magical drama of woman's maturation.

From the time of the handmade cloth dolls that serve as comforters and companions, Indigo is in motion. She has "a moon falling from her mouth," signifying the magic of the menstrual cycle. Indigo begins menstruating while visiting Sister Mary Louise Murray. The good church sister promptly classifies the child as one with roses. "There in the garden," she says, "you should spend these first hours. Eve's curse threw us out the garden. But like I told you, women tend to beauty and children. Now you can do both. Take your blessing and let your blood flow among the roses" (19).

Indigo's formulas entitled "Marvelous Menstruating Moments" follow Sister Mary Louise's injunction. These formulas, which offer instruction and sanctification, are akin to the "Moon Journeys" encountered earlier in Shange's text. As *Sassafrass* explains them, such interposed textual moments are like spells of procurement and beneficence: "There wasn't enough for Indigo in the world she'd been born to, so she made up what she needed. What she thought the black people needed" (4).

The image of the magical child in the garden draws together myriad aspects of the narrative's beginning: "Indigo sat bleeding among the roses, fragrant and filled with grace" (19).

The "curse" of Eve is literally washed (and spoken) away by Sister Mary Louise. Women's grace includes the potential not only for children but also for the creation of beauty. The rosey and sanguinary image of Indigo provides a phantasmal and almost theatrical scene in itself.

The figures whom we encounter in Shange's narrative are less novelistic characters than actors in a mosaic of living tableaus. Every moment in the first stage of the narrative is in suspension until Indigo enters. It is the magic of the pubescent child/woman that moves these various landscapes. It is Indigo's making-in-transition that engages our attention. Moving from childhood and dolls (which she ventriloquizes), the girl/woman achieves not only the rich potentialities of childbearing, but also the difficult wisdom that "being a grown colored woman is hard" (52). Indeed, "being a grown colored

woman" marked by menstruation and magic brings not only
the creative grace of roses but also responsibilities of and for
"the folk."

When Indigo's mother, Hilda Effania, demands that she confine her dolls to the house and put away make-believe, it is Mr. Henderson the junkman (known as "Uncle John") who suggests a grown colored woman's alternative. He gives Indigo a fiddle, which she initially snubs. Not to be denied, Uncle John exposits the ethics and aesthetics of "the folk."

> "Listen now, girl. I'ma tell ya some matters of the reality of the unreal. . . . Them whites what owned slaves took everythin' was ourselves & didn't even keep it fo' they own selves. Just threw it on away, ya heah. Took them drums what they could, but they couldn't take our feet. Took them languages what we speak. Took off wit our spirits left us wit they Son. But the fiddle was the talkin' one. The fiddle be callin' our gods what left us/be givin back some devilment & hope in our bodies worn down and lonely over these fields and kitchen . . . you & me, we ain't the onliest ones be talkin' wit the unreal. What ya think music is, whatchu think the blues be, them get happy church musics is about, but talkin' wit the unreal what's mo real than most folks ever gonna know." (26–27)

~~~~~

Uncle John says, in effect, that the fiddle marks a productive, temporal folk relationship to the "reality of the unreal." Biological and aesthetic converge in an image of altered aesthetic practices. Uncle John bestows a heritage and a means of expression and defense on the girl/woman. "Indigo . . . carried that bow cross those fiddle strings . . . till the slaves who were ourselves made a chorus round the fire, till Indigo was satisfied she wasn't silenced. She had many tongues, many spirits who loved her, real & unreal" (28). Signaling defense, she "patted the violin by her bed exactly where Aunt Haydee kept her shotgun" (35).

~~~~~

Although others—including her mother—think of Indigo's untutored fiddling as "noise," the girl/woman knows that her sound is a spiritual bridgework akin to the voodoo pole in the hounfort. It is a connective between the everyday life of

Photographer's caption: "One of five Negro girls who entered the
first grade at two previously white New Orleans schools,
November 1960."

Charleston and "unreal" repositories of ancestral voices, spells, and curative wisdom. It bridges, as well, nature and society in a "wild" onomatopoeia:

> Indigo had mastered the hum of dusk, the crescendoes of the cicadas, swamp rushes in light winds, thunder at high tide, & her mother's laughter down the hall. Uncle John told her one time . . . he'd got this feeling . . . that . . . [she] was dwelling dangerous on the misery of the slaves who were ourselves, & this feeling directed him to march her toward the beauty of this world & the joys of those who come before us. Indigo couldn't get enough. No creature that moved escaped . . . [her] attention. (36)

The twelve-year-old Indigo moves through an instant to a new aesthetics of time and nature. The question of gender specificity is complicated, however, by the girl/woman's relationship to the young boys who confront her.

Indigo's interaction with Spats and Crunch does not transform her into a superwoman. Rather, her newly projected folk status seems to augur the gender complexity and complication of identity suggested by Kristeva and discussed earlier.

Spats and Crunch call themselves "Junior Geechee Capitans," miniatures of the gang that controls the black underground at Sneeds Bakery. They put a "twig" (with shades of *Sula*) between Indigo's legs and attempt to intimidate her with infantile titles: "What's your name, sweetheart?" Later they strip to the waist and do a "cock walk" around her. Aggressively male and potentially dangerous, they revive the ominous threat of Mr. Lucas, the pharmacist who leeringly sells Indigo her first "feminine napkins."

Art and aggression, aesthetics and gender come together as the girl/woman summons falcons and panthers into her fiddle. Energizing the shotgun implications of an earlier image, she "shoots" the boys down. Leaning over their crouching forms, she taps them on the head with her fiddle bow and says: "What's your name, sweetheart?"

Rather than domination by the black woman as folk artist, what follows Indigo's successful defense is her initiation into the Junior Geechee Capitans and—cross dressing. Gender boundaries dissolve as Indigo is outfitted with a man's Stetson hat, a leather belt with switchblades inscribed on it, and a leather carrying strap for her fiddle.

The girl/woman's allegiance to the JGCs signals her absorption not only of unexpected gender energies but also of class responsibilities. The "Geechees" are, in Sister Mary

Louise's estimate, the heathens of the islands. To Cypress, Indigo's sister, they are southern versions of New York's thugs. But for Indigo the geechees belong to the cultural category of "the wild," the marginal. They are outlawed, nonstandard; they constitute the nearest link to "the slaves who were ourselves."

Inhabitants of the coastal islands, geechees are also speakers of a peculiar dialect; they are practitioners of a unique way of life, from cuisine to religion. Indigo, thus, taps further into a special world of colored signification when she allies herself with the JGCs.

There are caverns beneath Sneeds Bakery where the sporting colored people gather for pleasure. It is here that Indigo performs. She expresses in her fiddling the "souls" of those who inhabit the social room. Ironically, it is the leader of the Geechee Capitans, Pretty Man, who decides that Indigo needs to change her aesthetics. Buying records of violinists from Yehudi Menuhin to Papa John Creach, Pretty Man offers to pay Indigo for each "classical arrangement" she masters. From this imitative aesthetics, disaster follows.

People desert the underground. Indigo is dissatisfied. The entire experiment ends in violence. Mabel, Pretty Man's girlfriend, is hurt. Escaping through the caverns, Indigo realizes for the first time how much and how badly "the Colored had been hurt" (49). Her epiphany is accompanied by a hatred for Pretty Man, a deep sympathy for Mabel and all colored women, and a sound of cavern walls singing.

She suddenly knows "her calling": VIZ., to ease the pain of "the Colored," who "had been hurt enough already." Two formulas appear at this point and add to Shange's polyvocal enterprise; both are proposed remedies for seen and unseen wounds.

In the interest of time, it seems sufficient to use *Sassafrass, Cypress and Indigo*'s own narrator's words to describe the full temporal image of Indigo's achieved aesthetics: "She was particularly herself. She changed the nature of things. She colored & made richer what was blank and plain. The slaves who were ourselves knew all about indigo & Indigo herself" (40).

It seems almost predictable, given our previous analyses, that the youngest daughter of Hilda Effania becomes the conjure woman and resident midwife of Difuskie Island.

The writing of an Afro-American woman's time as biology, folk aesthetics, and curative wisdom entails, for Shange, a formal multiplicity that can only be described as improvisational. In part, this is a result of the composition and process of *Sassafrass, Cypress and Indigo*. A stitching was required in order to achieve the work's tripartite title.

Shange's novella *Sassafrass* was first published by California's Shameless Hussy Press in 1976. With its interpolated poems, italicized fantasies of black blues singers, recipes, letters from Hilda Effania, and "revues" of blackmale artists, *Sassafrass* the novella both set the textual form for the expanded work and demanded additional text.

Sassafrass, Cypress and Indigo is, thus, imagistically reflective insofar as its own making contains a "before" and an "after" (respectively, Indigo and Cypress). Furthermore, the generative power of the aesthetics that produced the novella can be deduced from the impressive resonances of what has been added. Time is not displayed as a simple chronological order, but rather as an instant created and occupied by and susceptible to aesthetic practices. That is to say, every making modifies Afro-American woman's time and can bring a new aesthetic and ethical clarity. Although she is Sassafrass's younger sister and subsequent (as text) to the oldest child, Indigo is placed first by Shange. The last becomes first. Temporal determination—in the last instance—is, actually, wisdom gained from the productivity of the *latest* instant.

~~~~~

Significantly, it is Cypress who is last. She is the middle child chronologically and, thus, generationally suspended. Her suspension results in her assimilationist instinct to be a ballerina, despite her mother's caveat that "ballet is for white girls . . . your ass is too big and your legs are too short" (134). She is the inheritor of her father Alfred's wanderlust and strays farthest into what her mother calls "experimental living."

While she is titularly in the middle, however, Cypress is textually last, and least, in the wisdom of her mother and sisters. The fact that she comes late to "Soil and Soul," the final dance troupe that she joins, is not surprising.

Sassafrass, Cypress and Indigo's discontinuous production is textually mirrored by the manifold seams that are part of the work's show. The work's episodic emergence is matched by its polyvocalic and multiply focused story of three sisters, each of whom offers an image of timed release.

Indigo's roses, fiddling, conjuring, and dead certainty of her calling complement a definition of production that marks

Hilda Effania's Charleston home front. When Sassafrass and
Cypress return from a New England prep school and a New
York dance school, respectively, to enjoy Christmas at home,
Shange's work provides a stunning depiction of what might
be called an "aesthetics of the domestic."

~~~~~~

Domestic aesthetics in *Sassafrass, Cypress and Indigo* are
best exemplified by Hilda Effania's craft; she only weaves for
"useful" purposes. Furthermore, her letters to her daughters, which are interspersed throughout the narrative, are conservative calls to homely virtues. Juxtaposed with her un-
pretentious craft economy are the antics of a black southern
middle class. The three sisters receive and accept an invitation to a "Christmas Eve Wassail" sent by Eugene Alphonso
Schuyler III.

Hilda Effania's work is precapitalist productivity. It is precisely "outside" the mainstream economics that make possible rich doctors' families like the Schuylers. Her weaving is
a redaction, in fact, of codes of slave production. She is dependent on the Fitzhugh family that enslaved her forebears. Her
daughters have grown up in a house "full of spinning wheels,
table and floor looms, and . . . [Hilda Effania] always busy
making cloth because the Fitzhugh family never wore anything but hand-woven cloth . . . until they couldn't afford it
any more" (91).

Mrs. Fitzhugh is rather like a duchess (a white complement to Robert Johnson of Frances Harper's *Iola Leroy*) who
philanthropically influences her subjects' lives. Only a subversion of her control—or an economic and aesthetic escape
from it—can produce independence: "Being a grown colored
woman ain't easy." Rather than a middle-class assimilation to
gain currency, this independence occurs as a domestic aesthetics conceived in spiritual, ancestral terms.

The image of such a subversive recognition and employment of Afro-American woman's power occurs when Hilda
Effania recognizes all of the vestments worn by Mrs. Fitzhugh
as her designs. Indigo's response is more forceful: "She felt
some huge anger coming over her. Next thing she knew, Miz
Fitzhugh couldn't keep her hat on. There was a wind justa
pushin, blowing Miz Fitzhugh out the door" (71).

There are also other acts of subversion, such as Hilda's recipes.

These recipes are recurrent items in the narrative. They are

spirit work (p. 76)

wisdom transmitted from generations past; they are, also, present instruction for nourishment. While they may seem passive texts, or mere pastiche, they may also be compared to the *verver* of voodoo. Written sometime in meal or flour the *verver* are signs of habitation made on the floor of the hounfort to welcome loa or ancestors.[17] One of the rules of Cypress's house in San Francisco reads "Don't touch the altar for the Orishas" (102). Similarly, Hilda Effania might enjoin: "Don't tamper with my recipes."

Designed for a nurturance that can only be "activated" by the recipient, her texts are phenomenological. They are altars in themselves, transforming the raw into the culturally cooked—into home cooking.

Weaving, conjuring, recipes, letters are all products of Hilda Effania's domestic space. In her quarter of Charleston, *making* is always in progress. Beyond its subsistence function, this making seeks to transform the lives of black women. "Hilda Effania had some dreams of her own. Not so much to change the world, but to change her daughters' lives" (57). Mother/daughter bonding, a pre-Oedipal alliance that promotes intimacy, is ultimately the productive relationship of Hilda's instant in *Sassafrass, Cypress and Indigo*.

After the domestic instant, Sassafrass's Los Angeles home of tenor-saxophone solos and revolutionary appliqués seems outrageously stylized. In comparison with Indigo's fiddle and conjuring contact with secrets of the folk, Sassafrass's elaborate hopes for a "New Afrikan" aesthetics seem virtually satirical. The crumbling Victorian house in Los Angeles that she shares with Mitch has walls plastered with black poster art. Mitch is a drug addict and ex-convict who dictates aesthetic mottoes for Sassafrass to weave into appliqués. Yet he chides her for her failure to apply herself as a writer.

We are, it seems to me, decisively on satirical ground.

For we are told by the narrator that "Sassafrass believed it was absolutely necessary to take black arts out of the white man's hands; to take black people out of the white man's hands" (77). Her difficulties as an artist and an Afro-American woman, however, have everything to do with Afro-American men and nothing at all to do with "the white man's hands." Shange knows this.

While the middle section of *Sassafrass, Cypress and Indigo* is set in a house of "Black Art," the real drama of the section involves a woman weaver's transition from subservience to a

sense of her own power. By any characterization available
from the second section, "Sassafrass," Mitch is a self-centered,
undisciplined artistic poseur. Sassafrass, however, accepts him
as her "cosmic lover" and artistic mentor. The results are viv-
idly displayed when his fellow black artists, Otis and Howard
Goodwin Smith, appear. The three artists, who seem terribly
akin to Black Aestheticians of the 1960s, insist on performing
a revue for Sassafrass, whom they place in a barber chair. The
text of this revue is Otis's poem *Ebony Cunt,* dedicated to all
the women of the world and especially to the women Otis
claims to have exploited sexually during his adolescence. Like
her sister Indigo, Sassafrass is more than equal to this crass
chauvinistic attempt to place a twig between *her* legs.

In response to the men's attempts to intimidate her with a
cock walk, she shouts:

> "god damn it, I don't haveta listen to this . . . I am not
> interested in your sick, sick, weakly rhapsodies. . . . I
> don't like it. I am not about to sit here and listen to a
> bunch of no account niggahs talk about black women.
> . . . don't you ever sit in my house and ask me to cele-
> brate my inherited right to be raped" (89).

It comes as no surprise that Otis and Howard, who are bla-
tantly contemptuous of black women, have white wives. Nor
is it surprising that Howard's paintings are "contorted phallic
symbols dipped in Afrikan mystique and loaded with latent
rapist bravado" (85). Nor does it come as a total shock when
Mitch beats Sassafrass with an "accordion shaped" rubber
tube (a junkie's accoutrement), hitting her over and over and
over again.

The daughter's response is not confined to a curse. She
also has her own visions and productive instruments for
countering a Black Male Aesthetic. Billie Holiday and a chorus of dancing Afro-American women appear before her early
in the middle section of *Sassafrass, Cypress and Indigo.* They
provide an italicized instance that connects her with the blues
in the same way that singing cavern walls connect her younger
sister to sounds of "the slaves who were ourselves." Both lyrical instants are powerful in their feelings of black women
bonding against pain and despair.[18] In her epiphanic moment,
Sassafrass learns from Lady Day that

> "It's the blues, Sassafrass that's keepin' you from your
> writing, and the spirits sent me because I know all
> about blues . . . that's who I am. . . . Don't ya know
> we is all sad ladies because we got the blues, and joyful

women because we got our songs? Make you a song, Sassafrass, and bring it out so high all us spirits can hold it and be in your tune. We need you, Sassafrass, we need you to sing best as you can; that's our nourishment, that's how we live." (81)

In addition to her blues lineage, which is instanced again in a later italicized encounter with Mamie Smith, we learn that in her childhood Sassafrass garnered the wisdom of the folk. She transmits recipes, weaves cloth, and carries the magic from a childhood season when she said to the old folks: "i'ma be a conjuh" (109). The folks' response: "you awready a gee-chee/how much more magic you want?" The answer: As much as it takes to move into a new *now*.

━∿∿∿━

When Mitch beats her, Sassafrass remembers a stormy night in Charleston when her father, Alfred, dragged Hilda Effania down the stairs and beat her. The mother's wisdom on the matter was "you got to leave room for the fool in everybody" (99). This, however, is not Sassafrass's wisdom. Finding Mitch nodding out when she returns from a sleepless night away from home, she pronounces an accurate judgment on the blackmale artist: "You're a lousy, stinkin' junkie, Mitch. I haveta go now" (100). The pronouncement is that of a woman in possession of making powers.

As Sassafrass steps into a new *now* and looks toward a utopian future, her tutelary spirits in the instant of transition are ancient deities of the New World. Breaking her apprenticeship to a cosmic Black Aesthetic lover, she recalls the aesthetics of her youth when

> she wrote songs of love and vindication for
>   all the african
> & indian deities disgraced by the coming of
>   the white
> man/& loss of land/& cities reflectin' respect
>   for
> livin' things
>   "i am sassafrass/my fingers behold you
>   i call upon you with my song you teach
> me in my sleep/i am not a besieger of yr
> fortress/ i am a crusader/for you are
> all my past/i offer you my body to
> make manifest yr will in this dungeon
> of machines & carolina blues/ i wanna

Photographer's caption: *"Read by candlelight. No electricity in house."*

sing yr joy/& make present our beauty/
spirits/black brown/find yr way
thru my tainted blood/make me one of
yr own/ i am yr child in the new world/
i am yr fruit/yet to be chosen for
a single battle in yr behalf/come to
& thru me/i am dazzled by yr beneficence
i shall create new altars/new praises
& be ancient among you/

~~~~~

If in her moment of motion, Sassafrass summons and
states an aesthetics that constitutes a logical space, the *now*
into which she steps at her sister's home in San Francisco is
clearly nonlogical. *Sassafrass, Cypress and Indigo* is at its "hip-
pest" and most bejeweled in the pages devoted to Cypress.
Perhaps the cosmopolitan settings of San Francisco, New
York, and Europe (where Leroy McCullough, the jazz musi-
cian, triumphs) call forth the dense texture of artistic allusion,
dance reviews, critiques of jazz performances, and gushing
rhapsodies about Afro-American pictorial art. In any case,
there is about the Cypress section a general air of the *artiste*
that would have made even the Huysmans of *A Rebours* blush.

What, though, constitutes a reasonable explanation for
this exuberant excess?

The Cypress section of *Sassafrass, Cypress and Indigo* explores—no matter how "hiply"—a full array of issues that
make being a "grown up colored woman" *and a professional
artist* difficult in the United States. Commencing with Cypress's desire to emulate the aesthetics of ballet, this section
traces the daughter's sometimes outlawed, occasionally fre-
netic, and often heartbreaking attempts to make herself into
the "original/aboriginal dancin' girl" (158).

Her initial ambition is "to dance as good as white folks and
to find out the truth about colored people's movements"
(135). She wants to master the aesthetics of the best that has
been danced in Western ballet and to convert her mastery into
a unique practice of black dance. Which means, of course, that
she must suffer the virtues, as well as the horrors, of the entire
dance cosmos—the entire cosmopolitan world of dance—in
order to move from a *now* of unskilled, or, at best, raw desire
to a black dance that is really cooking.

Further, since she begins her quest when she is only sixteen years old, Cypress has both biological *and* aesthetic

growth to achieve. Her youthful exuberance and inexperience find their mirror in the "wildness" of her San Francisco parties and her eager acceptance of Ariel Moroe's invitation to join his troupe, The Kushites Returned. Ariel, who is gay, introduces the first gender complexities into the Cypress section. When in New York Cypress becomes associated with the lesbian dance troupe Azure Bosom, gender is further complicated. The first time she experiences passionate love, Cypress does so with the lesbian dancer Idrina.

Shange, thus, creates an extraordinarily heavy burden for black dance to bear. Under such weight, the Cypress section shows more than one flaw. Nevertheless, Shange manages to keep her changes and riffs interesting by introducing an authentically talented (if not "cosmic") lover for Cypress in the character of Leroy McCullough.

Leroy's life story is too contrived to be compelling, but the story of his search for a music that expresses the souls of black folk is complementary to Cypress's quest. Like Cypress, Leroy's initial ambition is to master Western concert music and European traditions. In addition, he wants to achieve a music that is a "force" (159). He "wanted the blood of . . . [Afro-American] culture, the songs folk sing, how they move, what they look at, the rhythms of their speech; that was the blood Leroy was after. Blackening up America" (189).

The complementary passions of Leroy and Cypress result in a fiercely sexual relationship that frees her to dance "aboriginally," and that inspires him to European triumphs akin to those of John Coltrane and Miles Davis. The couple is planning marriage when the Cypress section concludes. Cypress has become a member of a politically active dance troupe that is touring the same circuit as the Black Panthers, Rap Brown, and Ralph Featherstone—all advocates of militant black activism. From such a state of affairs, we might construct an image of the black woman dancer as a politically correct and culturally achieved bride of jazz. The image would represent a wedding in life and person of the improvisational (jazz) and the moving singularity (danced poetry) that Shange considers the only aesthetic moment worthy of the name *Black Aesthetic*.

Matters, however, are not as purely romantic and unproblematic as such a construct suggests. For in the concluding pages of *Sassafrass, Cypress and Indigo,* dystopian images outweigh those of temporal success. One thinks of Ariel Moroe with keloidal scars, revealing a battered mouth, and appearing desperately thin—a victim of vicious homosexual violence in return for his own voracious exploitations of young boys during the migrations of the Kushites. Or, one calls to mind the

rank crassness and crude sexual economics of the lesbian
world of Azure Bosom. The process of making—at its essentialist, danced, corporeal foundations—is scarcely idealized.

Cypress has a nightmare of a feminist community that is
little more than a rewriting (what Kristeva would call a
second-generation counterinvestment) of male hegemony.
White women assume the title of "Mother," while black and
hispanic serfs do the actual childbearing. (O, shades of Mary-
beth Whitehead.) Captured males are used exclusively to produce sperm. In the nightmare, Cypress sees both her mother
and father in humiliating postures. Her dream (though future
directed) is akin to Indigo's cavern experience. It also re-
sembles Sassafrass's encounter with the blues of Billie Holiday
and Mamie Smith.

Finally, in the work's concluding pages we witness a community of New Afrikan artists as an elaborate, muddy, hierarchical, ritualistic assembly of poseurs. Mitch is present.
Having impregnated Sassafrass, he dreams sacrilegiously on
Shango's birthday of city days and drug addiction. The activities of the New World Found collective seem to verify the
assessment of the Baton Rouge community: the commune is
a group of "crazy fanatic niggahs out there."

~~~~~

The dystopias envisioned by *Sassafrass, Cypress and Indigo*
are representations of the disastrous consequences of agit-
prop art. A quest for "engaged" aesthetic universals—whether
New Afrikan or Radical Feminist—can only result in a brutal,
confused topsy-turvydom. Shange has, of course, told us:
"we assume a musical solo is a personal statement/we think
the poet is speakin for the world/ there's something wrong
there, a writer's first commitment is to the piece itself."
Hence, *Sassafrass, Cypress and Indigo* refuses a universalist,
"political" conclusion. It privileges, instead, a momentary
poetics, an image of a specifically Afro-American woman's
time that returns the daughters to a domestic *now*. This domestic space has itself been changed, however, by Hilda Effania.

In a letter to Sassafrass, she writes: "Send me the other
patterns you've been working on. I was trying to see if I could
set up my warps like yours to make 'art' things for Christmas
sales to Mrs. Fitzhugh's friends. Charleston doesn't have the
sophistication of California, but things change, even your
mama" (133). When she urges Sassafrass to come home, the

Poetic images such as house *serve as analytical tools. They allow us not only to map a topography of intimate human space but also to follow moments of human consciousness (p. 51).*

mother further elaborates a plan for her and her eldest daughter to establish a business. The *now* to which the daughters return, then, is not only a realm of folk aesthetics and domestic culture, but also a universe of commerce and culture. Everything is in flux. Geechees are selling their land to grand white hotel builders. Black men and women in the United States are raising hell over their rights. The mirror for such transitions is the temporal transformations of Sassafrass, Cypress and Indigo.

Through aesthetic making, the daughters have all been creating a logical space of black woman's time. They have all maintained, or achieved, an allegiance with black folk ancestors and ancestral spirits that enables them to transform an instant into an energetic *after.* And the "after," thus, resonates a new *now* and a perduring *before.*

〜〜〜

The space that most fittingly represents the transformed ethics and aesthetics of "the slaves who were ourselves" is a black southern home. Here, a childbearing mother reigns supreme in her craft and in her knowledge. Sassafrass's woven hanging given to Hilda Effania as a Christmas gift says it all: "You Know Where We Came From, Mama."

The daughters do return to and are *a return upon* the mother's productive knowledge. In the concluding scene, Sassafrass's baby is being delivered by the midwife Indigo, who is now a permanent resident of Difuskie. The youngest daughter is a lineal descendant of Blue Sunday, the patroness of women who dare to birth free children. Cypress is also in attendance, lending support and awaiting her own wedding to Leroy.

〜〜〜

The time of *Sassafrass, Cypress and Indigo* is, finally, not so much the space-time of theories of relativity as the place-time of Bantu philosophy. In this philosophy, time is neutral until it is marked by an event; it then becomes the "time of that event." But events do not occur in a void; they occur in particular places. The sign *Hantu* expresses this localizing being, or place-time. In *Sassafrass, Cypress and Indigo,* the place of localizing being is the family home conceived as both memory and "correspondent" (Hilda's letters) domestic economy. A southern home, one might say, is coextensive with all of the narrative's aesthetic events.

The mother's domestic space and her letters constitute a lyrical space (one activated by reading and recall) that serves to represent the daughters' conceptualization of time and change. Space and place merge in the event of the mother. She is a sustaining place-time. Place-time yields a memorialized (if not a monumental) universe where Mother is indeed supreme, but also very, very local. The daughters' capacity for *change* is like the species-specific human capacity for language. The girls have "the South" *in* them by way of origin. "You Know Where We Came From, Mama." The comma in this phrase might be replaced by the query "don't you?" Such a substitution would make *Mama* the answer to the question of origins rather than an object of direct address. The very last words of *Sassafrass, Cypress and Indigo* sweep the temporality of the work into a signal place-time: "Mama was there."

～～～～

The question remains whether this concluding *there* signals the place and time of a discrete category of Afro-American women's writing called, as I earlier proposed, the *Timed Book*. As I have suggested earlier, such a work captures a liberational entry into and modification of the very concept of time accomplished by women's aesthetic practices. Without carrying the present discussion beyond reasonable temporal boundaries, let me suggest what I consider features and representative examples of such a genre. Distinctive features include: an absent or severely enervated father, husband, or lover; a community or a single representative of aesthetically talented black women (storytellers count here); a lineage of younger men and women to be instructed; a vivid, reverential sense of the black folk past in which conjure is greatly valued; a setting in a time of social transformation when traditional verities are under siege; the inscription of an *instant of crisis* for the black woman protagonist; formal experimentation in a psychological or meditative vein that takes language apart "to the bone." Representative examples include Hurston's *Their Eyes Were Watching God*, Morrison's *Sula*, Toni Bambara's *The Salt Eaters*, and Paule Marshall's *Praisesong for the Widow*. Each of these works has clear generational incumbencies borne by black women in the making—women whose men are gloriously dead like Hilda Effania's Alfred or Avey Johnson's Jay (in *Praisesong for the Widow*), seriously absent like Eva's BoyBoy and Nel's Jude, or lacking in the will and power to get on with life like Sassafrass's Mitch. The protagonist of each of the texts mentioned is a singer, adventurer, conjurer, storyteller, blues woman, weaver, or aesthetic lover. Further, these protagonists are productive black women uniquely responsible for time.

Their solutions and sojourns carry them from a static instant of crisis to a new *now*. And their achieved *now* is held to be salvific for "The Race," and, by implication, for humankind as a whole. At the end of her sojourn, Marshall's Avey is a womanist ancient mariner. Having passed through her crisis of widowhood, she is dedicated to arresting and instructing young people wherever she finds them, passing on to them the restorative wisdom of her great-aunt Cuney—inhabitant of the Geechee regions of the South.

In *The Salt Eaters*—the entire action of which occupies but a half-hour and raises intriguing issues of simultaneity—the concluding lines witness the "coming through" of Velma. The healing of this young black woman by the conjurer Minnie Ransom is paradoxically simultaneous with the apocalypse that threatens throughout the work. "No need for Minnie's hands now so the healer withdraws them, drops them in her lap just as Velma, rising on steady legs, throws off the shawl that drops down on the stool a burst cocoon" (295).

The *time* of the protagonists in the books that I have cited is, in a word, the logical space of a new and salvific ethics. The aesthetic practices that produce such Timed Books as well as the books' images of Afro-American women signal the space of a third generation.

~~~~~~~

Upon encountering such works, a poetics of Afro-American women's writing must suggest an adequate analytical framework for their expansiveness and difference. Third-generation Afro-American women writers have achieved their status by adhering to the wisdom implicit in Hilda Effania's injunction: "Whatever ideas you have that're important to you, write down . . . but write them down so your enemies can't understand them right off" (110). Only understanding *in time,* through the lived life, makes such writing the localized being of a new order. The general formal questions motivated by Timed Books are captured in words of Cypress's poem devoted to the sounds and motions of black folk:

> what does it mean that blk
> folks cn sing n dance?

its how we remember what
cannot be said/
that's why the white folks say [black folks'
                    singing and dancing] ain't got no
form
        what was the form
        of slavery/what was the form of jim crow/& how
        wd they
        know . . .

Perhaps the aesthetic form that Shange has in mind for the souls of black folk is either the choreopoem—or the Timed Book.

In any case, the form of *Sassafrass, Cypress and Indigo* and those of the other examples considered here are most fully realized in the image of a black woman in the changing instant of her aesthetic practice. The "lady in red" of *for colored girls* states it simply:

        i wanted to jump up outta my bones
        & be done wit myself
        leave me alone
        & go on in the wind

        ·   ·   ·   ·   ·

        i found god in myself
        & i loved her/ loved her fiercely.

A new aesthetic. A new ethics of the Timed Book. An Afro-American woman's time.

If we all find god in *her*self, then we shall learn to love *our*selves—one another. ALL, perhaps, in time.

One thing is certain. The products of Afro-American women writers in time will never have the passively ocular character of Tennyson's Lady of Shalott, who seems made, or cursed, exclusively for aesthetic viewing by spectator males:

        But Lancelot mused a little space;
        He said, "She had a lovely face;
        God in his mercy lend her grace,
        The Lady of Shalott."[19]

By way of temporal and dynamic contrast, we return to a response to a Timed Book meant for a woman's hearing that we have already cited: " 'Lawd!' Pheoby breathed out heavily, 'Ah done growed ten feet higher from jus' listenin' tuh you Janie.' "

Not satisfied with herself in the instant of her utterance, Pheoby announces her intention to step into a new *now*.

~~~~~

We can do no less. Our task is to figure our way out of history in order to create a theoretical future. Such a future would refuse glib pronouncements that, say, *Sassafrass, Cypress and Indigo* is too "romantic" or merely a "return upon the mother's body." How can the dynamics of a traditional abjection work if there is no black LAW, nor Afro-American Phallus—veiled or otherwise—allowed by economies of white domination?[20]

Alfred is dead; Jay is dead; BoyBoy is among the permanently "missing."

In such economies of absence the role of both mothers and daughters is not a horrifying struggle to escape the mother and her body but a figurative endeavor to provide new *productive* (not traditionally [re]productive) terms for aesthetic practices.

The daughters' task is to shotgun the instant in a collective aesthetics of defense rather than individualistically to enter symbolizations of a phallic order. Shange's boogie-woogie landscape does not offer an apolitical romance of the domestic, but a polyvocal and courageous book of black woman's *time-future*—if only we as readers allow it to mirror *US*.

The Timed Book is crafted not principally for male viewing but for women's hearing, which is, of course, also the hearing of women. Like Zora's Janie, Shange's women in her choreopoems and in her Timed Book of Southern mothers and daughters provide changing instants that carry Afro-American women's poetics toward new ethical and aesthetic dimensions.

Toward the Iterability of ONE

THOUGH WE ARE always embroiled with theory, we need not claim for any theory a validity beyond its powers to move and inform us. The poetics that I have proposed in the foregoing pages are but a single gesture; they are presented as both a theoretical challenge and a contribution to the efforts of contemporary scholars who are articulating a new order of expressive cultural understanding. The intended goal of my project is not an exhaustive naming and description of a vast array of Afro-American women's texts. Rather, my aim is to provide horizon-shifting accounts of certain imagistic fields. The texts that I have chosen do not comprise an ideal order unto themselves. I am not proclaiming a three-part "new" tradition or anything of the kind. As presented, the texts that I have analyzed make no claim for a decipherable chronology or an old literary history of influence among themselves. And though we acknowledge the wisdom that Zora Neale Hurston's productions represent a distinguishably modern line, we are nonetheless obliged to add that Toni Morrison has stated on more than one occasion that she did not read Hurston during her creative apprenticeship nor prior to her emergence as a successful novelist.

The harmony among the texts I have chosen is not then a historical accord but a poetical adherence. Each work is spiritually resonant in its presentation of at least one operative territory of Afro-American women's expressivity. Further, each demands articulation—a theoretical figuring out, as it were—of a sui generis analytical horizon for its comprehension. Hence, the texts are at once phenomenologically endowed and phenomenologically demanding. Their power is derived, at least in part, from their returns upon a suppressed lineage of creative mothers and grandmothers. Unlike some turn-of-the-century and Harlem Renaissance productions of departed daughters, they site themselves—in indisputably energetic ways—at the locus of the black neighborhood, the maternal home front, or the southern vernacular community. All three project strong, older, idiosyncratic black women characters as guides to the territories they map—Kitty Brown's space, Eva Peace's and Irene's places, and Hilda Effania's time. And they all tap poetically into the resources of conjure as a pivotal space of Afro-American women's power. Finally, all are products of poetically adept, deeply original, and courageously nonconformist authors. Hurston, Morrison, and Shange are, in themselves, like the images they present. They are incomprehensible via strictly causal accounts.

While we can adduce folklore, vernacular crafts, magical realism, jazz, and other performative models as "influences" in their lives, their productions outstrip any one of these domains. Moreover, their expressive import is so specifically and poetically womanist that it leads, not to a general genealogy of black creative forms, but to a distinctive order of black women's expressive consciousness in its projections of space, place, and time.

We arrive, with these closing reflections, at the end of a critical trilogy that began with *Modernism and the Harlem Renaissance*. But if one view of experience is captured by the maxim "the end is in the beginning and lies far ahead," then an alternative view is invoked by the notion that the beginning is always in the end and lies far behind. Though it only makes its appearance in this third volume, a woman's issue was the beginning of my work. And in a project devoted to Afro-American expressive cultural criticism of an autobiographical stamp, it would be remiss—indeed countermethodological—to leave the personal beginnings "far behind" or unstated. The motivation for my project was not, in any honest accounting, the fathers' proper inscription, but a woman's violation. The trilogy is, in a very real sense, the product of my own attempt to (re)create the cosmos after such a violation, to (re)discover a voice after a menacing silence, to discover and articulate the force in Afro-American tradition of that *spirit work* which binds us all together and ensures our fierce survival. I called the names of the fathers initially because women's dynamics and sitings were unsayable at the beginning.

The story of the beginning is one of woman's violation—and of my own subject position. A colonial siting provides an entry to this narrative and raises a preeminent question of the entire trilogy: "Who speaks here?"

━━━━

"I" am indisputably an-other, but I am also "not I." I do not occupy, for example, the same subject position as "the colonizer"—a sign that we shall employ for dominant and dominating authority.

In the colonizer's discourse the prototypical utterance is "*I* tell *you* this." The utterance is initiated by prototypical personhood. It is channeled through language to a similarly prototypical *you*. In the third position (or third "person," for the colonizer) are the "he" and "she" of distinction. "I" may be the "she" listening.

Grammatical categories—pronoun chartings, as it were—thus initiate the colonizer's speaking and engender personhood.

In her astute reflections on gender and language, Mary Jacobus writes: "If there is no literal referent to start with, no identity or essence, the production of sexual difference can be viewed as textual, like the production of meaning."[1] Extending this observation, one may say that the beginning of all difference, as has been earlier suggested, lies in the symbolic order and its categorical enclosures. Paraphrasing Anna Julia Cooper, we might ask "*Where* and *when* does an-other enter?" The answer—like personhood in a colonizer's discourse—is to be sought among pronouns. They tell us that an-other is a third, but not of distinction. An-other's position is the neuter "it." An-other is "it." The conversational consequence of this position is disabling muteness. The colonizing "I" cannot, for example, speak to an African slave as a prototypical "you"; and by the logic of categorical exclusion, the African—as colonized "it"—cannot initiate verbal exchange as prototypical "I." Rather than a cultural and conversational personhood, the "it" of an-otherness signifies instrumental "thingness," without gender distinctions of "he" and "she." In the third position, an-other becomes not a distinguishable "he" or "she" but a *tertium quid*. And "thingness" legitimizes enduring servitude.

What manner of "thing" were these things of labor dubbed "chattel"? The most common answer given by Europeans is suggested by observations of Leo Africanus recorded some four hundred and fifty years ago. Africanus writes, "The Negroes likewise lead a beastly kind of life, being ut-

terly destitute of the use of reason, of dexterite of wit, and of
all arts. Yea, they so behave themselves, as if they had contin-
ually lived in a Forrest among wild beasts. They have great
swarmes of Harlots among them; whereupon a man may easily conjecture their manner of living."[2]

"Conjecture," indeed—engaging in scandalous inference
based on trumped-up evidence—that is what Europe did.
And the colonial law inscribed a singularly libidinous zone of
occupancy for an-other's "it." African men were bestial crea-
tures of insatiable lust—the "it-rapes."

This inscription offered grounds for European, male empowerment—and profit. As we have earlier noted, laws of
southern states of the United States mandated that the offspring of enslaved Africans were to follow the condition of the
womb of "accessible women." The colonizer's—the whitemale master's—lechery could, thus, legally yield an-other
"thing" subject to enduring servitude. Here, surely, was a colonial repetition and reward through the control of *différance.*

〰

We are speaking here of the male colonial prerogative of
"rape," drawing out implications of that prerogative discussed
in our analysis of Afro-American women's place. This prerogative brings about a necessary inversion in the projectional
world of an-other. The most telling fact of the inversion is that
distinctions between "he" and "she" are brutally elided. The
space between African man and African woman is recuperated
by their common and legally inscribed, libidinal "it-ness."
"Normal sexuality" (socially constructed, or otherwise) is
subsumed by an economics, politics, and symbolic projection
of rape.

"Thingness," therefore, cancels gender and writes a different pronominal law. The results of this law are enslaved mu-
lattoes and frenzied lynchings. Thousands upon thousands of
both mark the space and place of ungendered "it-ness." The
situation is not unlike the enforced historicizing of the black
body discussed earlier.

And the present-day black man and woman who hope to
write a useful and empowering subject position must first site
themselves at this initiatory "it-ness" with all its abject entailments. For in the achievement of a fully expressive self and
culture, it cannot be ignored; it, alone, denotes the colonizer's
control of boundaries of human discourse—a control that in-
sures domination. When this historically determinate siting

assumes a ruthlessly personal form, then the horror of the subject position of an-other can be nearly unendurable. My own siting and the very beginning of this present trilogy were personal.

~~~~~

Not so many years ago, a best friend of mine was raped, and I entered with her the horrifying world of a woman violated. I watched a trusting, resourceful woman become a dazed victim of tawdry justice and tranquilizers. Powerless— we were both suddenly implicated in economics, politics, and symbolic distortions that previously we had only intellectualized. We were literally dumb before such horror.

Somehow speech returned. But, among the many other things I could no longer do, I could not teach *Native Son* for years, and only then as a deeply flawed book. I discovered (I believe now, to my survival) a convergence between Women's Liberation and Black Power signified by Afro-American women's writing. The creativity of black women became a space for framing, sublimating, and, yes, taming down some of the murderous rage I felt toward an American economics and politics of rape. The instability of my first semester teaching black women's writing was a baptism by fire.

Who was "I" to enter a classroom and speak of brutality? Wasn't "I," in fact, the designated rapist? To receive my self in my role as "an-other" was jolting in the person of Grange Copeland and "Pa" who is not Pa. But I found solace and instruction in the brilliant understanding accorded Shadrack, Jay Johnson, and Harriet Jacobs's first choice of a husband, her father, her brother—in Milkman Dead and Guitar's studied seriousness and love. If personhood in the moment of "itness" is to be determined, then let the depth of black women writers' judgments prevail. Especially if such judgments are communally aided by the conversations of a friend, fellow travelers, black women critics.

While reading, studying, and teaching black women's creativity for the first months, I moved with my friend through unimaginably filthy corridors of City Hall. I reviewed the ceaseless coffles of manacled young blackmale "offenders" paraded there. The common discourse of survival that my friend and I evolved included the words and works of black women writers to whom we had both turned as a way of re-apprehending—re-articulating the world. From these

works and words of black women and from our conversations, the awareness grew that what we were facing was but a shadow text of the ancient agonies of all women's positions in courts of male power.

Only such writings as those of Hurston, Morrison, Shange—and many, many, many others—compelled me honestly and ineluctably to confront the full horror of a neutering discourse of power and, at the same time, to acknowledge with awed and grateful respect the indisputable comprehension, containment, and conquest of such powers of horror by black women's own uncanny powers of resistance. There can be no easy, complex, subtle, or labyrinthian path of evasion for an-other—nor for the colonizer—who grants a hearing to these expressive resistances of Afro-American women's talking books.

The texts of Afro-American women writers became mine and my friend's harrowing but sustaining path to a new, common, and, we thought, empowering discourse and commitment. To "victim," in my friend's semantics, was added the title and entitlement "survivor." Are we not all only that? Victim/Survivors?

<hr>

Who, then, now speaks here? Who speaks is, finally, ONE—not (and never again, one thinks) "it." Who speaks is ONE who has discovered the necessity to reject as deception and scandal a colonizer's vocabulary of distinctions. Such pronoun chartings not only subject me and such friends as I have to brutal victimization, but also institute as a *normal* division (and divisiveness) a two-ness of gender that has never been the privilege of an-other. Who can *he* or *she* possibly be in an economy governed by a Law of "thingness," an inhuman exclusiveness of "it"? *He* and *She* can only be ONE in their wounding—at least that is the way it seems to the "me" who speaks here.

Gender divisions, as Jacobus's observation forcefully implies, are grammatical disguises of power; they are masterful veils of colonial powers of horror. Present-day African American men and women have a lesser distance to travel, ONE thinks, in redesigning such grammatical fashions because they share a common "it-ness" which can be transformed into a common—and, here, I am grateful to Phil Lewis for the word—into a common *iterability*:

it.er.ate "To say or perform."

WE can speak as ONE out of an-other and brutalized commonality of "it-ness." WE can speak about the sources and sig-

Conclusion   natures of our wounding. Knowing the third status of "thing-ness" which is the powerful marker of our mutual estatelessness, we can lay pens of a new self's presentation in the fissures of our life among the colonizers and *perform*.

Who is it, then, who speaks, finally, here? It is the possibility, ONE thinks, of a new Afro-American writing—a poetics, shall WE say, of Afro-American discourse that may lead us through provinces of the fathers, revisions of Harlem and the Black Aesthetic, but whose terrible beginnings in "it-ness" are only effectively comprehended and transformed through an attentive, theoretical refiguration of Afro-American women's expressivity. Such an end was the beginning of this trilogy, and lends resonance now, I think to what WE must all come to know. A selective contribution to such knowledge is the only wisdom that these concluding poetics claim.

AFTERWORD

It would be uncharitable and a betrayal of the communal spirit of my project if I were to neglect to thank fellow travelers who encouraged and supported the composition of the present work. I have reserved such thanks for an afterword, since this placement at the conclusion clearly separates the generosity of friends from the responsibility for errors in my foregoing discussions.

First, I extend gratitude to Professor Mary Helen Washington, who trusted me in those early months of my reading of Afro-American women's expressivity and invited me to the University of Massachusetts at Boston to talk on Phillis Wheatley at the dedication of a building in the poet's name. The invitation spurred my thinking on architecture, space, and Afro-American women's writing. I also wish to thank Professor Sue Houchins, who was kind enough to attend three—ever-expanding—presentations of my formulations on conjure and space, to help me get it right.

Students in my graduate and undergraduate classes at the University of Pennsylvania and at Haverford and Bryn Mawr Colleges were generous in their contributions to my knowledge and understanding of Afro-American women's writing. Michele Rubin and Jonathan Gross stand out in this regard. Professors Susan Lanser and Michael Ragussis provided an opportunity for me to share my work on Afro-American women writers at the Georgetown Literary Criticism Conference in 1985. And Professors Elizabeth Meese and Alice Parker provided an opportunity for me to deliver a lecture on *Sula* at the University of Alabama symposium "The Difference Within."

Participants in my seminar at the 1987 School of Criticism and Theory taught me a great deal about feminist criticism and literary theory. Professor Mae Henderson offered a critique of my project that led to an expanded definition of the "felicitous" image. Colleagues at the University of Ibadan in 1989 were generous and instructive in their responses to my lectures on literary theory and Zora Neale Hurston.

The most outstanding occasions for presentation and instruction were provided through the gracious collegiality of Professor Henry Louis Gates, Jr., who was responsible for an invitation from Cornell University to deliver the spring 1988 Messenger Lectures. These six lectures were attended by supportive colelagues who offered helpful suggestions and posed challenging questions. Professor Dominick LaCapra was especially notable in this respect. With the sterling assistance of Sharon Adams and Maggie and Liza Gates, Professor Gates made the Messenger moment a memorable and instructive one.

The type of engagement with Afro-American women's writing that grew out of my interactions with Professor Michael Awkward cannot be described in full. It is fair to say, however, that Professor Awkward not only challenged my prejudices, but also corrected and qualified my enthusiasms. Similar intellectual engagement was provided by Jeffrey Decker of Brown University, who read a substantial portion of the present work and posed important questions.

My editor, Alan Thomas, has been forbearing and intellectually supportive from the beginning.

My greatest gratitude goes, as always, to my wife, Charlotte Pierce-Baker, and to my son Mark. If any two people deserve the ancient spiritual's inscription about trouble seen, it is they.

A last word: the phototext is the artistry of two young scholars. Their complementary text is a rich enhancement of the present work, and I cannot thank Elizabeth Alexander and Patricia Redmond enough for their collaboration. It seems to me that the intertextuality represented by their effort makes the present work more engaging than it would otherwise have been. My initial idea was that such a text would comprise a type of countercurrent of signification, soliciting always my own words, qualifying their "maleness." What emerged from the labors of Redmond and Alexander, however, is a visualization of an Afro-American women's poetics. Eyes and events engage the reader/viewer in a solicitous order of discourse that asks: "Who reads here?" The phototext is not a countering bulwark, but a complementary action, invoking and demanding attention. It offers felicitous images in motion. Such textual energy suggests, at least phenomenologically, not clo-   sure, but a womanist, poetical art of living. It is highest praise, therefore, to designate the present study a "pictured book." One can read the space, place, and time of Afro-American women by simply beginning again—right now—with the first illustration in the phototext and following its sightings through an amazing imagistic field of representation. To begin again is, of course, the first order of phenomenology and of the present study's self-direction.

N O T E S

INTRODUCTION

1. Anna Julia Cooper, *A Voice from the South* (New York: Oxford University Press, 1988), 11.

2. Houston A. Baker, Jr., *Modernism and the Harlem Renaissance* (Chicago: University of Chicago Press, 1987).

3. Houston A. Baker, Jr., *Afro-American Poetics: Revisions of Harlem and the Black Aesthetic* (Chicago: University of Chicago Press, 1988).

4. See, for example, Roseann P. Bell, Bettye J. Parker, and Beverly Guy-Sheftall, eds., *Sturdy Black Bridges: Visions of Black Women in Literature* (Garden City: Anchor Books, 1979); Mary Helen Washington, ed., *Blackeyed Susans: Classic Stories by and about Black Women of Color* (Garden City: Anchor, 1975); Barbara Smith, ed., *Home Girls: A Black Feminist Anthology* (New York: Kitchen Table-Women of Color Press, 1983); Mary Helen Washington, ed., *Midnight Birds: Stories by Contemporary Black Women Writers* (Garden City: Anchor Books, 1980); Mary Helen Washington, ed., *Invented Lives: Narratives of Black Women 1860–1960* (Garden City: Doubleday, 1987), Gloria T. Hull, Patricia Bell Scott, and Barbara Smith, eds., *All the Women Are White, All the Blacks Are Men, But Some of Us Are Brave: Black Women's Studies* (Old Westbury, N.Y.: The Feminist Press, 1982); Deborah McDowell, "New Directions for Black Feminist Criticism," in *The New Feminist Criticism: Essays on Women, Literature and Theory,* Elaine Showalter, ed. (Pantheon, 1985); and Hazel Carby, "It Jus' Bes That Way Sometimes: The Sexual Politics of Women's Blues," *Radical America* 20 (1986): 9–22.

5. Cherrie Moraga and Gloria Anzaldua, eds., *This Bridge Called My Back: Writings by Radical Women of Color* (Watertown, Mass.: Persephone Press, 1981).

6. Notable recent reprintings include The Schomburg Library's series of writings of nineteenth-century black women — thirty volumes under the general editorship of Henry Louis Gates, Jr., published in 1988 by Oxford University Press; the Black Women Writers Series of Beacon Press, with Deborah E. McDowell as Series Editor;

and the reissue in 1988 of Nella Larsen's *Quicksand* and *Passing* as part of the American Women Writers Series of Rutgers University Press.

7. See Alice Walker, *In Search of Our Mother's Gardens* (New York: Harcourt Brace, 1983).

8. The clearest articulation of the claim that I know of came during Morrison's public lecture at Washington College in March of 1987.

9. Barbara Smith, "Toward a Black Feminist Criticism" in *All the Women Are White, All the Blacks Are Men, But Some of Us Are Brave* Gloria T. Hull, Patricia Bell Scott, and Barbara Smith, eds. (Old Westbury, New York: The Feminist Press, 1982), 157–175.

10. Hortense J. Spillers, "Mama's Baby, Papa's Maybe: An American Grammar Book," *Diacritics* 17 (Summer 1987): 67.

11. Lerone Bennett, *Before the Mayflower: A History of Black America* (Chicago: Johnson Publishing Co., 1969), 137.

12. Bennett, *Before the Mayflower,* 137.

13. Valerie Smith, *Self-Discovery and Authority in Afro-American Narrative* (Cambridge, Mass.: Harvard University Press, 1987).

14. Valerie Smith, "Gender and Afro-Americanist Literary Theory and Criticism," in *Speaking of Gender,* Elaine Showalter, ed. (New York: Routledge, 1989), 56–70.

15. Sacvan Bercovitch, "Afterward," in *Ideology and Classic American Literature,* Sacvan Bercovitch and Myra Jehlen, eds. (Cambridge: Cambridge University Press, 1986), 419.

16. Houston A. Baker, Jr., *Blues, Ideology and Afro-American Literature* (Chicago: University of Chicago Press, 1980). See "Discovering America: Generational Shifts, Afro-American Literary Criticism, and the Study of Expressive Culture."

17. Harriet Jacobs, *Incidents in the Life of a Slave Girl* (New York and London: Harcourt, Brace, Jovanovich, 1973), 163–64. All citations are from this edition and are hereafter noted by page numbers within the text.

18. Harriet Wilson, *Our Nig, or Sketches from the Life of a Free Black In a Two-Story White House, North: Showing That Slavery's Shadows Fall Even There* (New York: Random House, 1983).

19. Pauline Hopkins, *Contending Forces* (rpt. Carbondale and Edwardsville: Southern Illinois University Press, 1978). All citations refer to this edition and are hereafter noted by page numbers in parentheses.

20. Hazel Carby, *Reconstructing Womanhood: The Emergence of the Afro-American Woman Novelist* (New York: Oxford University Press, 1987).

21. Richard Wright, "Blueprint for Negro Writing," in *The Black Aesthetic,* Addison Gayle, Jr., ed., (Garden City: Doubleday, 1971), pp. 333–345.

22. Robert G. O'Meally, "Frederick Douglass' 1845 Narrative: The Text Was Meant to Be Preached," in *Afro-American Literature: The Reconstruction of Instruction,* Dexter Fisher and Robert B. Stepto, eds. (New York: The Modern Language Association of America, 1979), pp. 193–211.

23. Paula Giddings, *When and Where I Enter: The Impact of Black Women on Race and Sex in America* (New York: William Morrow, 1984), 108. All citations refer to this edition.

24. Evelyn Brooks-Higginbotham, "Beyond the Sound of Silence: Afro-American Women in History," *Gender and History* 1 (March 1989): 50–67.

25. Jacqueline Jones, *Labor of Love, Labor of Sorrow: Black Women, Work and the Family, From Slavery to the Present* (New York: Random House, 1985), 80. All citations refer to this edition.

26. The phrase is Richard Wright's, in "Blueprint for Negro Writing" (see note 21).

27. Frances E. W. Harper, *Iola Leroy* (Boston: Beacon, 1987), 153. All citations refer to this edition and are hereafter marked by page numbers in my text.

28. *Cabin* is one of the more energetic motion pictures with virtually all-black casts that have figured prominently as race-exploitation epics to keep Hollywood affluent.

29. Anna Julia Cooper, *A Voice from the South by a Black Woman of the South* (New York and Oxford: Oxford University Press, rpt., 1988). All citations refer to this edition.

30. The black humor of such signs is, surely, enhanced by their second line, which read "If you can't read, run anyhow!"

31. See Nella Larsen, *Quicksand* and *Passing* (New Jersey: Rutgers University Press, 1986) and Jessie Fauset, *Plum Bun* (London: Pandora Press, 1985).

32. See Priscilla Ramsey, "A Study of Black Identity in 'Passing' Novels of the 19th and Early 20th Century," *Studies in Black American Literature* 7 (Winter, 1976): 1–7. Also see Amrijit Singh, *The Novels of The Harlem Renaissance: Twelve Black Writers 1923–1933* (University Park: Pennsylvania State University Press, 1976).

33. The allusion is, of course, to Alice Walker's poem "Revolutionary Petunias."

34. Susan Willis, "Eruptions of Funk: Historicizing Toni Morrison," in *Black Literature and Literary Theory,* Henry Louis Gates, Jr., ed. (New York: Methuen, 1984), 263–83.

35. Toni Morrison, *Beloved* (Knopf, 1987). All citations are to this edition.

CHAPTER ONE

1. For a discussion of the expressive cultural, or ritual, responses of Africans to the trade, see: Sterling Stuckey's *Slave Culture* (New

York: Oxford, 1987). See also: Lawrence W. Levine, *Black Culture and Black Consciousness* (New York: Oxford, 1977).

2. For a discussion of Afro-American autobiography, see: Houston Baker's "Autobiographical Acts and the Voice of the Southern Slave," in *The Journey Back* (Chicago: University of Chicago Press, 1980). See also: William Andrew's *To Tell a Free Story* (Urbana: University of Illinois Press, 1986).

3. *The Poems of Phillis Wheatley,* ed. Julian Mason (Chapel Hill: University of North Carolina Press, 1986). All citations refer to this edition.

4. *Narrative of the Life of Frederick Douglass,* ed. Houston A. Baker, Jr. (New York: Penguin, 1982), 58. All citations refer to this edition.

5. See *New Literary History,* XVIII (1986–87) for Joyce Joyce: see also R. Baxter Miller, ed., *Afro-American Literature and Humanism* (Lexington: University of Kentucky Press, 1978).

6. "The Blackness of Blackness: A Critique of the Sign and the Signifying Monkey," in *Black Literature and Literary Theory,* Henry Louis Gates, ed. (New York: Methuen, 1984), 285–321.

7. *Beautiful Theories* (Baltimore: Johns Hopkins University Press, 1979).

8. "Tradition and the Individual Talent," in *Selected Essays* (New York: Harcourt, 1950), 10.

9. Chicago: University of Chicago Press, 1978.

10. *The Poetics of Space,* Maria Jolas, trans. (Boston: Beacon, 1969), xix. All citations are to this edition and are hereafter marked by page numbers in parentheses.

11. Alice Walker, "In Search of Our Mothers' Gardens," *Ms* (May 1974), and in *In Search of Our Mothers' Gardens: Womanist Prose* (San Diego: Harcourt, Brace, Jovanovitch, 1983).

12. Edmund Husserl, *Phenomenology and the Crisis of Philosophy,* trans. Quentin Lauer (New York: Harper, 1965). Lauer's extensive introduction was very helpful for my project. Hereafter, all Husserl citations refer to this edition of his work, which contains two seminal essays: "Philosophy as Rigorous Science" and "Philosophy and the Crisis of European Man."

13. "Philosophy as Rigorous Science," (see note 12), 89.

14. Martin Heidegger, *The Basic Problems of Phenomenology* (Bloomington: Indiana University Press, 1982). All citations refer to this work and are hereafter marked by page numbers in parentheses.

15. Trans. David B. Allison (Evanston: Northwestern University Press, 1973). All citations refer to this edition and are hereafter marked by page numbers in parentheses.

16. *Ibid.,* 86.

17. In Husserl, *Phenomenology and the Crisis of Philosophy* (see note 12), 40–41.

18. Toni Morrison, *Sula,* (New York: Knopf, 1974).

19. Zora Neale Hurston, *Their Eyes Were Watching God* (Urbana: University of Illinois Press, 1978).

20. Michael Awkward, *Inspiriting Influences* (New York: Columbia University Press, 1989).

21. Gayl Jones, *Corregidora* (New York: Random House, 1975).

22. Toni Morrison, *The Bluest Eye* (New York: Washington Square Press, 1972).

23. The school of critics known as "The Black Aesthetics" was preeminent in such charges.

24. Alice Walker, *The Color Purple: A Novel* (New York: Harcourt, Brace, Jovanovitch, 1982).

25. See Barbara Smith, "Toward a Black Feminist Criticism," in *All The Women are White, all the Blacks are Men, but Some of Us are Brave: Black Women's Studies,* Gloria T. Hull, Patricia Bell Scott, and Barbara Smith, eds. (Old Westbury, N.Y.: Feminist Press, 1982), 157–75.

26. Zora Neale Hurston, *Mules and Men* (Bloomington: Indiana University Press, 1978).

27. Ntozake Shange, *Sassafras, Cypress and Indigo* (New York: St. Martin's Press, 1982).

CHAPTER TWO

1. Gaston Bachelard, *The Poetics of Space,* Maria Jolas, trans. (Boston: Beacon Press, 1969), 220. All citations refer to this edition and are hereafter marked by page numbers in parentheses.

2. By "trope" I mean an unusual rhetorical figure or the pressing into figural service of a type or form from a general cultural repertoire. The "signifying monkey," who is the verbal folk trickster of Afro-American folklore, serves as an analytical trope for the critic Henry Louis Gates in his essay "The Blackness of Blackness: A Critique of the Sign and the Signifying Monkey," in *Black Literature and Literary Theory,* Gates, ed. (New York: Methuen, 1984). I use the Afro-American *blues* as such an analytical trope in my book *Blues, Ideology, and Afro-American Literature* (Chicago: University of Chicago Press, 1984). A defining site for tropological criticism is: Hayden White, *Tropics of Discourse* (Baltimore: Johns Hopkins University Press, 1978).

3. Minneapolis: University of Minnesota Press, 1977. All citations refer to this edition and are hereafter marked by page numbers in parentheses.

4. New York: Perennial Library, 1970. All citations refer to this edition and are hereafter marked by page numbers in parentheses.

5. In *Selected Essays* (New York: Harcourt, Brace, 1950), 3–11. All citations refer to this edition and are hereafter marked by page numbers in parentheses.

6. Defined as: a compulsion to embroider the truth, to exaggerate, to tell lies.

7. In *Pathologie de l'imagination et de l'émotivité* (Paris: Payot, 1925). Dupré's work first alerted me to the possibilities of the term "mythomania." I discovered Dupré through the work of Louis Mars.

8. In *The Crisis of Possession in Voodoo* (Berkeley, Calif.: Reed, Cannon, and Johnson, 1977).

9. *Ibid.*, 46–47.

10. In *God's Trombones* (New York: Viking, 1955), 17–20.

11. Hayden's poem is found in *Selected Poems* (New York: October House, 1966), 75–77. Professor Traylor delivered her insights on the poem at a conference for the Institute for the Black World in Atlanta, Georgia, in 1981.

12. Hayden, *Selected Poems,* 75.

13. *Invisible Man* (New York: Vintage, 1972). All citations refer to this edition and are hereafter marked by page numbers in parentheses. Bledsoe is the chief adversary in the southern college episodes of the novel found in chapter 2.

14. Marcel Mauss, *The Gift,* Ian Cunnison, trans. (New York: Norton, 1967).

15. Charles W. Chesnutt, *The Conjure Woman* (Ann Arbor: University of Michigan Press, 1969).

16. John Blassingame, *The Slave Community* (New York: Oxford University Press, 1972), 45.

17. Chicago: Encyclopedia Britannica, Inc., 1951. Vol. 23: 254.

18. In Newbell Niles Puckett, *Folk Beliefs of the Southern Negro* (Chapel Hill: University of North Carolina Press, 1926), 183. All citations from Puckett refer to this edition and are hereafter marked by page numbers in parentheses.

19. Michel S. Laguerre, *Voodoo Heritage* (Beverly Hills, Calif.: Sage, 1980).

20. Puckett, *Folk Beliefs* (see note 18).

21. Mr. Blockson is the curator of the Blockson Collection at the Temple University Library of Philadelphia, Pennsylvania. His remarks on Prosser occurred during a personal conversation in the summer of 1985.

22. Harry M. Hyatt, *Hoodoo, Conjuration, Witchcraft, Rootwork: Beliefs Accepted by Many Negroes* and *White Persons These Being Orally Recorded among Blacks and Whites,* memoirs of the Alma Egan Hyatt Foundation, 5 volumes, Washington, D.C.: Distributed by the American University Bookstore, 1970.

23. Berkeley, Calif.: Turtle Island, 1983. All citations refer to this edition of *Tell My Horse* and are hereafter marked by page numbers in parentheses.

24. Puckett, *Folk Beliefs,* 189.

25. Hyratt, *Hoodoo, Conjuration . . . ,* (see note 22), epigraph to vol. 1.

26. My colleague Roger Abrahams, who made a personal, extensive, and generous response to the present discussion, greatly enhanced my knowledge of Franz Boas and his pluralistic, liberal, indeed revolutionary work in establishing a rigorous discipline of folklore in the United States. My account of Hurston's practice is not an attempt to break faith with such fine scholarly human activity, but to maintain a faithful scrupulosity with respect to *Mules and Men*'s textuality and status as a medium of transmission of the image "conjure." Earlier than Abrahams, Professor Sue Lanser expressed concern about the negotiations of the terms "Jew" and "Jewish" in the present discussion. Again, my circulation and attention to the terms is textually determinate. Still, there is always the question of critical tone, and on that score I think Zora Hurston's circulation of the terms is tonally consonant with the historical problematics of Afro-American/Jewish relations in the United States. There are, one knows, myriad affective and cognitive blind spots in the eyes of both parties to these relations. But Hurston was scarcely an anti-Semite, or ungrateful for the gigantic efforts of Boas on her behalf. Nonetheless, she was also a genius who understood the propensity of a dominant scholarly elite — as Ellison's Bledsoe puts it — to "give orders" and to assume expertise vis-à-vis "other" cultures. The project of the Afro-American spirit worker is always, then, in double jeopardy of white disapproval and Afro-American rejection. A kind of "nativism" on the part of dominant-culture scholars engenders hopes that "native scholars" will never become more "complex" than the material of their group would seem — to the dominant culture — to warrant. There are, for example, folklorists and anthropologists of the dominant culture who believe that a postmodernist or theoretical attention is a *mishandling* of black culture. Similarly, there are Afro-American scholars who claim that such theoretical attention invalidates, *tout à fait,* any claim to genuine cultural knowledge of the *real* or *actual* lore. I think this situation could be called the "Hurstonian pinch." That Zora "signifies" on it in *Mules and Men* provides, if nothing else, an occasion for a reprise on the Afro-American scholar's situation. Given the history of colonialism in our era, it seems a paradoxical situation indeed when scholars of the dominant (colonizing) traditions accuse the native of a misappropriation of either *soul* or *souls*.

27. In *Dissemination* (Chicago: University of Chicago Press, 1981), 61–171. All citations refer to this edition and are hereafter marked by page numbers in parentheses.

28. I am indebted to Dominick LaCapra for his suggestion that Hurston's mastery consists in her ability to move inside both the formal, disciplinary and the vernacular discourses. I am grateful to Professor Barbara Babcock for word of the women anthropologists who surrounded Boas in the 1920s and 1930s.

29. New York: Harcourt, Brace, Jovanovich, 1970.

30. See Intro., note 18.

31. New York: Alfred A. Knopf, 1977.

32. New York: G. P. Putnam's Sons, 1983.

33. Puckett, *Folk Beliefs* (see note 18), 239.

34. Old Westbury, N.Y.: The Feminist Press, 1973.

35. Langston Hughes, *The Big Sea* (New York: Hill and Wang, 1963).

36. Urbana: University of Illinois Press, 1984.

CHAPTER THREE

1. *Invisible Man* (New York: Vintage, 1972); *Native Son* (New York: Harper and Row, 1966). All citations from the novels refer to these editions and are hereafter marked by page numbers in parentheses.

2. The phrase is the title of Leo Marx's justly celebrated work *The Machine in the Garden,* which explores the expressive effects of technology in American writing.

3. Jacques Lacan, "The Insistence of the Letter in the Unconscious, in *The Structuralists,* Richard and Fernande DeGeorge, eds. (New York: Anchor, 1972), 287–323.

4. *12 Million Black Voices* (New York: Arno Press and the *New York Times,* 1969). All citations refer to this edition and are hereafter marked by page numbers in parentheses.

5. Michel Fabre and Ellen Wright, eds., *Richard Wright Reader* (New York: Harper and Row, 1978), 144.

6. In her introduction to *The Body in Pain* (New York: Oxford University Press, 1985), Elaine Scarry says: "Physical pain does not simply resist language but actively destroys it, bringing about an immediate reversion to a state anterior to language, to the sounds and cries a human being makes before language is learned" (p. 4). What is useful about her observation for the present discussion is the implicitly precultural state to which pain reduces its carrier and sufferer. The precultural can be considered, as well, a cultural death. Reduced, stripped of a "language" for a new, agonizing, and horrible pain, the African "gives up" African culture in its pre-pain discursive specificity.

7. In Eric Williams, *Capitalism and Slavery* (New York: Capricorn Books, 1966), 35. Citations to Williams's work refer to this edition and are hereafter marked by page numbers in parentheses.

8. George Kent, "Richard Wright: Blackness and the Adventure of Western Culture," in *Blackness and the Adventure of Western Culture,* Kent (Chicago: Third World Press, 1972), 76–97.

9. "Middle Passage," in *Selected Poems* (New York: October House, Inc., 1966), 68.

10. Williams, *Capitalism and Slavery* (see note 7) 19.

11. *Ibid.*, 7.

12. *Ibid.*

13. *Uncle Tom's Cabin* (New York: Collier, 1962), 74.

14. Pages 68–73 of a 143-page narrative.

15. The observation belongs to Charlotte Pierce-Baker on seeing the huge towers in Chicago that Mayor Jane Byrne moved into for a week in a symbolic show of identification with the inhabitants.

16. "And high above me now the bridge seemed to move off to where I could not see, striding like a robot, an iron man, whose iron legs clanged doomfully as it moved. And then I struggled up, full of sorrow and pain, shouting, 'No, no, we must stop him!' " *Invisible Man* (see note 1), 558.

17. Adrienne Rich, *Of Woman Born* (New York: Bantam, 1981). All citations refer to this edition and are hereafter marked by page numbers in parentheses.

18. I have in mind Roland Barthes's "Historical Discourse," In *Introduction to Structuralism,* Michael Lane, ed. (New York: Basic Books, 1970). I have also found White's *Tropics of Discourse* (see chapter 2, note 2) useful in thinking about the composition of history. A great deal of the work of the poststructuralists is devoted as well to a revisionist view of the nature and force of historical discourse.

19. Richard Wright, "Blueprint for Negro Writing," in *The Black Aesthetic,* Addison Gayle, Jr., ed. (New York: Doubleday, 1971), 333–45. All citations of the essay refer to this version and are hereafter marked by page numbers in parentheses. The essay originally appeared in the single issue of the magazine *New Challenge* that was published. The year was 1937, and the issue included, among other contributors, Ralph Ellison.

20. Bettina Aptheker, *Woman's Legacy Essays on Race, Sex, and Class in American History* (Amherst: University of Massachusetts Press, 1982), 112. Bare statistics suggest that Wright's perception of an absence of "women in the making" in industry was not exclusively a function of his own imagination. In 1940, only 13 percent of black women in the labor force served as either white- or blue-collar workers, while 74 percent of white women served in such capacities. Further, 70 percent of black women in the labor force served in 1940 as "service workers"; 60 percent of that number were, in fact, "private household workers."

21. Until 1935 and the Seventh World Congress in Moscow, the Communist Party of the United States endorsed the notion of a black nation within America, calling for "self-determination in the Black Belt" as a goal. The League of Struggle for Negro Rights and the *Negro Liberator* were agencies designed to secure such a nationalist end. With the coming of the Popular Front, however, designed to curb the powers of Nazi Germany and the spread of fascism, the nationalist program for American blacks was abandoned, leading to a sense of betrayal on the part of some black Communist Party sup-

porters. Mark Naison's *Communists in Harlem During the Depression* (New York: Grove, 1983) contains an account of the shifting policies of the CPUSA during the 1930s.

22. Sigmund Freud, *The Interpretation of Dreams* (New York: Avon, 1965), James Strachey, trans., 429. All citations from the text refer to this edition and are hereafter marked by page numbers in parentheses.

23. *Ar'n't I a Woman? Female Slaves in the Plantation South* (New York: W. W. Norton, 1985), 63. All citations refer to this edition and are hereafter marked by page numbers in parentheses.

24. The immediacy of pain surely differentiates a woman's response from the "astonishment" expressed by Olaudah Equiano as recorded in *The Life of Olaudah Equiano, or Gustavus Vassa, The African Written By Himself,* in *Great Slave Narratives,* Arna Bontemps, ed., (Boston: Beacon, 1969), 27.

25. In Angela Y. Davis, *Women, Race & Class* (New York: Random House, 1981), 3–29. Further citations refer to this edition and are marked by page numbers in parentheses.

26. A paraphrase of Adrienne Rich's *Of Woman Born* (see note 17).

27. In his still controversial essay in definition of the "protest novel" entitled "Many Thousands Gone," Baldwin writes of a "necessary dimension" that has been excluded from black life by *Native Son* — "this dimension being the relationship that Negroes bear to one another, that depth of involvement and unspoken recognition of shared experience which creates a way of life. . . . [with the eradication of this dimension, we are] led . . . to believe that in Negro life there exists no tradition, no field of manners, no possibility of ritual or intercourse, such as may, for example, sustain the Jew even after he has left his father's house" (35–36). In Baldwin, *Notes of a Native Son* (Boston: Beacon, 1955).

28. In Lewis S. Feuer, ed., *Marx and Engels, Basic Writings on Politics and Philosophy* (New York: Anchor, 1959), 320–48. All citations refer to this edition and are hereafter marked by page numbers in parentheses.

29. "Classic" blues are those that were scored and orchestrated for and by such women singers as Clare, Mamie, and Bessie Smith, Victoria Spivey, and Gertrude "Ma" Rainey during the decade of the 1920s. Recording labels such as Vocalion and Okeh, Victor and Gennett, made the classic blues (a refiguration of blackmale, country blues from, among other places, the Mississippi delta region) into a very profitable commodity, sometimes selling as many as 10,000 copies of a single release in a week. Radio helped to disseminate these "classics" to a wide and diverse audience.

30. Toni Morrison, *Sula* (New York: Alfred A. Knopf, 1974). All citations refer to this edition and are hereafter marked by page numbers in parentheses. The "Bottom" is the name of the fictive community that Morrison constructs in her novel.

31. "'Intimate Things in Place': A Conversation with Toni Morrison," in *Chant of Saints,* Michael S. Harper and Robert B. Stepto eds. (Urbana: University of Illinois Press, 1979), 213–29.

32. It seems important at this juncture to differentiate Morrison's "intimate" place from the spaces of confinement described in the magnificently suggestive study of women writers and the nineteenth-century literary imagination offered by Sandra M. Gilbert and Susan Gubar. Gilbert and Gubar write in *The Madwoman in the Attic* (New Haven: Yale University Press, 1979) as follows: "literally, women like Dickinson, Brontë, and Rossetti were imprisoned in their homes, their father's houses; indeed, almost all nineteenth-century women were in some sense imprisoned in men's houses. Figuratively, such women were, as we have seen, locked into male texts, texts from which they could escape only through ingenuity and indirection. It is not surprising, then, that spatial imagery of enclosure and escape, elaborate with what frequently becomes obsessive intensity, characterizes much of their writing" (83). The thesis of Gilbert and Gubar stresses "escape" by imprisoned women authors as a writing of the "madwomen," the mad double who is id energy or the wantonness of the unlawful. Bertha of *Jane Eyre* is the *ur*-madwoman double. She, in Gilbert and Gubar's view, expresses the anxiety of authorship of Brontë and other women writers and represents, as well, the woman's escape from patriarchal houses and male texts into a peculiarly woman's imaginary. The specifically Victorian and white Western psychosexual orientation of this thesis—and responsible for its resonant clarity and persuasiveness—seems to remove it from the type of ancestral, folk codifications of space and place implied by Morrison's writing.

33. I am referring back, of course, to the historian Deborah White's observation that African women who were victims of the European slave trade were not confined to the holes of ships but were allowed to go unshackled on the half and quarter decks.

34. *Purity and Danger, An Analysis of the Concepts of Pollution and Taboo* (London: Routledge and Kegan Paul, 1966). All citations refer to this edition and are hereafter marked by page numbers in parentheses.

35. In *Literature and the Urban Experiences,* Michael C. Jaye and Ann Chalmers Watts, eds. (New Brunswick: Rutgers University Press, 1981), 35–43. Further citations are marked by page numbers in parentheses.

36. In *The Souls of Black Folk,* which in turn appears in *Three Negro Classics,* John Hope Franklin, ed. (New York: Avon, 1965), 233–34.

37. The discussion of the joke that follows relies heavily upon the observations of Sigmund Freud in *Jokes and Their Relation to the Unconscious,* James Strachey, trans. (New York: W. W. Norton, 1960).

38. In *Purity and Danger* (see note 34), Douglas writes: "[O]ur pollution behavior is the reaction which condemns any object or idea

likely to confuse or contradict cherished classifications. We should now force ourselves to focus on dirt. Defined in this way it appears as a residual category, rejected from our normal scheme of classifications" (36).

39. "Then Nebuchadnezzar came near to the mouth of the burning fiery furnace, and spake, and said, Shadrach, Meshach, and Abednego, ye servants of the most high God, come forth, and come *hither.* Then Shadrach, Meshach, and Abednego, came forth of the midst of the fire." *Daniel,* iii, 26 (Bible). The ironic resemblance that Morrison's antihero bears to the biblical Shadrach lies in his seeming idolatry before the power of death, while the Shadrach of the book of *Daniel* is condemned by the king for his refusal to worship the golden image. Insofar as Morrison's character is a partisan of an *ordering* ritual, however, he does construct an alternative to the capitalist disorder of war.

40. New York: Pocket Books, 1972.

41. New York: Alfred A. Knopf, 1977. The three women who work in the Dead house are Ruth (the wife) and the two daughters of Macon Dead—Magdalene called Lena and First Corinthians.

42. Otto Rank reports and interprets a dream as follows in the *Interpretation of Dreams* (see note 22): "If we bear in mind that Freud's researches into sexual symbolism . . . have shown that stairs and going upstairs in dreams almost invariably stand for copulation, the dream becomes quite transparent" (405).

43. Shadrack's followers increase yearly; the first to join his inversive parade are Tar Baby and the Deweys.

44. Dorothy Sterling, ed., *We Are Your Sisters, Black Women in the Nineteenth Century* (New York: W. W. Norton, 1984), 57.

45. "'Intimate Things in Place'" (see note 31), 218.

46. Jean Toomer, *Cane* (New York: Liveright, 1977). All citations refer to this edition and are hereafter marked by page numbers in parentheses. *Cane* was first published in 1923.

47. In "The Blackness of Blackness: A Critique of the Sign and the Signifying Monkey," in *Black Literature and Literary Theory* (see chapter 2, note 2), 285–321. Gates refers to the quality of Toomer's and Hurston's prose as "lyrical" (295) and goes on to designate what he calls a "speakerly" text (the Afro-American equivalent of Barthes's "writerly" text), 296. Hurston's work, then, like Toomer's would consist of the lyrical production of talking books.

48. For valuable accounts of the PHALLUS in the work of Freud and Lacan, see Juliet Mitchell and Jacqueline Rose, eds., *Feminine Sexuality: Jacques Lacan and the école freudienne* (New York: W. W. Norton, 1982); Juliet Mitchell, *Psychoanalysis and Feminism: Freud, Reich, Laing and Women* (New York: Vintage Books, 1975; Jane Gallop, *The Daughter's Seduction: Feminism and Psychoanalysis* (Ithaca, N.Y.: Cornell University Press, 1982).

49. *The Reproduction of Mothering: Psychoanalysis and the Sociology of Gender* (Berkeley: University of California Press, 1978), 140. Further citations are marked by page numbers in parentheses.

50. In Gloria T. Hull, Patricia Bell Scott, and Barbara Smith, eds., *All the Women Are White, all the Blacks Are Men, But Some of Us Are Brave: Black Women's Studies* (see Intro., note 4), 157–75. Adrienne Rich, in her essay "Compulsory Heterosexuality and Lesbian Existence," also speaks of *Sula* as a novel of "lesbian existence," Rich's essay appears in *The Signs Reader,* Elizabeth Abel and Emily K. Abel, eds. (University of Chicago Press, 1983).

51. *The Bluest Eye* begins as follows: Here is the house. It is green and white. It has a red door. It is very pretty. Here is the family. Mother, Father, Dick, and Jane live in the green-and-white house. They are very happy." Quickly, however, the normal spacing and typeface are run together, and, finally, reduced to mere strings of letters. The novel, thus, begins with a deconstruction of the representation of "traditional" (read: **WHITE PATRIARCHAL**) family structures that greeted so many of us as we were just learning to read. Morrison's artistry suggests another (a **BLACK**) reading of the family.

52. In *The Newly Born Woman,* Betsy Wing, trans. (Minneapolis: University of Minnesota Press, 1986), 3–59. The Minnesota edition is a re-release of a 1975 work; included in the book is Hélène Cixous's "Sorties: Out and Out: Attacks/Ways Out/ Forays." Further references are marked by page numbers in parentheses.

53. In *Invisible Man* (see chapter 3, note 1) the final scene before the "Epilogue" is a nightmare vision of castration in which the protagonist's testes are launched into the air by his male adversaries and false guides and hang floating over a technological civilization as possible salvation (556–58).

54. *Of Woman Born* (see note 17), 11. " 'Vous travaillez *pour l'armeé, madame?'* ('You are working for the army?'), a Frenchwoman said to me early in the Vietnam war, on hearing I had three sons."

55. Juliet Mitchell and Jacqueline Rose, eds., *Feminine Sexuality,* (see note 48) and Jane Gallop, *The Daughter's Seduction* (also note 48), are excellent sources for a discussion of the Lacanian problematic, as is Luce Irigaray, *This Sex Which Is Not One* (Ithaca, N.Y.: Cornell University Press, 1985; first published in 1977).

56. Quoted from Michel de Certeau, *Heterologies: Discourse on the Other* (Minneapolis: University of Minnesota Press, 1986), 56. Further references are marked by page numbers in parentheses.

57. *Ibid.*

58. Bessie Smith, "Back Water Blues."

59. Bernard C. Nalty, *Strength for the Fight: A History of Black Americans in the Military* (New York: The Free Press, 1986), 143. I must thank my extraordinary research assistant, Claire Satloff, for

this reference and for her very dedicated work in securing sources necessary for the completion of this entire essay.

60. Paula Giddings, *When and Where I Enter: The Impact of Black Women on Race and Sex in America* (New York: Bantam Books, 1984). Giddings's history seems to me essential reading for anyone interested in feminist, or Afro-American, or general historical contours of the United States of America. Her account of Walker is my source for the discussion that follows.

61. The poem is from Miller's volume *Where Are the Love Poems for Dictators* (Washington, D.C.: Open Hand, 1986).

62. Bo Chatman, "Arrangements for Me — Blues." For my blues citations, I have relied on the remarkable work of Michael Taft, *Blues Lyric Poetry* (New York: Garland, 1983).

CHAPTER FOUR

1. "Women's Time," in *Feminist Theory: A Critique of Ideology,* Nannerl O. Keohane, Michelle Z. Rosaldo, and Barbara C. Gelpi, eds. (Chicago: University of Chicago Press, 1982), 31–54. All citations are marked hereafter by page numbers in parentheses.

2. The perception of woman only in her (re)appearance or (re)production is, in part, a function of a psychology that defines her in terms of "lack." It is, as well, a function of an economics that refuses or fails to cite her at the site of production.

3. *Jouissance* is "a word with *simultaneously* sexual, political and economic overtones. Total access, total participation, as well as total ecstasy are implied. At the simplest level of meaning — metaphorical—woman's capacity for multiple orgasm indicates that she has the potential to attain something more than Total, something extra — abundance and waste (a cultural throwaway), real and unrepresentable." From the "Glossary" of Hélène Cixous and Catherine Clement, *The Newly Born Woman,* Betsy Wing, trans. (Minneapolis: University of Minnesota Press, 1986), 165.

4. *Their Eyes Were Watching God* (Urbana: University of Illinois Press, 1978), 134–35. All citations refer to this edition.

5. This is Aristotle's definition in Book Delta of the *Physics.*

6. G. E. R. Lloyd, "Views on Time in Greek Thought," in *Culture and Time* (Paris: Unesco Press, 1976), 139.

7. The phrase is from "A Defense of Poetry": "A man cannot say, 'I will compose poetry.' The greatest poet even cannot say it; for the mind in creation is as a fading coal, which some invisible influence, like an inconstant wind, awakens to transitory brightness."

8. Toni Morrison, *Sula* (see chap. 3, note 30), 92.

9. Bas C. van Fraassen, *An Introduction to the Philosophy of Time* (New York: Random House, 1970), 104.

10. The "dozens" are traditionally a male game. They consist of the trading of verbal insults between participants until one concedes

the victory, or until an eager audience acknowledges a victor in the competition.

11. In *three pieces* (New York: St. Martins, 1981), 115. All citations refer to this edition and are hereafter marked by page numbers in parentheses.

12. Quoted from *Culture and Time* (see note 6), 143.

13. *Sassafrass, Cypress and Indigo* (New York: St. Martins, 1982). All citations refer to this edition.

14. In *See No Evil* (San Francisco: Momo's Press, 1984), 21.

15. In *nappy edges* (New York: St. Martins, 1978), 88.

16. In *See No Evil* (see note 14), 31.

17. "signs or habitations made on the floor of chapel, 'bood,' or hounfort to welcome gods, spirits, loa, powers, ancestors": from "Notes" to *Mother Poem* by Edward Kamau Brathwaite (Oxford: Oxford University Press, 1977), 120.

18. Professor Abena Busia of Rutgers University was kind enough to point out to me the added significance that folk-rootedness has in the lives of the three daughters as a function of gender. They are not only champions of the folk, but adept champions of and heralds for Afro-American women as folk.

19. From: *Poetry of the Victorian Period,* Jerome Buckley and George Woods eds. (Chicago: Scott, Foresman, 1965), 119.

20. My reference here is to Kristeva's *Powers of Horror: An Essay on Abjection* (New York: Columbia University Press, 1982).

CONCLUSION

1. *Reading Women* (New York: Columbia University Press, 1986), 4.

2. In Winthrop D. Jordan, *White over Black* (Baltimore: Penguin, 1968), 34.

ILLUSTRATION

SOURCES

The photographs on pages ix, x, xi, 3, 4, 5, 6, 7, 8, 162, 177, 185 (photograph of Pearl Primus), 189, 195, and 216 are reproduced with the permission of the Schomburg Center for Research in Black Culture at the New York Public Library (Astor, Lenox, and Tilden Foundations).

Those on pages xii and xiii (three photographs of Zora Neale Hurston), xiv (top), 65, 131, 134, 163, 184, and 194 are reproduced with the permission of the Moorland-Spingarn Research Center at Howard University (Mary O'H Williamson Collection, Prints and Photographs Department).

Pages xv, 46–47, and 179: Photographs by Roland L. Freeman, © 1990.

Photographs on pages 27 and 198 are reproduced by permission of the *Washington Post*.

Photographs on pages 172–73, 183, 193, 196, 197, and 214 are reproduced by courtesy of the Library of Congress.

Photographs on pages 135 and 176 are reproduced with the permission of AP/Wide World Photos.

The photograph on page xiv (bottom) is reproduced by courtesy of Elizabeth Alexander.

INDEX